A Scottish Postbag

A Scottish Postbag

Eight centuries of Scottish letters

edited by
George Bruce and Paul H. Scott

Published in association with the Saltire Society

Chambers

Published by W & R Chambers Ltd Edinburgh

© George Bruce and Paul H. Scott 1986

British Library Cataloguing in Publication Data

A Scottish Postbag
 I. Bruce, George, *1909*- II. Scott, Paul Henderson
 826'.008'0941 PR1342

ISBN 0 550 20490 3

The Saltire Society has been active since 1936 in the encouragement of everything that might improve the quality of life in Scotland and restore the country to its proper place as a creative force in European civilisation.

Printed by Martin's of Berwick.

Contents

The Parliamentary Union of 1707

The Forty-Five

David Hume *(continued)*

Introduction

The editors claim no credit for the idea behind this book, although, as is usual with good ideas, it is difficult to understand why nobody thought of it before. Very appropriately for a collection of Scottish letters, the proposal came from the Scottish Post Office Board. Martin Cummins of the Board called one day at the Saltire Society and asked if we would be interested in arranging for the collection and publication of outstanding Scottish letters from all periods and all kinds of people. He suggested that a book of this kind would reveal both the extraordinary range of the Scottish contribution to our common civilisation and the versatility and power of the letter as a means of communication. The Board was ready to help with the cost of publication if the Society would do the rest. Of course, the Society responded with enthusiasm because the proposal accorded perfectly with one of our main objectives, 'to make the nation conscious of its heritage'. We agreed to make the collection and edit the book, and we found a very co-operative publisher in W & R Chambers.

Since we have both spent long years on the highways and byways of Scottish history and literature, we knew from the beginning that mountains of splendid letters were readily available. The difficulty would not lie in finding enough letters full of wit, passion and life, but in agonising decisions about what to leave out. In our first discussion about the project, we drew up a list of letters which we remembered from printed sources that were obvious candidates for inclusion, and there were already enough of them to fill a book. We began a systematic search through the published collections of letters and biographies and the like where letters are quoted. Many of these books were familiar friends on our own shelves, but in Edinburgh we are fortunate in the accessibility of great libraries that are always ready to help, the National Library of Scotland, Edinburgh University Library, and the admirable Scottish Room in the Central Library on George IV Bridge.

Many friends with special knowledge came to our aid: Ian Campbell, for example, with his intimate familiarity with the Carlyle correspondence (the edition on which he is working will amount to 40 volumes), Douglas Mack who is editing the letters of James and Margaret Hogg, and Alan Bell who knows more than anyone else about Cockburn's letters and will, we hope, publish an edition before long. As a result of some publicity on the BBC and in the press, people were good enough to volunteer letters in their own possession. When we turned to unpublished manuscript sources, we found enthusiastic allies in the entire staff of the Manuscript Department of the National

Library of Scotland. They could not have been more generous of their time and scholarship in guiding us through the vast resources of their holdings which are full of revelation and delight. The Scottish Record Office, which is rich in manuscript correspondence, also came to our aid.

So we had happy months of discovery. We tried the patience of our households with long and frequent telephone calls about our latest unexpected find. We were nearly drowned in a sea of letters. Obviously, if we were to produce a balanced and representative collection of acceptable length, we should have to omit the less interesting passages of the longer letters. (Omissions are indicated by . . . in the text.) We decided that it was better to give as much space as possible to the letters themselves and therefore to keep introductory and explanatory material to the bare minimum. In spite of this, we have had to omit scores, if not hundreds, of letters for which we had no space. This is a rich and largely unexplored field which could produce many more volumes. We can offer only an aperitif to the feast.

G.B., P.H.S.   *Edinburgh July 1986*

☆   ☆   ☆

Acknowledgements

We gratefully acknowledge the help of many people who brought letters to our attention or gave us the benefit of their expert knowledge. They include:

A. J. Aitken; Marinell Ash; L. L. Ardern; J. P. C. Bannerman; Joyce Barrie; Alan Bell; John Blair; David Bruce; Iain G. Brown; Meg Burgess; Athole Cameron; Ian Campbell; Robert Clark; Peter Cook; A. C. Davis; Gordon Donaldson; Rev. A. Ian Dunlop; Lindsay Errington; Alexander Fenton; William Ferguson; Tom Fleming; Charles Fraser; John Gibson; Valda Grieve; H. Forsyth Hardy; Alexia Howe; Jean Jones; Kenneth Lawson; Leah Leneman; Peter Liddle; Maurice Lindsay; Malcolm Macdonald; Douglas Mack; Sorley Maclean; Iseabail Macleod; Rosalind K. Marshall; Ronald Mavor; Olivia Mitchell; R. M. Mitchison; W. J. Bruce Munro; David Murison; J. B. Pick; Ian Rae; Sarah Stevenson; A. R. Turnbull; Bruce A. Tyrie; Norman Wilson; Ian S. Wood.

In addition to the National Library of Scotland, Edinburgh University Library, the Scottish Room in Edinburgh Central Library, the Scottish Record Office, also of great assistance have been the Dartmouth College Library, Peter Liddle's 1914–18 Archive, Sunderland Polytechnic, New College Library, Edinburgh, the Royal Observatory, Edinburgh, the Council of the Scottish History Society, and the Science Museum, Fox Talbot Collection, London.

Every effort has been made to contact all copyright holders, but if there are any omissions we shall be glad to make amends at the earliest opportunity.

Editorial Note

We have reproduced our sources as accurately as we can, including their spelling and punctuation. The letters are arranged chronologically by date of birth, except where writers are grouped together under subject headings.

William Wallace (c. 1270-1305)
and
Andrew Moray (? -1297)

Andrew Moray or Sir Andrew Murray started a rising against the English in Moray and went on to join forces with Wallace at the Battle of Stirling Bridge in 1297. The victory secured freedom of entry to the Forth. The letter written immediately after the battle to assure the merchants of Lübeck and Hamburg that they may 'now have safe access' to all the harbours of Scotland is more sanguine than the facts merited. Andrew Moray died from wounds after the battle.

1. The recovery of the Kingdom

(Original in Latin)

*To the Senate and Commoners
of Lübeck and Hamburg*   *Haddington 11 October 1287*

Andrew Moray and William Wallace, leaders of the Scotch army, and the commonwealth of the same kingdom send to the prudent and discreet men, our good friends, the Senate and the commoners of Lübeck and of Hamburg greeting and a continuous increase of sincere affection. We have been informed by trustworthy merchants of the said kingdom of Scotland, that you on your own behalf have been friendly in counsel and deed in all things and enterprises concerning us and our merchants, though our own merits did not occasion this. We are therefore the more beholden to you, and wishing to prove our gratitude in a worthy manner we ask you to make it known among your merchants that they can now have safe access with their merchandize to all harbours of the Kingdom of Scotland, because the Kingdom of Scotland has, thanks be to God, by war been recovered from the power of the English. Farewell. Given at Hadsington (Haddington) on the eleventh day of October in the year of Grace one thousand two hundred and ninety seven.

We also pray you to be good enough to further the business of John Burnett and John Frere, our merchants, just as you might wish that we should further the business of your merchants. Farewell, Given as above.

The Declaration of Arbroath (1320)

The document known as the Declaration of Arbroath, the most important and best known in Scottish history, was a letter, if of a specialised kind. It was a diplomatic communication from the barons and 'whole community of the realm' of Scotland to Pope John XXII, remarkable both for its eloquence and persuasiveness and for the boldness and originality of its ideas. Long before such conceptions were found elsewhere in Europe, it spoke for the whole community and asserted the ideas that the independence of the nation was worth defending for its own sake and that rulers exist to serve the community and not the reverse. The following is part of a translation by Sir James Fergusson from the Latin original.

2. 'For freedom alone'

To Pope John XXII   *The Monastery of Arbroath*
6 April 1320

. . . The high qualities and deserts of these people, were they not otherwise manifest, gain glory enough from this: that the King of kings and Lord of lords, our Lord Jesus Christ, after His Passion and Resurrection, called them, even though settled in the uttermost parts of the earth, almost the first to His most holy faith. Nor would He have them confirmed in that faith by merely anyone but by the first of His Apostles — by calling, though second or third in rank — the most gentle Saint Andrew, the Blessed Peter's brother, and desired him to keep them under his protection as their patron for ever.

The Most Holy Fathers your predecessors gave careful heed to these things and bestowed many favours and numerous privileges on this same kingdom and people, as being the special charge of the Blessed Peter's brother. Thus our nation under their protection did indeed live in freedom and peace up to the time when that mighty prince the King of the English, Edward, the father of the one who reigns today, when our kingdom had no head and our people harboured no malice or treachery and were then unused to wars or invasions, came in the guise of a friend and ally to harass them as an enemy. The deeds of cruelty, massacre, violence, pillage, arson, imprisoning prelates, burning down monasteries, robbing and killing monks and nuns, and yet other outrages without number which he committed against our people, sparing neither age nor sex, religion nor rank, no one could describe nor fully imagine unless he had seen them with his own eyes.

But from these countless evils we have been set free, by the help of Him Who though He afflicts yet heals and restores, by our most tireless Prince, King and Lord, the Lord Robert. He, that his people and his heritage might be delivered out of the hands of our enemies, met toil and fatigue, hunger and peril, like another Maccabaeus or Joshua and bore them cheerfully. Him, too, divine providence, his right of succession according to our laws and customs which we shall maintain to the death, and the due consent and assent of us all have made our Prince and King. To him, as to the man by whom salvation has been wrought unto our people, we are bound both by law and by his merits that our freedom may be still maintained, and by him, come what may, we mean to stand.

Yet if he should give up what he has begun, and agree to make us or our kingdom subject to the King of England or the English, we should exert ourselves at once to drive him out as our enemy and a subverter of his own rights and ours, and make some other man who was well able to defend us our King; for, as long as but a hundred of us remain alive, never will we on any conditions be brought under English rule. It is in truth not for glory, nor riches nor honours that we are fighting, but for freedom — for that alone, which no honest man gives up but with life itself.

Therefore it is, Reverend Father and Lord, that we beseech your Holiness with our most earnest prayers and suppliant hearts, inasmuch as you will in your sincerity and goodness consider all this, that, since with Him Whose vice-gerent on earth you are there is neither weighing nor distinction of Jew and Greek, Scotsman or Englishman, you will look with the eyes of a father on the troubles and privations brought by the English upon us and upon the Church of God. May it please you to admonish and exhort the King of the English, who ought to be satisfied with what belongs to him since England used once to be enough for seven kings or more, to leave us Scots in peace, who live in this poor little Scotland, beyond which there is no dwelling-place at all, and covet nothing but our own. We are sincerely willing to do anything for him, having regard to our condition, that we can, to win peace for ourselves.

The Chancellor and Thrie Estatis of the Realme of Scotland

With a boy king (James V), an English queen mother working against her adopted country, and her fighting strength greatly weakened at Flodden, Scotland might have seemed in no condition in 1522* to defy England. But her spirit of resistance is evident in this reply to the demands of Henry VIII.

3. Reply to an ultimatum 1522

To Henry VIII   *Edinburgh 11 February 1522*

. . . Giff this your Querell be Just or Resonable God be the Juge, sen it may be na better, for we have alwais desirit and desiris to leiff with your Grace in gude Amyte and Pece, giff We may have it without extreme Inconvenientis. Howbeith We ar resolute that, or We suld consent to do sa grete hurt to *the King* our Soverane Lord and the Common Weill of his Realme, sa grete Dishonour to our selff, and sa grete Wrang to our said *Lord Governour*, as to amove him furth of this Realme and leiff in Divisioun and dailie Truble amang our selff, as this lang tyme bipassit we have done, he being in France; We will with his Presence take our Aventure of Pece or Were as sall pleys God to send it; Assuring Youre Grace that, for the Caus above specifyt, and utheris enew quhilk We sall schaw in tyme and Place, We nouther may nor will at requeist of Youre Grace, nor ony uthir Prince, consent nor suffer in ony maner that oure said *Lord Governour* depart furth of this Realme during the King oure Soverane Lordis Minorite and lesse Age.

And giff, for this Cause, We happin to be Invadit, quhat may we do bot tak God to oure gude Querell in Defens, and do as oure Progenitouris and Forbearis has bene Constrenyt to do, for the Conservatioun of this Realme heretofore.

Geven under oure Soverand Lordis Prive Sele at Edinburgh the xi day of Februare the Yeir of God One Thousand Five Hundred and Twenty one Yeris.

Your humble Oratouris and Servandis with all lauthful service

THE CHANCELLOR AND THRIE ESTATIS OF THE REALME OF SCOTLAND

*New Style

George Buchanan (1506 – 82)

George Buchanan was regarded throughout Europe as one of the greatest scholars and poets of his age. He wrote almost exclusively in Latin, not only his neo-classical tragedies but even his history of Scotland and his treatise on Scottish constitutional practice. His history 'superabounded in patriotism' but, by modern standards, was uncritical, although Buchanan said that he sought to purge it of 'Inglis lyis and Scotis vanite'. He was tutor to James VI who became in consequence one of the most scholarly of kings. Buchanan's letters, like his other writing, were mostly in Latin. The following is one of only two of his letters in Scots which have survived. It was addressed to Thomas Randolphe, 'maister of postis to the queenis grace of Ingland', who had been English Ambassador to Scotland.

4. 'Writyng of our historie'

To Thomas Randolph   *Stirling 25 August 1577*

Maister, I haif resavit diverse letters frome you, and yit I have ansourit to naine of thayme; of the quhylke albeit I haif mony excusis, as age, forgetfulnes, besines, and disease, yit I wyl use nane as now, except my sweirness, and your gentilnes; and geif ye thynk nane of theise sufficent, content you with ane confession of the falt, w^tout fear of punitioun to follow on my onkindnes. As for the present, I am occupiit in writyng of our historie, being assurit to content few, and to displease mony thar throw. As to the end of it, yf ye gett it not or thys winter be passit, lippin not for it, nor nane other writyngs from me. The rest of my occupation is wyth the gout, quhilk haldis me besy both day and ny^t. And quhair ye say ye haif not lang to lyif, I traist to god to go before yow, albeit I be on fut, and ye ryd the post; praying you als not to dispost my hoste at New werk, Jone of Kelsterne. Thys I pray you, partly for his awyne sake, quhame I tho^t ane gud fellow, and partly at request of syk as I dar no^t refuse. And thus I take my leif shortly at you now, and my lang leif quhen God pleasis, committing you to the protection of the almy^tty. At Sterling xxv. day of August, 1577.

Yours to command w^t service,

G. BUCHANAN

James V (1512 – 42)

James V was only one year old when his father, the brilliant Renaissance prince, James IV, was killed on the disastrous field of Flodden. He had a difficult time during his minority, although Sir David Lyndsay of The Thrie Estaites *was for a time his tutor. He seems to have looked for consolation to a succession of mistresses; by the age of 20 he had three illegitimate sons (and subsequently at least four more), all by different mothers.*

5. The royal bastards
(Original in Latin)

To Pope Clement VII   *27 February 1532/3*

. . . As I have three illegitimate sons (two of them being the children of an unmarried father and mother, the third of an unmarried father only), I am obliged to confess to your Holiness that the fault is my own (although it might indeed easily be attributed to youth), and I acknowledge the error of human weakness. Yet that natural fatherly affection, common to all creatures, which nature prompts, urges every man to have regard for the welfare of his offspring as of himself; for to be a father and yet not be moved by concern for the care of his children would be at once ungrateful and unnatural. We therefore beg your Holiness, of your clemency and courtesy (which we have hitherto experienced in every matter) to dispense with those our sons, by the grace of your apostolic authority, that, notwithstanding their defect of birth, they may, when their age allows, be duly promoted (outwith the terms prescribed by law) to all holy orders, even that of priesthood, and that at present, notwithstanding their minority as well as their defect of birth, they may, after receiving the clerical character, hold any church dignities whatsoever, either secular or regular of any order, in title or commend, even two, three, four or more incompatible benefices, and greater dignities *post pontificales** in cathedral and metropolitan churches and the first dignities in collegiate churches, and also monasteries, abbeys and priories (deputing coadjutors therein until they reach mature years). Let your Holiness grant also that hereafter it be not necessary to narrate their defect of birth in apostolic impetrations for any of them, and that their letters seem not on that account to be surreptitious. Finally, let your Holiness grant that when they attain their twentieth year they may be able to be promoted to the dignities of archbishop, primate and bishop . . .

*dignities inferior to that of a bishop

(In response to this petition, the pope provided Lord James Stewart, elder, to the abbeys of Kelso and Melrose, Lord James, younger (later the Regent Moray), to the priories of St Andrews and Pittenweem, and Lord Robert, elder, to the abbey of Holyrood. Subsequently another son, Lord John, was provided to the priory of Coldingham.)

Mary, Queen of Scots (1542-87)

Mary, after eighteen years of imprisonment in England, was beheaded in Fotheringay Castle on 8 February 1587, on a warrant signed by Queen Elizabeth of England. This was the last letter that Mary wrote; she finished it at 2 a.m., six hours before her execution. It was addressed to Henri III, King of France, younger brother of her first husband, Francis II.

6. The last letter of Mary, Queen of Scots
(Original in French)

To King Henri III of France   *Fotheringay 8 February 1587*

Queen of Scotland

Royal brother, having by God's will, for my sins I think, thrown myself into the power of the Queen my cousin, at whose hands I have suffered much for almost twenty years, I have finally been condemned to death by her and her Estates. I have asked for my papers, which they have taken away, in order that I might make my will but I have been unable to recover anything of use to me or even get leave either to make my will freely or to have my body conveyed after my death, as I would wish, to your kingdom where I had the honour to be queen, your sister and old ally.

Tonight, after dinner, I have been advised of my sentence: I am to be executed like a criminal at eight in the morning. I have not had time to give you a full account of everything that has happened, but if you will listen to my doctor and my unfortunate servants you will learn the truth, and how, thanks be to God, I scorn death and vow that I meet it innocent of any crime, even if I were their subject. The Catholic faith and the assertion of my God-given right to the English crown are the two issues on which I am condemned, and yet I am not allowed to say that it is for the Catholic religion that I die, but for fear of interference with theirs. The proof of this is that they have taken away my chaplain, and, although he is in the building, I have not been able to get permission for him to come and hear my confession and give me the Last Sacrament, while they have been most insistent that I receive the consolation and instruction of their minister, brought here for that purpose. The bearer of this letter and his companions, most of them your subjects, will testify to my conduct at my last hour. It remains for me to beg Your Most Christian Majesty, my brother-in-law and old ally, who have always protested your love for me, to give proof now of your goodness on all these points: firstly by charity, in paying my unfortunate servants the wages due them — this is a burden on my conscience that only you can relieve: further, by having prayers offered to God for a queen who has borne the title Most Christian, and who dies a Catholic, stripped of all her possessions. As for my son, I commend him to you in so far as he deserves, for I cannot answer for him. I have taken the liberty of sending you two precious stones, talismans against illness, trusting that you will enjoy good health and a long and happy life. Accept them from your loving sister-in-law, who, as she dies, bears witness of her warm feeling for you. Again I commend my servants to you. Give instructions, if it please you, that for my soul's sake part of what you owe me should be paid, and that for the sake of Jesus Christ, to whom I shall pray for you tomorrow as I die, I be left enough to found a memorial mass and give the customary alms.

Wednesday, at two in the morning.

Your most loving and most true sister.

MARY R

To the Most Christian King, my brother and old ally.

John Knox (1512?-72)

For his pulpit deliveries and rhetorical style of writing John Knox was well described as 'the thundering Scot'. His pamphlet, The First Blast of the Trumpet against the Monstrous Regiment of Women *(meaning that the rule of women was unnatural), is in this vein. But Knox's style responded to the situation in which he found himself. After the publication of* The First Blast, *Elizabeth, Queen of England, took him to task. Knox wilted, and in his reply to the Queen's accusations he turns politician, seeking to limit the damage his characteristic outburst has done to the relationship.*

7. An apology for The Blast

To Elizabeth, Queen of England   *Edinburgh 1559*

. . . As your Grace's displeasure against me, most unjustlie conceaved, hath beene, and is to my wretched hart a burthein greevous, and almost intollerabill; so is the testimonie of a cleene conscience to me a stay and uphold, that in desperation I sink not, how vehement that ever the temptation appear: for in Goddis presence, my conscience beareth me record, that maliciouslie nor of purpose I never offended your Grace, nor your realme; and, therefore, howsoever I be judged of man, I am assured to be absolved by Him who onelie knoweth the secreates of hartes. I cannot denie the writting of a booke against the usurped Authoritie and unjust Regiment of Women; neyther yit am I mynded to retreate or to call backe anie principall point, or propositioun of the sam, till truthe and veritie doe farther appear. Bot why, that eyther your Grace, eyther anie such as unfainedlie favour the libertie of England, sould be offended at the author of suche a worke, I can perceave no just occasioun: For, first, my booke tuichest not your Grace's person in especiall, neyther yit is it prejudiciall to anie libertie of the realme, if the time and my writing be indifferentlie considered. How could I be enemie to your Grace's person, for deliverance quhairof I did more study, and interprised farther, than anie of those that now accuse me? And, as concerning your Regiment, how could I, or can I, envy that which most I have thristed, and the which (als oblivion will suffer) I render thanks unfainedlie unto God? That is, it hath pleased Him of his eternall goodnes to exalt your head there (who sometime was in danger), to the manifestatioun of his glorie, and extirpatioun of idolatrie?

. . . God is witnesse, that unfainedlie I both love and reverence your Grace; yea, I pray that your raigne may be long, prosperous, and quiet; and that for the quietnes which Christ's members, before persecuted, have receaved under you . . .

8. Epistle to a mother-in-law

Knox was evidently on the defensive in the letter to Queen Elizabeth, but in his letters to his mother-in-law, Mrs Bowes, his guard is down and we see the much less confident private man. The life-long friendship began when he was thirty-seven and she was over fifty. In 1555 Knox married her fifth daughter, Marjorie. Mrs Bowes had fifteen children. The extract is from the first letter to her.

To Mrs Elizabeth Bowes　　　　　　　　　　　*London 23 June 1553*

. . . Since the first day that it pleasit the providence of God to bring yow and me in familiaritie, I have alwayis delytit in your company; and when labouris wald permit, ye knaw I have not spairit houris to talk and commune with yow, the frute whairof I did not than fullie understand nor perceave. But now absent, and so absent that by corporall presence nather of us can resave comfort of uther, I call to mynd how that oftymes when, with dolouris hartis, we haif begun our talking, God hath send greit comfort unto baithe, whilk now for my awn part I commounlie want. The expositioun of your trubillis, and acknawledging of your infirmitie, war first unto me a verie mirrour and glass whairin I beheld my self sa rychtlie payntit furth, that nathing culd be mair evident to my awn eis. And than, the searching of the Scriptures for Godis sueit promissis, and for his mercies frelie givin unto miserable offenderis, (for his nature delyteth to schew mercie whair maist miserie ringeth,) the collectioun and applying of Godis mercies, I say, wer unto me as the breaking and handilling with my awn handis of the maist sueit and delectabill ungementis, whairof I culd not but receave sum comfort be thair naturall sueit odouris.

But now, albeit I never lack the presence and plane image of my awn wreachit infirmitie, yit seing syn sa manifestlie abound in al estaitis, I am compellit to thounder out the threattnyngis of God aganis obstinat rebellaris; in doing whairof (albeit as God knaweth I am no malicious nor obstinat synner) I sumtymes am woundit, knawing my self criminall and giltie in many, yea in all, (malicious obstinacie laid asyd,) thingis that in utheris I reprehend. Judge not, Mother, that I wrait theis thingis debassing my self uther wayis than I am; na, I am wors than my pen can express. In bodie ye think I am no adulterer; let sa be, but the hart is infectit with foull lustis, and will lust, albeit I lament never sa mekill. Externallie I commit na idolatrie; but my wickit hart luffeth the self, and can not be refranit fra vane imaginationis, yea, not fra sic as wer the fountane of all idolatrie. I am na man-killer with my handis; but I help not my nedie brother sa liberallie as I may and aucht. I steill not hors, money, nor claithis fra my nychtbour; but that small portioun of warldlie substance I bestow not sa rychtlie as his halie law requyreth. I beir na fals witnes aganis my nychtbour in judgement, or utherwayis befor men; but I speik not the treuth of God sa boldlie as it becumeth his trew messinger to do. And thus in conclusioun, thair is na vyce repugnyng to Godis halie will, expressit in his law, whairwith my hart is not infectit.

Ninian Winzet (c. 1518-92)

The scholar, Ninian Winzet, was dismissed from his post of Master at the Grammar School, Linlithgow (c.1551) for publishing criticisms of the reformed faith. He fled to the continent, first to Antwerp, and finally to Germany, where he became Abbot of Ratisbon. His chief target was John Knox. He attacked him not only for his theology, but also for his tendency to anglicise his native Scots in his writings.

9. A great impediment

To John Knox   *Antwerp 27 October 1563*

It appears to me, Brother, that ye haif sum grete impediment, quhareby ye ar stoppit to keip promise tueching your anssuering to this our tractate, eftir sa lang advisement. Gif ye persave your fall*, *Quid tardas converti ad Dominum?*** Bot gif my handwritt peradventuir hes nocht bene sa legible as ye wald, please resave fra this beirar the samin mater now mair legible. Gif ye, throw curiositie of novationis, hes forget our auld plane Scottis quhilk your mother lerit you, in tymes cuming I sall wryte to you my mynd in Latin, for I am nocht acquyintit with your Southeroun . . .

---

*   *duty*   ** *Why do you hesitate to turn to the Lord?*

James VI (1566-1625)

The following letters were written by James shortly after he had received the news on 23 February 1587 of the execution of his mother, Queen Mary. The first is a reply to a letter from Queen Elizabeth of England in which she sought to deny personal responsibility. James expresses disapproval without going so far as to jeopardise his chances of succeeding to the English throne. The second, summoning a meeting of the Estates, is more outspoken. The third, to his Secretary, about his solitary withdrawal from the Court, may perhaps reflect his private grief.

10. 'Yon unhappy fact'

To Queen Elizabeth of England   *late February 1587*

Madame and dearest sister,

Whereas by your letter and bearer Robert Carey, your servant and ambassador, ye purge yourself of yon unhappy fact, as on the one part considering your rank, sex, consanguinity, and long professed goodwill to the defunct, together with your many and solemn attestations of your innocency, I dare not wrong you so far as not to judge honourably of your unspotted part therein. So on the other side, I wish that your honourable behaviour in all times hereafter may fully persuade the whole world of the same. And as for my part I look that ye will give me at this time such a full satisfaction in all respects as shall be a mean to strengthen and unite this isle, establish and maintain the true religion, and oblige me to be, as of before I was, your most *loving and dearest brother.*

JR

This bearer hath somewhat to inform you of in my name, whom I need not desire you to credit for ye know I love him.

11. 'Dolorous and cruel death'

To James Stewart, Earl of Moray   *Dalkeith 15 March 1587*

Right trusty cousin, we greet you well.

The strait wherein this recent news of the Queen our mother's most dolorous and cruel death has cassin us, both in honour and estate being the greatest that befell us ever since our nativity, and wherein we have greatest need of the assistance and advice of our nobility and Estates to take such resolution as may be to the preservation of God's true religion, our honour, and the quietness of our estate, we have therefore thought meet to assemble our Estates at Edinburgh, upon the 20th day of April next, and to the same effect will desire you most affectuislie that in any ways ye fail not to be present with us the said day and place, as ye will testify unto us your willing mind to do us service and will deserve therefore our special thanks.

Thus we commit you to God, from Dalkeith, the xv day of March, 1587.

JAMES R

We look that ye will come accompanied with 24 persons allanerlie, according to our proclamation.

12. 'My pilgrimage'

To Sir John Maitland   *early 1587*

. . . Because I am making now to my pilgrimage, I must remember you that is resident to garr keep good order and watch in this town during my absence and have good intelligence of any folk is steiring be south oure hande. As for me, I will flit every two or three days anis as I told you yestereen. Retain all folks by public or pri[vate] command from coming to trouble me. And garr them await upon my coming every two or three days anis to this town for doing of business. As for the horsemen, let them wait on in some places near me, but forbid them to remain directly with me. I recommend to your memory and diligence all my affairs, especially remember the stay of Gray where he is.

JAMES R

☆   ☆   ☆

The Covenanters

Alexander Leslie (c. 1580-1661)

Alexander Leslie trained as a soldier under Gustavus Adolphus, and served in many campaigns in Europe with him. In 1632 he assisted the king at the taking of Frankfurt. Later that year he shared in the victory of Lutzen, in which battle Gustavus Adolphus was killed. Leslie was a reticent Scot, not given to expressing emotion, but in the letter he wrote to the Marquis of Hamilton, who joined with Leslie in levying troops for the Swedish service, his grief is plain. That victory could in no way compensate for the loss of a friend, nor for the greater loss to the Protestant cause. In 1636 Leslie was made a field marshal in the Swedish army. In 1642 he was made the first Earl of Leven.

13. The death of Gustavus Adolphus

To the Marquis of Hamilton   *Stade 26 November 1632*

I have thought it expedient to mak your Excellencie this sad narration of the lamentable death of our most valarouse and worthie chiftaine, who in the sixt (16th) of November, did end the constant course of all his glorious victories with his happie lyffe, for his Majestie went to farre on with a regiment of Smolandis horsemen, who did not second him so well as they showld, at the which instant ther came so thick and darke a mist, that his owin folkis did lose him, and he being seperate from his owin amongst his foes, his left arme was shote in two, after the which whill he was lying, one asked him, whate he was, he answeared, King of Sweddin, wherupon his enemies that did compasse him thought to have carried him away; but in the mean while, his own folkis comeing on, striveing in great furie to vindicate his Majestie out of ther handis, when they saw that they most quite him againe, he that before asked what he was, shote him through the heade; and so did put ane end to his dayes, the fame of whose valoure and love to the good cause sal nevir end. When his corpes were inbalmed ther waes found in them fyve shottes and nyne woundis, so ar we to our unspeakable griefe deprived of the best and most valorouse commander that evir any soldiours hade, and the church of God with hir good cause of the best instrument under God . . .

your Excellencies faithfull servant till death

A. Leslie

Robert Baillie (1599-1662)

In 1638 Leslie returned to Scotland to command the army of the Covenant. In 1639 Robert Baillie was chaplain of that army at Duns Law, where he had the opportunity to observe Leslie. The letter to his cousin, The Rev. William Spang, minister of a Scots congregation at Campvere in Holland, shows Baillie's concern that Leslie should make a favourable impression on the Scottish nobles.

14. 'That old, little, crooked souldier'

To William Spang   *28 September 1639*

. . . We were feared that emulation among our Nobles might have done harme, when they should be mett in the fields; bot such was the wisdome and authoritie of that old, little, crooked souldier, that all, with ane incredible submission, from the beginning to the end, gave over themselves to be guided by him, as if he had been Great Solyman. Certainlie, the obedience of our Nobles to that man's advyces was as great as their forbears wont to be to their King's commands; yet that was the man's understanding of our Scotts humours, that gave out, not onlie to the nobles bot to verie mean gentlemen, his directions in a verie homelie and simple forme, as if they had been bot the advyces of their neighbour and companion; for as he rightlie observed, a difference would be used in commanding sojours of fortune and sojours voluntars, of which kinde the most part of our camp did stand . . .

Samuel Rutherford (1600-61)

Samuel Rutherford was a Covenanting minister who refused to accept the rule of bishops, as a consequence of which he was removed from his ministry at Anwoth. The success of the Covenanters restored him to his parish, from where he went to St Andrews to become Professor of Divinity at St Mary's College and, in 1651, Principal. Despite Rutherford's antipathy to the ritual and ceremony of the Episcopal church, his letters abound in imagery which flows uninhibited from his pen.

In this letter he comforts and exhorts John Fenwicke, an English puritan, who had associated himself with the Covenanters at Duns Law in 1639 where the Covenanting army faced King Charles's army, but did not engage in battle.

15. 'The breath of faith'

To John Fenwicke   *St Andrews 13 February 1640*

Much honoured and dear friend,

Grace, mercy and peace be to you . . .

Oh if I could help you, and if I could be master-conveener to gather an earth-full and an heaven-full of tongues dipped and steeped in my Lord's well of love or his wine of love, even tongues drunken with his love, to raise a song of praises to him betwixt the east and west end and furthest points of the broad heavens! If I were in your case (as alas! my dry and dead heart is not now in that garden) I would borrow leave to come and stand upon the banks and coasts of that sea of love and be a feasted soul to see love's fair tide, free love's high and lofty waves, each of them higher than ten earths, flowing in upon pieces of lost clay. O welcome, welcome, great sea! O if I had as much love for wideness and breadth as twenty outmost shells and spheres of the heaven of heavens, that I might receive in a little flood of his free love! Come, come, dear friend, and be pained that the King's wine cellar of freelove and his banquetting house (O so wide, so stately! O so God-like, so glory-like!) should be so abundant, so overflowing, and your shallow vessel so little to take in some part of that love. But since it cannot come in you for want of room, enter your self in this sea of love, and breath under these waters and die of love and live as one dead and drowned of this love.

But why doe ye complain of waters going over your soul and that the smoke of terrors of a wrathfull Lord doeth almost suffocate you and bring you to death's brink? . . .

Either now or never let God work. Ye had never since ye was a man such a fair field for faith, for a painted hell and an apprehension of wrath in your Father is faith's opportunity to try what strength is in it. Now give God as large a measure of charity as ye have of sorrow. Now see faith to be faith indeed if ye can make your grave betwixt Christ's feet and say, 'Though he should slay me, I will trust in him. His beleeved love shall be my winding-sheet and all my grave-cloaths. I shall roll and sowe in my soul, my slain soul, in that web, his sweet and free love. And let him write upon my grave, "Here lieth a beleeving dead man, breathing out and making an hole in death's broad side, and the breath of faith cometh forth through the hole . . ." '

Janet Lintoun (fl. 1685)

Janet Lintoun was imprisoned in Dunnottar Castle in 1685 on account of her adherence to the faith of the Covenanters. She wrote to her husband from prison.

16. The faith of a Covenanter

To my husband   *Dunnottar Castle*

My dear heart, bless the Lord on my behalf that ever it should hav pleased such a holy God to have looked upon such an unworthy sinner as I am, or to hav honoured the like of me to suffer anay thing for his name's saik, or bear his cross in a day when ther is so few longing to wear his livery . . . The Lord has made all things easy to me and he has been soe kind to my soul somtyms since I came to prison, that I counted all things nothing in comparison of him . . . *Now*, my dear, ye are dear, indeed, to me, bot not soe dear as Christ . . . My love, I ken not what the Lord will doe with me; bot I think I will see you although I should be banished out of my nativ land. Although enemies have separat our bodies, they shall never separat my love from you . . .

☆　☆　☆

Michael Young (fl. 1654)

Michael Young was tutor to the two eldest sons of William Kerr, the third Earl of Lothian. By the mid-seventeenth century travel was deemed an important aspect of a gentleman's education. Young left Montrose for the Netherlands on 20 March 1651 with his two charges, Lord Kerr, aged 15 and Sir William, aged 12. Three years later, Young reports on the progress of his students.

17. The education of Scottish gentlemen

To Lord Lothian   *Saumur January 1654*

. . . In the study of history and geography they have made some progress, and in these they go on (having had a little beginning of logic and philosophy at Leiden) when their other exercises permit. In the morning from 7 till 8, besides the scriptures which they read in French and in English, they read a little for the French language in books proper for that use, either a romance or the grammar. From 8 till 9 they fence. After breakfast they dance till half-eleven; and these exercises they do with as great commendation (to say no more) as any that practise with them. At half-eleven cometh a master for the French, that they may learn the true accent so far as possible. A little after eleven cometh the lute master for my Lord (for he desireth to learn a little upon it) till 12. At that time Sir William writeth. After dinner Sir William learneth upon the guitar till 2 o'clock. From 2 till 3 they have a master for designing, in which they both profit very well, but Sir William's inclination runneth most that way — as my Lord's doth to instrumental music. From 3 till 4 we had bespoken a master for singing and the great viol but he is for present sick. After 4 o'clock they practise in one thing or another prescribed by their masters; and being now forbidden the tennis (though they never used it but very soberly) we walk in the fields. At night they go on in Plutarch or Cluvier for geography and history . . . The master of the mathematics who was here being lately dead, there is as yet none come in his place. So soon as any cometh they are to follow that study. There is also here an occasion for riding, but the horses are altogether naught.

Sir Thomas Urquhart of Cromarty (1611-60)

Sir Thomas Urquhart is famed especially for his translation of Rabelais, in which he easily outdoes the original in numbers of adjectives per noun by many, the translation being nearly twice as long as the original. Like the poet Dunbar, he delighted in extravagant language and ideas; he traced his pedigree back to Adam and included the Queen of Sheba in the list. He fought against the Covenanters and was forced to flee to England, then later supported the cause of Charles II. He gloried in the idea of himself as duellist. In the letter he challenges his cousin for 'unnatural and cannibillyk proceedings'. It was reported that he died of 'an excessive fit of laughter' on hearing of Charles II's restoration to the throne.

18. Fair warning

To the Laird of Cromartie   *Midlebrugh 1 July 1658*

... Iff it prove uther wayes and that you altogither slight the honorable motiones proposed by me for the saving off your own reputation then have I in that caise given ordor to breake up a certaine box ... and out of It to take the double off this letter that copies theiroff may be dispersed over all whole the kingdome off Scotland with ane incitement to Scullions, hogge rubbers, kenell brakers and all others off the meanist sorte of rascallitie, to spit in your face, kicke you in the breach, to tred on your mushtashes, as also to all those that know yow to curse yow with all the execrations mentioned in the Psalmes off David and uther prophets in the old testament and with all to hold them in littell better reputatione nor yor selfe that will keipe any kynd off freindly correspondence with yow Iff yow thinke that this will prove a very thraldome and troublsum bondage to yow for that from thence furth no honest man will offer to eat drinke or converse with yow nor any above the degre of a hangmans varlet to serve yow nor any tennent of yours to pey yow the value off halfe ane penny with out a hunderethe thousand curses to atendit ...

    Souldiers of als good birthe as yow and off greather worthe doe very frouardly hazard ther lives every day all most for a smaler pay and less pittance and shall yow shrinke for the gaining of ane ancient and considerable estaite to quhich with out my consent yow have no right at all to adventure a personall conflict for the space of one halfe houre yow are unworthy of the name of a man iff yow did, and fitter to be called ane *amphibian animall*, that is, of a mixed nature, betwein the oule and the asse, then a rationall creature Nevertheless (suspending my Judgement of yor Cowardise untill I hear either off or from yow In quhat may concerne your answer heirto) I doe promise quhen all lets shall be removed after the manner above specified that then I will not only forgive quhat yow have done unto me, but withall Subscrive my selfe

Midlebrugh the i off July, 1658

Youer Loving and affectionat freind and Cosen

SIR THOMAS URQUHART

Alexander Munro (fl. 1691)

Alexander Munro, Professor at St Andrews University at the end of the seventeenth century, was a golf enthusiast. Though The Society of St. Andrews Golfers was not founded until 1754 — it became the Royal and Ancient in 1834 — the Professor could refer to St Andrews as 'the metropolis of Golfing' in 1691. The letter accompanied a gift of clubs and balls to John Mackenzie of Delvine, whose two sons were to be students at St Andrews.

19. 'The metropolis of Golfing'

To John Mackenzie   *University of St Andrews 1691*

. . . Receive from the bearer, our post, ane sett of Golfe-clubs consisting of three, viz. an play club, ane scraper, and ane tin fac'd club. I might have made the set to consist of more, but I know not your play, and if you stand in need of more, I think you should call for them from me. Tho I know you may be served there, yet I presumed that such a present from this place, the metropolis of Golfing, may not be unsuitable for these fields, especially when it's come from a friend. Upon the same consideration I have also sent you ane dozen of Golfe balls which receive with the clubs. I am told they are good, but that will prove according to your play and the fields. If the size do not suite, were you so free with me I would mend it with the next . . .

Archibald Pitcairne (1652-1713)

Pitcairne was one of the most celebrated medical doctors of his day in the whole of Europe, for a time Professor of Physic at the University of Leyden and one of the founders of the College of Physicians in Edinburgh. He was also an accomplished Latin poet and a lively satirist in Scots, a Scots European humanist of the old school, episcopalian, Jacobite and a supporter of Scottish independence and the alliance with France. At his death his library was bought by Peter the Great and it still survives in Leningrad.

The first of these letters is a joke at the expense of the Gregories, a remarkable family who (like the Munros in Edinburgh) supplied professors to several universities for generation after generation. The second is a protest against one of the consequences of the Union, a tendency for government patronage to give important posts in Scotland to men from south of the Border.

20. 'Murder, adulterie &c.'

To the Earl of Mar,
Principal Secretary of State   *16 May 1706*

My Lord,

    I bless myself That I have nothing to write about Yo^r Lady's health or yours. I hear with great satisfaction Yee are both in good health. Next to Yo^r Lordships and The Countesses good health, I presume to wish Your Lordship may be pleas'd to mind the good education of our gentrie. I know no better occasion for Yo^r Lo/ to shew your power and good will to the people of Scotland Than what now presents itself. The rascal Liddel that was Professor in Mathematics at Aberdeen is depos'd for murder, adulterie &c. The fund is 50 lib st. a year. No mortal is able to stand against Dr Bower, if Your Lo/ will be pleas'd to patronize him. I know there is a child to be set up against him.

    I humblie beg Your Lo/ wold consider That our education is more than ruin'd already by raw, ignorant boys; And that it makes not one sufficient for a Mathematical Professor by having the sirname of Gregorie. Dr Gregorie is my worthie friend, but I hate monopolies.

    I am
        Your Lo/s
            most oblidged and most
                humble servant   A PITCAIRNE

My Lord, I can assure Yo^r Lo/ yee can not doe a thing worthier of Yo^r self and character than to prefer Th. Bower. I speak freelie, for I'm half fou.

To the Earl of Mar   *10 February 1708*

Most noble Patron,

    I presum'd to recommend Your owne Mathematical Professor Mr Charles Gregorie of St Andrews. That Colledge will not receive him, and laughs at her Majesties patent. What to doe I know not.

    But, My Lord, there is a thing in Your Lordship's power,, independentlie of Council or presbyterie, for our friend James Hamilton. It is a post no man in the nation (I mean now the Island) can behave so well in as he can. I beg Yo^r Lordship may be forward in it, least some insignificant Southerne put in for it. Our Surgeons are abler far than our neighbours, And it is just wee should be serv'd by the best of our owne. Yo^r Lo/s

A Pitcairne

Andrew Fletcher of Saltoun (1653-1716) and his nephew

Known from his own lifetime simply as 'The Patriot', Fletcher was a leading opponent of the Treaty of Union in the session of the Scottish parliament from 1703 to 1707. He was widely respected even by his political opponents for his courage, integrity and the brilliance and clarity of his political thought. He was, for example, much in advance of his time in advocating a European system of decentralised autonomy combined with co-operation for trade and defence. Unfortunately, his private papers have mostly disappeared and few of his letters have survived. Perhaps they were sent to Rousseau who promised Boswell that he would write a biography.

22. A prisoner in Stirling Castle

When there was a scare of a Jacobite invasion from France in 1708, the Privy Council in London ordered the arrest of a number of people in Scotland. They included Fletcher who was certainly no Jacobite, but this does not seem to have dampened his spirits.

To the Earl of Mar   *Stirling Castle 14 April 1708*

My Lord:

    Your friendship shows itself by effects not words. My Lady Mar has put herself to so much trouble about me as gives me more than my confinement. But my greatest mortification was from the civilitys I received from Collonel Ariskin to whom of late I never showed common ones. All that I could say for myself was that my prejudices were never personal. You see what uneasyness one falls under by imprisonment, when even kind things done him turne to be of a different nature, especialy to a man who sees himself in no capacity to returne them. You may tell my Lord Colvin we are not locked up here at night, and that we drank all yesternight of the Collonel's good wine and continued till this morning, that he can find no such company in Scotland, and that for his excuse we shall perswade the Collonel to say that he is confined. I am with great sense of your obligations, my Lord, your most humble servant,

FLETCHER

23. Fletcher's last letter

When the Treaty of Union was finally approved by the Parliament in Edinburgh in 1707, Fletcher is said to have left with the remark that Scotland 'was now fit only for the slaves who had sold it'. It is clear from his letters, however, that his concern for his country moved him to the end. In September 1716, he fell ill when he was travelling in France, and he died on the 15th in London on his way home. This is his last letter.

To his brother, Henry   *September 1716*

. . . My recovery being not only uncertain but almost desperate I thought fit whatever might happen to send you this. I design to make no formal will seeing what I have will naturally go to you, I only desire that Two Hundred Pounds sterling value may be employed in relieving the most necessitous poor Scots prisoners or others who are rendered miserable by the late Rebellion. I have desired your son to bestow in this Town a third or fourth part of the forsaid soume to the said use in the most charitable way he can. I likewise for the love and favour I bear to Mr Alexander Cunningham to whom I have been much obliged and from whom I have received many kind services these many years, and to whom your Son has been much obliged and may still be more; for these reasons I desire you would pay to him at Martinmass nixt one Hundred Pound sterling. I have left no other paper than this, having sufficient confidence that you will not neglect to perform this my request.

A. FLETCHER

As a postscript, the following is part of a letter from his nephew, also called Andrew Fletcher, who was with him when he died.

24. 'My poor Countrey'

To Henry Fletcher   *London 15 September 1716*
                                              at past 10 o'clock

. . . My Uncle continues still to grow weaker and weaker, he has had two convulsive fits this day, in both which we were affraid that he should have expired. Dr Arbuthnott does not believe its possible he can live many hours. Some days ago I asked him if he would see Doctor Clark, minister of our paroch Church St James's, with whom I was told he was well acquaint and for whom he had a great kindness, but he shifted it, I was very sorry for it because it might give some people occasion to make reflections but yesterday to my great satisfaction about 4 o'clock in the afternoon he called upon Mr Cunningham, Mrs Duras, our landlady, his servant and the Nurse, and upon me, and desired us to come near that he had something that was very serious to tell us and called for some water to wash his mouth that we might understand what he said the better; lest (says he) I turn afterwards so weak as not be able to speak; I take all of you to witness that I dye in the believe of the only true God and in hopes to be saved by the merites of Jesus Christ in whom alone I have confidence. Then he stopped a little, and Mr Cunningham beginning to retire thinking he had done, he says Pray, Mr Cunningham, stay, I hadn't done, then he said, And I leave my blessing to my Brother, his Lady and to all their Children, and recommend my spirit to my God; after he called for me and gave me his blessing and spoke some things none of us could understand. I thought he said I forgive everybody I wish everybody may forgive me; about a quarter of an hour thereafter he said distincly, Lord have mercy on my poor Countrey that is so barbarously oppressed . . .

I must say I always esteemed him highly but now I admire him, and should be more ambitious of his Constancy in going out of the world than the Reputation he had while he has been in it. If it had pleased God to allow him have come home I have reason to know that he would have lived with us all in the greatest love and affection imaginable which I am sure is the greatest . . . *freinds can have in this side of . . .*

* Paper torn in the original

The Parliamentary Union of 1707

The proposals for the Union of the two Parliaments were strongly opposed all over Scotland, but were eventually carried in the Scottish Parliament by intimidation and pressure of various kinds, especially bribery.

Duke of Argyll (1680-1743)

25. 'An offer of a reward'

The Duke of Argyll, who was with Marlborough's army in Flanders, replies to the Earl of Mar's request that he should return to Scotland to help to push the treaty through Parliament.

To Mar   *Camp at St Luis le Tere 18 July 1706*

. . . I should have receiv'd your letter before Ostend, but so it is I had it only this morning. I am extremely sorry that all my friends should desire me to doe what for aught I can as yet see I shall not be able to comply with. My Lord, it is surprising to me that my Lord Treasurer, who is a man of sense, should think of sending me up and down like a footman from one country to another without ever offering me any reward. Thier is indeed a sairtin service due from every subject to his Prince, and that I shall pay the Queen as fathfully as any body can doe; but if her ministers thinks it for her service to imploy me any forder I doe think the proposall should be attended with an offer of a reward. But I am so fare from beeing treated in this manner that I cannot obtain justice even in the army, where I doe flatter my selfe I have dun the Queen as much service, to say no more, as any body in my station. My Lord, when I have justice dun me here and am told what to expect for going to Scotland, I shall be reddy to obey my Lord Treasurer's commands. Till then I hope my friends will think it fitt I stay here, unless I have sum body put over my head; and in that cais I shall lett my Lord Marlboro give my post to sumbody, who chances to be more to his mind, which will be a very noble reward for my service and I'll goe and hear Camilla in her own country.

Earls of Seafield (1663-1730) and Glasgow (1666-1733)

26. Burn when read

Queensberry, Lord High Commissioner of the Scottish Parliament which approved the Treaty of Union, was asked by Godolphin, the English Lord Treasurer, to provide receipts for the distribution of £20,000. The following letter was all that the responsible members of the Scottish administration, the Earls of Seafield, and Glasgow, were prepared to reveal. Godolphin evidently insisted on keeping it as evidence because it remained in his family papers until it was sold to the British Museum in 1892.

To Queensberry   *Edinburgh 20 July 1707*

May it please your Grace,
You have one accompt signed by the Earle off Glasgow, how the twenty thousand pounds advanced by my Lord Treasurer was disposed off, wee would doe anything that is in our power, to procure it to be reimbursed to his Lop. and for a consider part of it, it may be done and stated upon the Equivalent. Your Grace's Equipage & dayly allowance will amount to betwixt twelve and thirteen thousand pounds and it is already stated as owing to your Grace, and that being a preferable debt to most off the debts on the civill List, my Lord Treasurer may reckon upon it, but it is impossible for us to doe more, for what was given to the Duke of Atholl, Marquis off Tweedale, Earles off Roxburgh, Marchmont, Bellcarray, Dunmore, Cromerty and singly or evenly others in small soumes, its impossible to state these soumes without discovering this haill affair to every particular person that received any part of the money, which hath been hitherto keeped secret, and its more than probable, that they would refuse to give a signatory if they were demanded of them, so the discovering of it would be of no use, unless it were to bring discredit upon the managdement off that parliament; and all that will be loosed is about seven thousand pounds, if your Grace please, you may Lay this befor my Lord Treasurer with that secrecy that this affair requires, wee are with all respect,

Ede 20 Jully,   May it please your Grace,
1707   your Graces most faithfull & most
                                    obedient humble servant.
                                                    SEAFIELD
                                                    GLASGOW
your Grace may be pleased to burn this
Letter when you have read it to my Lord Treasurer.

Earl of Mar (1675-1732)

27. 'Wearie of the Union'

The Earl of Mar had been active in promoting the Union in the Scottish Parliament; but it was not long before he, and others of his kind, regretted it.

To his brother, the Justice Clerk   *London 17 January 1711/12*

. . . We are in a harder state than you imagin. Tho' both parties be wearie of the Union, they will upon no tearmes that I can yet see quitt with the Union in a legall way. They are so wearie and abominate the elections of our peers so much that they (I apprehend) will never restore the Q[ueen] to her hability and us to our capacity without we quitt with them. If we shou'd agree to this, I'm affraid they wou'd not come near that number of our peers to be made heritablie (which is the only way they will hear of) as wou'd satisfie us, so what we can do God knows, and I wish He may direct us. To go peacablie home and rebell, as the Irishman said, is but a bad remidie, and yet it is impossible for us to lay under this hardshipe. If we saw a possibility of getting free of the Union without a civill warr we wou'd have some comfort, but that I'm affraid is impossible. They all (I mean the English) agree that the elections cannot be altred without the consent of the Scots peers (I do not mean of the sixteen only), and how that can ever be gott is more than I can tel. Here you have the desease, and I wish you could find the remidie, but that is not so easilie found as the desease is. However, 'tis impossible to give anybody a true and just vew of this affair, and to make them comprehend the difficulties in it at a distance. As to this affair of ours, there is nothing so like a Whige as a Torie and nothing so like a Torie as a Whige — a cat out of a hole and a cate in a hole.

Notwithstanding many dissapointments I have mett with in the Union, I have yet some hopes that if this of our elections were altred to both our contents, they wou'd come to treat us more like one people; but as long as they last they have such an apprehension of the acquisition of strenth the Crown gets by us, and as it were in opposition to both their parties, that they will ever treat us as enimies, Whige and Torie being alike affraid of the power of the Crown.

I must own to you that I think its possible to find out an expedient in the matter of our elections more for the intrest of our nobility and Scotland in generall, and what wou'd be thought so there if they judged impartially; but I know the bent of that country is so much for the dissolution of the Union, that they will not harken to any expedient of this kind with patience, thinking it is to confirme that which they hate; so one must be very cautious how they go into anything of this kind . . . With you I have no doubt but the dissolveing of the Union is thought to be possible and pritty easie in a Parliamentary way; but that I cannot conceave, and I fear it will be found so, and I wish our countrymen could be made understand this . . .

☆   ☆   ☆

Allan Ramsay (1684-1758)

Ramsay was a kenspeckle figure in the Edinburgh of the early eighteenth century, a man of multifarious interests and influence. From wig-making he changed to bookselling and opened a circulating library, said to be the first in Britain. He opened a theatre at a time when the Kirk was still strongly opposed to all theatre. His editions of early Scottish poetry and his own poems stimulated the vernacular revival which prepared the way for Fergusson and Burns. He was the father of the other Allan Ramsay, the portrait painter.

28. Prelude to the Porteous Riot

To Duncan Forbes of Culloden   *Edinburgh 14 April 1736*

... On the Sunday preceeding (viz) the 11th, the two condemn'd criminalls Wilson & Robertson were taken as usual by four sogers out of prison to hear their Last Sermon and wer but a few minutes in their Station in the Kirk when Wilson who was a very strong fellow took Robertson by the headbands of his Breeks and threw him out of the seat held a soger fast in each hand and one of them with his Teeth while Robertson got over & throw the pews, pushed over the Elder & Plate at the door made his escape throw the parlt Clos doun the Back Stairs got out of the Poteraw port before it was shut the mob making way & assisting him, got friends money and a swift Horse and fairly got off nae mair to be heard of or seen — this made them take a closser care of Wilson who had the best character of them all (till his foly made him seek reprisals at his own hand) which had gained him so much pity as to raise a report that a great mob would rise on his execution day to relieve him which noise put our Magestrates on their Guard and maybe made some of them unco fleyd as was evidenced by their inviting in 150 of the Regement that Lys in the Cannongate who were all drawn up in the Land Market while the criminal was conducted to the Tree by Capt Portous and a strong party of the City Guard; all was hush Psalms sung, prayers put up, for a long hour and upwards and the man hang'd with all decency & quietnes; after he was cut doun and the guards drawing up to go off some unlucky Boys threw a stone or two at the Hangman, which is very common on which the Brutal Portuos (who it seems had ordered his party to load their Guns with Ball) let drive first himself amongst the Inocent Mob and commanded his men to folow his example which quickly cleansed the street but left three men a Boy and a woman dead upon the spot besides several others wounded some of whom are dead since after this first fire he took it in his head when half up the Bow to order annother voly & killd a Taylor in a window three storys high, a young gentlewoman, & a son of Mr Mathison the Minister's and several more were dangerously wounded and all this from no more provocation than what I told before, the throwing of a Stone or two that hurt no body — believe this to be true for I was ane Eye witness and within a yard or two of being shot as I sat with some Gentlemen in a Stablers window oposite to the Galows — after this the Crazy Brute marchd with his ragamuffins to the Guard as if he had done nothing worth noticing but was not long there till the Hue & Cry rose from them that had lost friends & servants demanding Justice he was taken before the Councill where there aboundance of witnesses to fix the guilt upon him the uproar of a Mob encreased with the loudest din that ever was heard and would have torn him, council, & guard all in pieces if the Majestrates had not sent him to the Tolbooth by a strong party and told them he should be tryd for his Life which gave some satisfaction and sent them quietly home — I could have acted more descretly had I been in Portous's place. . .

29. The poet in old age

To John Smibert
Boston, New England   *Edinburgh 10 May 1736*

My dear old friend,

Your health and happiness are ever ane addition to my satisfaction. God make your life ever easy and pleasant — half a century of years have now row'd o'er my pow; yes, row'd o'er my pow, that begins now to be lyart; yet thanks to my Author, I eat, drink, and sleep as sound as I did twenty years syne; yes, I laugh heartily too, and find as many subjects to employ that faculty upon as ever: fools, fops, and knaves, grow as rank as formerly; yet here and there are to be found good and worthy men, who are an honour to human life. We have small hopes of seeing you again in our old world; then let us be virtuous, and hope to meet in heaven . . . My good auld wife is still my bedfellow; my son, Allan, has been pursuing your science since he was a dozen years auld — was with Mr Hyssing, at London, for some time, about two years ago; has been since at home, painting here like a Raphael — sets out for the seat of the Beast, beyond the Alps, within a month hence — to be away about two years . . . I'm

sweer to part with him, but canna stem the current which flows
from the advice of his patrons, and his own inclinations . . . I have
three daughters, one of 17, one of 16, one of 12 years old, and no
walydragle among them, all fine girls. These six or seven years past I
have not wrote a line of poetry; I e'en gave o'er in good time, before
the coolness of fancy that attends advanced years should make me
risk the reputation I had acquired.

> Frae twenty-five to five-and-forty
> My Muse was nowther sweer nor dorty;
> My Pegasus wad break his tether;
> E'en at the shakking of a feather,
> And through ideas scour like drift,
> Streaking his wings up to the lift,
> Then, then my saul was in a low,
> That gart my numbers safely row,
> But eild and judgment gin to say,
> Let be your sangs, and learn to pray.

I am, Sir, your friend and servant,

ALLAN RAMSAY

30. 'A braw new House' for the players

To Sir Alexander Dick
Rainbow Coffee House, London   *Edinburgh 28 June 1737*

Dear Doctor,

Why have you been so unkind as never to honour me with a line
since you came to Brittain. I would have paid my respects sooner
but was in hopes to have got all your Italian cracks sooner by word
of mouth. Deil tak a' Qurks of Law, say I that keeps you sae lang
frae Cross-de-orphine Hill and friends that lang to see ye, I have
been in pain for my poor Allan since ye left him, whae has he now
to converse with but un ho' saes the seed of antichrist; after he has
laid by his pencill I see him dandering about lonely, with a great
length of under lip, among the antique ruins, striving to divert his
melancholy while he thinks on his separation from his good ffriend.
I begin already to weary sair and wish for a Quick cerculation (of)
the ensuing year O Doctor ye dinna ken what it is to be a father of
ane only that has merit — but ther is a good time coming.
    We of Edr have been (as many of us think) sore handled about
the Raskall Porteous which makes ane unervasall grumble, but I am

particularly attacked by a certain act against our publick Theatres having a set of players under my management I should be sory to see them driven to Beggary now, when I had last year got a braw new House for them.

Soon as this comes to hand get the act if printed or an exact coppy of it in manuscript and send it to me with a short hint of the generall opinion about it if a licence from the Ld Chamberlane can be had and the method of procuring it, or if the act puts it out of his power to grant one; there is likewise a new Play called the Projectors please if it be not too troublesome, to get two covers from some parliament man, to case it in and send it to me — Happy the man that can live independant on his ain tho small income and frae the leeside of that little Bield wrapt in his virtue can look smiling on the contentions of the great and little vulgar meditating all the arts of throatcutting.

For as much as our honest Provost Wilson* was slighted yet at this present writing 5 o'clock tusday afternoon he dines at John Steel's with great numbers of his friends gone to meet and welcome him and the musick Bells are Playing exterordinary for Joy of his return.

God preserve you in health and chearfullness and send you soon hame my wife has her humble respects to you.

Command Sir yr humble Servt

ALLAN RAMSAY

*He had been summoned to London, deposed and disqualified, as a punishment for the Porteous Riot.

☆ ☆ ☆

The Forty-five

John Murray (1715-77)

John Murray of Broughton, son of a Peeblesshire laird, visited Rome in 1741 where he met Prince Charles Edward Stuart. He became a friend and later his secretary during the Jacobite rising of 1745-46. He immediately admired the Prince and described him in a letter to his sister.

31. Bonnie Prince Charlie at twenty-one

1741

. . . Charles Edward . . . is tall above common stature, his limbs are caste in the most exact mould, his complexion has in it somewhat of an uncommon delicacy; all his features are perfectly regular and well turned, and his eyes the finest I ever saw. But that which shines most in him, and renders him without exception the most surprisingly handsome person of the age, is the dignity that accompanies his every gesture; there is such an unspeakable majesty diffused through his whole mien as it is impossible to have any idea without seeing . . .

Charles Edward Stuart (1720-88)

Charles Edward Stuart, the Young Pretender, landed on Eriskay on 12th July 1745 with a view to restoring the crown of the United Kingdom to the Stuart line. On account of his failure to bring a force from France with him, and the doubt as to whether without it the clans would rise, he was advised to return to France. He refused the advice. From Perth he wrote to his father in Rome.

33

To James Francis (the Old Pretender)   *Perth 10 September 1745*

Sir,

Since my landing everything has succeeded to my wishes. It has pleased God to prosper me hitherto even beyond my expectations. I have got together 1300 men, and am promised more brave, determined men who are resolved to die or conquer with me. The enemy marched a body of regular troops to attack me; but when they came near they chang'd their mind, and, by taking a different rout, and making forced marches, have escaped to the north, to the great disappointment of my Highlanders. But I am not at all sorry for it. I shall have the greater glory in beating them when they are more numerous and supported by their dragoons.

I have occasion every day to reflect on your Majesty's last words to me — That I should find power, if tempered with justice and clemency, an easy thing to myself and not greivous to those under me. 'Tis owing to the observance of this rule, and to my conformity to the customs of the people, that I have got their hearts to a degree not to be easily conceived by those who do not see it. One who observes the discipline I have established would take my little army to be a body of pick'd veterans, and to see the love and harmony that reigns amongst us he could be apt to look upon it as a large well-ordered family in which every one loves another better than himself.

I keep my health better in these wild mountains than I used to do in the Campagnie Felice, and sleep sounder lying on the ground that I used to do in the palaces at Rome . . .

Mrs Anne Dott (fl. 1746)

September 1745 was a month of triumph for the Prince. He had captured Edinburgh with little resistance and Sir John Cope had been routed at the Battle of Prestonpans. To Mrs Anne Dott at that time 'Bliss was it to be alive', or so she conveyed in her letter of admiration to her friend in Edinburgh, Mrs Jennet Wilson at the head of Nedhereys Wynd.

33. 'Such a Loving Prince'

To Mrs Jennett Wilson   *September 1745*

Dear Madam,
I have the Pleasure to wish you much joy in your New Prince, and I
could wish all my heart to be sharing with you of that Happiness
which I presume to think you are in. Who would not be transported
with the Sight of such a Loving Prince, and seeing him sway his
Sceptre with such Power and at the same time mingled with Love
even to his Usurper's Subjects and make his Enemys subdue under
him and fly before him as pursued by the hand of Justice.
. . . I am not such a Whigg as you always persuaded me, for nothing
could give me more pleasure than to see this Valiant Prince plac'd
upon the Throne of his Ancestors: for I think as he is running the
Danger he should have the Reward. Now Madam I engage myself;
with you drinking his happy restoration, the thing which I have
often heard you wish for, but as I am unfit for speaking on such a
subject for it requires to be put in a more polite and fine stile, I end
this scrole and begs you will forgive me and I ask the favour you
will write me soon and your News. Mrs. Heres and Mrs. Frazer join
with me in their Complemts to you and Sisters and mine to the
Misses, and I am Madam in sincerity your Obedient Humble
Servant.

ANNE DOTT

Writer Unknown

*The events which gave happiness to Mrs Dott gave only foreboding to a writer
who witheld her (or his) signature to a letter, unaffected by the charisma of the
Prince, and which saw in prospect civil strife and suffering.*

34. A 'publick calamity'

To Miss Barclay at Edinburgh   *1 November 1745*

My Dr Peggie:
We had yours last week which was very acceptable. It is all we can
get of our friends at present and no small comfort it is in our
situation who are always so much afraid of what may happen and at

the same time so ignorant. We are much surprised your folk know so little of one another and I think in times of publick calamity friends shou'd be much with their endeavours to soften the present Evil and alleviate the fears for the future as much as possible. Ah, Peggie, what think you will become of all this? Our present prospect is extremely dismal — to be sure there must be a date of bloodshed and probably at the very gates of Edinr. War at any rate is terrible but a civil war a hundred times more so than any other. I'm glad to hear Lord G. is still beyond seas. Write me if Colonel Muir or Sandy be in the Army, that is coming down or Sandie Dunlop. I hope Roby Elliot is still in France. We hear the Highland army intends to march southward. I sincerely wish it may be so that the scene of Action may be a little removed. Let me know what your papa is doing all this time, I dare say he will have a very sore heart. I'm sorry for the domestick change it has occasioned you, but I hope it shall not continue. Write me of the Kelburn family. I hear Patie is in Scotland. Dear Pegie adieu, I am going next week to Caldwell if you can forward it, I beg you will.

The Rev. R.P. (fl. 1745)

The Rev. R.P.'s letter puts a different gloss on the presence of the Prince in Scotland, who is to R.P. 'the Pretr' and of little interest to him. He turns to his advantage the demand for a reason for his journey, which allows him to indicate his vocation with self-satisfaction.

35. 'Din'd plentifully at North Ferry'

To Professor George Stuart
at Edinburgh   *Aberdeen 4 November 1745*

Dr Friend;
There is so little entertaining in a journey from E to A that you may spare yourself the trouble of reading till you come to the two three last lines of this letter, the sum total being that I arrived here on Saturday night safely. Wednesday forenoon mounted stop'd on Cramon Bridge. Questions from whence, who are you? Where going from Edinr? You may see my Caracter in my Dress, I am going about the Dutys of my Office — He is certainly a Minister — Sir, you may pass when you please. But whence are you two other Gentlemen etc? I found my Band was of use not only to myself but to my two companions who were dismissed readily. At twelve was

happily conducted on board the Happy Jannett and happily dismissed with a volley from all her guns. I had more joy in thinking these were innocent blasts and could not hurt our boat than if they had been discharged in honour of the Pretr.

Din'd plentifully at North Ferry on Cakes and Ale because there was nothing else to be got, no not Butter and Eggs, nor Cheese. Mounted again with a Runner at my foot. By moon light fell in on the Road to Leslie with a young woman who was properly dressed and walked as stately thro' the Gutters as ever Diana did thro' the woods — Conversation — Have the Highland men been here? I fancy you ask that as being a favourer of theirs — It may be so, but pray who is Minister of this place (King Glassy) — May a one ask what they know full well — Really I know not his name — It is Mr. Currie honest man of whom every body has heard, he is a sweet preacher, I hear him every week — Have you no Minister at Leslie where Lord Rothes has his place?— O yes we have, and the one is a Seceder, but you know one likes to go where they are most edifyed (—Apart to my Boy) who is this Gentleman? — I know not but believe he is a Minister by his Coat.

By this time we were got to the Village and at parting realy I have been very luckie (said she) in good Company this time of night on the Road, I wish you good journey, Farewell.

My landlady received me kindly put on a fire made ready supper.

I drank a snaker with my Landlord who by the description the Boy had given him of the young woman told me that she was the only Wh—— in the Town. Slept sound — mounted, came without any remarkable to Arbroth Thursday night. Friday dismal rain and wind, keep'd the Coast road all the way to Bervie, wet to the skin, but found small pleasure in observing the vast huge Rocks, and seeing the foaming surges lash the sounding shore. Slept well at Bervie and next day got to Aberdeen. Not half an hour in Town when everybody heard of it in spite of my endeavours to conceal it. Messages, Company, etc. Sunday preach'd and *sic finitur tabula**.

I find I will get a feather Bed to purchase here and Blankets too. Shall write more at leisure to Mrs. Stuart. Must have good Chimney Tongs etc for a Dining Room, a small mirror for adjusting my wig and Band if to be had easily. Remember my Scrivitore and see that the Brushes and Locks be good. Any utensils for a kitchen, I desire Mrs. Stuart may have her eye on. I have writ you the above believing by this time your fears of poor Gibbie are quit over. Pray let me know how he is and learn first to submit and then to trust in Providence. All your news let me have. I hope the Coast is or will

* so finished the day

soon be clear. Send my Complements to Mr. Dunbar and tell him I am well. I forgott to speak of Bed And Table Linnen tho as necessary as anything.

I am etc. R.P.

Item, Pair good candlesticks (brass) and snuffers. I have some new shirts making at Dalkeith which will be sent to you, pray forward them with my books.

The Rev. George Innes (fl. 1750)

The Battle of Culloden brought to an end more than the Jacobite rising. It was followed by persecution by the Duke of Cumberland's forces and by oppressive legislation designed to destroy the Highland way of life. In the following letter, the Rev. George Innes of Forres describes the beginning of this process immediately after the battle.

36. After Culloden

To the Rev. Robert Forbes,
Bishop of Ross and Caithness   *27 February 1750*

... But the most shocking part of this woefull story is yet to come; I mean the horrid barbarities committed in cold blood after the battle was over. I do not now precisely remember how many days the dead bodies lay upon the field to glut the eyes of the merciless conqueror. But certain it is that there they lay till the stench oblig'd him to cause bury them. In the meantime the soldiers, like so many savages, went up and down knocking such in the head as had any remains of life in them, and except in a very few instances, refusing all manner of relief to the wounded, many of whom, had they been properly taken care of, wou'd undoubtedly have recover'd. A little house into which a good many of the wounded had been carried was set on fire about their ears, and ev'ry soul in it burnt alive, of which number was Collonel Orelli, a brave old gentleman, who was either in the French or Spanish service. One Mr. Shaw, younger, of Kinrara, in Badenoch, had likewise been carried into another hut with other wounded men, and amongst the rest a servant of his own who, being only wounded in the arm, cou'd have got off, but chose rather to stay to attend his master. The Presbyterian minister at Petty, Mr. Laughlan Shaw, being a cousin of this Kinrara's, had obtain'd leave of the Duke of Cumberland to carry off his friend in return to the good services the said Mr. Laughlan had done the Government. For he had been very active in disswading his parishioners and clann from joining the Prince, and had likewise, as I'm told, sent the Duke very pointed intelligence of all the Prince's motions. In consequence of this, on the Saturday after the battle, he went to the place where his friend was, designing to carry him to his own house. But as he came near, he saw an officer's command, with the officer at their head, fire a plattoon at fourteen of the wounded Highlanders whom they had taken all out of that house and bring them all down at once. And when he came up he found his cousin and his servant were two of that unfortunate number. . .

Their treatment of their prisoners may easily be guess'd at from what I have already said. And, indeed, history, I believe, can scarce afford a parallel to it. For some days it was dangerous for any person to go near them, or to pretend to give them the least relief; so that all of them, especially the wounded, were in a most dismal state. And after they were put on board the ships, numbers of them died every day and were thrown overboard like so many dogs; and several of them, I'm told, before they were really dead . . .

Flora MacDonald (1722-90)

After his defeat at the Battle of Culloden on 16th April 1746 Prince Charles Edward was hunted by government forces. But for the assistance of Flora MacDonald, who escorted the Prince disguised as her maid-servant to Skye, he might have been captured. Flora MacDonald was arrested and imprisoned finally in London and then released. In the early 1770s the MacDonalds — she married Allan MacDonald in 1750 — decided to emigrate to North Carolina. MacKenzie of Delvine agreed to take the MacDonald's youngest son, John, into his house to educate him.

37. Farewell to 'good natured bidable' Johnie

To Mr MacKenzie   *Flodigarry, Trotternish, Skye*
                                          12 August 1772

Dear Sir,
This goes by my Son Johnie who thank God tho I am misfortunat in other respects is happy in his haveing so good a freind as you are to take him under his protection, he seemed when here to be a good

natured bidable Boy, without any kind of Vices, make of him what you please and may the Blessing of the almighty attend you along with him which is all the return I am able to make for your many and repeated freindships shown to me and this family; of which there will soon be no remembrance in this poor miserable Island, the best of its inhabitants are making ready to follow their freinds to America, while they have anything to bring there, and among the rest we are to go, especially as we cannot promise ourselves but poverty and oppression, haveing last Spring and this time two years lost almost our whole Stock of Cattle and horses; we lost within these three years, three hundred and twenty-seven heads, so that we have hardly what will pay our Creditors which we are to let them have and begin the world again, anewe, in anothere Corner of it. Allen was to write you but he is not well with a pain in his Side these ten days past. Sir I beg of you if you see anything amiss in the Boys conduct to let me know of it as some Children will stand in awe of their parents more than any body Else.

I am with my respects to you and Mrs. MacKenzie,
> Sir with esteem
> Your most obedient
> humble servant
> FLORA MCDONALD

☆   ☆   ☆

David Hume (1711-76)

Hume was one of the greatest of philosophers, carrying scepticism to the ultimate, and a considerable historian and economist. By all accounts, he was also the most delightful of social companions. Robert Adam's mother described him as 'the most innocent, agreeable, facetious man I ever met with'. All of these qualities appear in his admirable letters, including his mock indignation over an indiscretion by Boswell and his very real, and constantly repeated, irritation over the attitudes of London.

38. 'The indispensable requisites of life'

To John Clephane   *Riddal's Land, Edinburgh*
                                       5 January 1753

. . . I must now set you an example, and speak of myself. By this I mean that you are to speak to me of yourself. I shall exult and triumph to you a little, that I have now at last — being turned of forty, to my own honour, to that of learning, and to that of the present age — arrived at the dignity of being a householder. About seven months ago, I got a house of my own, and completed a regular family; consisting of a head, viz myself, and two inferior members, a maid and a cat. My sister has since joined me, and keeps me company. With frugality I can reach, I find, cleanliness, warmth, light, plenty, and contentment. What would you have more? Independence? I have it in a supreme degree. Honour? that is not altogether wanting. Grace? that will come in time. A wife? that is none of the indispensable requisites of life. Books? that *is* one of them; and I have more than I can use. In short, I cannot find any blessing of consequence which I am not possessed of, in a greater or less degree; and without any great effort of philosophy, I may be easy and satisfied.

As there is no happiness without occupation, I have begun a work which will employ me several years, and which yields me much satisfaction. Tis a History of Britain, from the Union of the Crowns to the present time. I have already finished the reign of King James. My friends flatter me (by this I mean that they don't flatter me), that I have succeeded. You know that there is no post of honour in the English Parnassus more vacant than that of History. Style, judgement, impartiality, care — everything is wanting to our historians; and even Rapin during this latter period, is extremely deficient. I make my work very concise, after the manner of the Ancients. It divides into three very moderate volumes; one to end with the death of Charles the First; the second at the Revolution; the third at the Accession, for I dare come no nearer the present times. The work will neither please the Duke of Bedford nor James Fraser; but I hope it will please you and posterity . . .

So, dear Doctor, after having mended my pen, and bit my nails, I return to the narration of parliamentary factions, or court intrigues, or civil wars, and bid you heartily adieu.

DAVID HUME

P.S.
When I say that I dare come no nearer the present time than the Accession, you are not to imagine that I am afraid either of danger or offence; I hope, in many instances, that I have shown myself to be above all laws of prudence and discretion. I only mean, that I should be afraid of committing mistakes, in writing of so recent a period, by reason of the want of materials.

39. 'The People most distinguish'd for Literature in Europe'

To Gilbert Elliot of Minto   *Edinburgh 2 July 1757*

. . . I fancy our Friend Robertson will be able to publish his History next Winter. You are sufficiently acquainted with the Merit of that Work; and really it is admirable how many Men of Genius this Country produces at present. Is it not strange that, at a time when we have lost our Princes, our Parliaments, our independent Government, even the Presence of our chief Nobility, are unhappy, in our Accent & Pronunciation, speak a very corrupt Dialect of the Tongue which we make use of; is it not strange, I say, that, in these Circumstances, we shou'd really be the People most distinguish'd for Literature in Europe? . . .

40. 'Fury and Combustion'

To James Boswell   *Edinburgh 24 February 1763*

. . . You must know, Mr James Boswall or James Boswell Esq, that I am very much out of Humour with you and your two Companions or Co-partners. How the Devil came it into your Heads or rather your Noddles (for if there had been a Head among you, the thing had not happend; nor are you to imagine, that a Parcel of volatile Spirits, enclos'd in a Skull, make a Head) I repeat it, How the Devil came it into your Noddles to publish in a Book to all the World what you pretend I told you in private Conversation? I say, *pretend I told you;* for as I have utterly forgot the whole Matter, I am resolv'd utterly to deny it. Are you not sensible, that by this *Etourderie,* to give it the lightest Name, you were capable of making a Quarrel between me and that irascible little man with whom I live in very good Terms? Do you not feel, from your own Experience, that among us, Gentlemen of the Quill, there is nothing of which we are so jealous, not even our Wives, if we have any, as the Honour of our Productions; and that the least Touch of Blame on that head puts us into the most violent Fury and Combustion? I reply nothing to your Letter till you give me some Satisfaction for this offence; but only assure you that I am not Sir

Your most obedient & most humble Servant

DAVID HUME

41. 'The Barbarians who inhabit the Banks of the Thames'

To Hugh Blair   *Paris 26 April 1764*

. . . Our Friend, I mean, your Friend, Lord Kaims had much provokd Voltaire who never forgives, & never thinks any Enemy below his Notice. He has accordingly sent to the Gazette Literaire an Article with regard to the Elements of Criticism, which turns that Book extremely into Ridicule, with a good deal of Wit. I tryd to have it suppress'd before it was printed; but the Authors of that Gazette told me, that they durst neither suppress nor alter any thing that came from Voltaire. I suppose his Lordship holds that satiric Wit as cheap as he does all the rest of the human Race, and will not be in the least mortify'd by his Censure.

The Taste for Literature is neither decayd nor depravd here, as with the Barbarians who inhabit the Banks of the Thames . . .

42. 'Am I an Englishman?'

To Gilbert Elliot of Minto   *Paris 22 September 1764*

. . . From what human Motive or Consideration can I prefer living
in England to that in foreign Countries? I believe, taking the
Continent of Europe, from Peterburg to Lisbon, & from Bergen to
Naples, there is not one that ever heard my Name, who has not
heard of it with Advantage, both in point of Morals & Genius. I do
not believe there is one Englishman in fifty, who, if he heard that I
had broke my Neck to night, woud not be rejoic'd with it. Some
hate me because I am not a Tory, some because I am not a Whig,
some because I am not a Christian, and all because I am a Scotsman.
Can you seriously talk of my continuing an Englishman? Am I, or
are you, an Englishman? Will they allow us to be so? Do they not
treat with Derision our Pretensions to that Name, and with Hatred
our just Pretension to surpass & govern them? I am a Citizen of the
World; but if I were to adopt any Country, it would be that in
which I live at present, and from which I am determin'd never to
depart, unless a War drive me into Swisserland or Italy. . .

43. Invitation to Adam Smith

To Adam Smith   *James's Court, Edinburgh*
20 August 1769

Dear Smith,
I am glad to have come within sight of you, and to have a View of
Kirkaldy from my Windows; But as I wish also to be within
speaking terms of you, I wish we coud concert measures for that
purpose. I am mortally sick at Sea, and regard with horror, and a
kind of hydrophobia the great Gulph that lies between us. I am also
tir'd of travelling, as much as you ought naturally to be, of staying
at home: I therefore propose to you to come hither, and pass some
days with me in this Solitude. I want to know what you have been
doing, and propose to exact a rigorous Account of the method, in
which you have employed yourself during your Retreat. I am
positive you are in the wrong in many of your Speculations,
especially where you have the Misfortune to differ from me. All
these are Reasons for our meeting, and I wish you would make me
some reasonable Proposal for that Purpose. There is no Habitation

on the Island of Inch-keith; otherwise I should challenge you to meet me on that Spot, and neither [of] us ever to leave the Place, till we were fully agreed on all points of Controversy. I expect General Conway here to morrow, whom I shall attend to Roseneath, & I shall remain there a few days. On my Return, I expect to find a Letter from you, containing a bold Acceptance of this Defiance. I am Dear Smith Yours sincerely

DAVID HUME

44. The philosopher as cook

To Sir Gilbert Elliot   *Edinburgh 16 October 1769*

. . . I have been settled here two Months, and am here Body & Soul, without casting the least Thought of Regreat to London, or even to Paris. I think it improbable that I shall ever in my Life cross the Tweed, except perhaps a Jaunt to the North of England, for Health or Amusement. I live still, and must for a twelvemonth, in my old House in James's Court, which is very chearful, and even elegant, but too small to display my great Talent for Cookery, the Science to which I intend to addict the remaining Years of my Life; I have just now lying on the Table before me a Receipt for making *Soupe a la Reine,* copy'd with my own hand. For Beef and Cabbage (a charming Dish), and old Mutton and old Claret, no body excels me. I make also Sheep head Broth in a manner that Mr Keith speaks of it for eight days after, and the Duc de Nivernois woud bind himself Apprentice to my Lass to learn it. I have already sent a Challenge to David Moncrief. You will see, that in a twelvemonth he will take to the writing of History, the Field I have deserted: For as to the giving of Dinners, he can now have no farther Pretensions. I should have made a very bad use of my Abode in Paris, if I coud not get the better of a mere provincial like him. All my Friends encourage me in this Ambition; as thinking it will redound very much to my Honour.

I am delighted to see the daily and hourly Progress of Madness and Folly and Wickedness in England. The Consummation of these Qualities are the true Ingredients for making a fine Narrative in History; especially if followed by some signal and ruinous Convulsion, as I hope will soon be the Case with that pernicious People. He must be a very bad Cook indeed, that cannot make a palatable Dish from the whole. You see in my Reflexions and Allusions I still mix my old and new Profession together. I am Dear Sir Gilbert

Your most obedient humble Servant,

DAVID HUME

Edinburgh
16 of Octr 1769

P.S.

    I beg my Respects to Lady Elliot.

45. 'Restoration of the Government'

To William Strahan   *Edinburgh 25 October 1769*

Dear Sir

I never enjoyed myself better, nor was in better spirits, than since I came down here. I live as I please, spend my time according to my fancy, keep a plentiful table for myself and my friends, amuse myself with reading and Society, and find the generality of the people disposed to respect me more on account of my having been well receiv'd in greater and more renowned places: But tho' all this makes my time slide away easily, it is impossible for me to forget that a man who is in his 59th Year has not many more years to live, and that it is time for him, if he has common Sense, to have done with all Ambition. My Ambition was always moderate and confind entirely to Letters; but it has been my Misfortune to write in the Language of the most stupid and factious Barbarians in the World; and it is long since I have renounced all desire of their Approbation, which indeed coud no longer give me either pleasure or Vanity . . .

    You say I am of a desponding Character: On the contrary, I am of a very sanguine Disposition. Notwithstanding my Age, I hope to see a public Bankruptcy, the total Revolt of America, the Expulsion of the English from the East Indies, the Diminution of London to less than a half, and the Restoration of the Government to the King, Nobility, and Gentry of this Realm. To adorn the Scene, I hope also that some hundreds of Patriots will make their Exit at Tyburn, and improve English Eloquence by their dying Speeches . . .

46. 'Recourse to America'

Dear Sir

I was very glad to hear of your safe Arrival in London, after being expos'd to as many Perils, as St Paul, by Land and by Water: Though to no Perils among false Brethen: For the good Wishes of all your Brother Philosophers in this place attend you heartily and sincerely, together with much Regret that your Business wou'd not allow you to pass more time among them.

Brother Lin* expects to see you soon, before he takes his little Trip round the World. You have heard, no doubt, of that Project: The Circumstances of the Affair coud not be more honourable for him, nor coud the Honour be conferd on one who deserves it more.

I really believe with the French Author, of whom you have favour'd me with an Extract, that the Circumstance of my being a Scotchman has been a considerable Objection to me: So factious is this Country! I expected, in entering on my literary Course, that all the Christians, all the Whigs, and all the Tories shoud be my Enemies: But it is hard, that all the English, Irish, and Welsh shoud be also against me. The Scotch, likewise, cannot be much my Friends, as no man is a Prophet in his own Country. However, it is some Consolation that I can bear up my Head under all this Prejudice.

I fancy that I must have recourse to America for Justice. You told me, I think, that your Countrymen in that part of the World intended to do me the Honour of giving an Edition of my Writings; and you promisd that you shoud recommend to them to follow this last Edition, which is in the Press. I now use the Freedom of reminding you of it.

Pray, make my Compliments to Sir John Pringle, and tell him how much I wish for his Company; and be so good as give him a Description of the House I reserve for him in this Square. If you really go over to America, we hope you will not grudge us Sir John as a Legacy. I am

Dear Sir with great Truth and Regard,

Your most obedient humble Servant,

DAVID HUME

*He refers to James Lind (Letter 55).

*   *   *

Mrs Alison Cockburn (1712-94)

Born at Fairnilee on the Tweed, two miles from Scott's first home after his marriage, Alison Rutherford, married to the brother of John Cockburn of Ormiston, became the uncrowned queen of eighteenth-century Edinburgh society. Amongst other distinguished persons, she entertained the philosopher David Hume, the eccentric judge Lord Monboddo and the Rev. John Home, author of Douglas: A Tragedy. *The sparkle of her wit and the acuteness of her observation sound out in her letters as if she had spoken her words aloud. In one letter she recollects meeting the boy Scott.*

47. The boy Walter Scott

To the Reverend Dr Robert Douglas   *Edinburgh 15 November 1777*

. . . He was reading a poem to his mother when I went in. I made him read on. It was the description of a shipwreck. His passion rose with the storm: he lifted his eyes and hands. 'There's the mast gone,' says he, 'crash it goes, they will all perish.' After his agitation he turns to me, 'That is too melancholy,' says he, 'I had better read you somewhat more amusing.' I preferd a little chat, and asked his opinion of Milton and other books he was reading, which he gave me. Wonderfull indeed one of his observations was — how strange it was that Adam, just new come into the world, should know everything! 'That must be the poet's fancy,' says he; but when he was told he was created perfect by God Himself, he instantly yielded. When he was taken to bed last night, he told his aunt he liked that lady. 'What lady?' says she. 'Why, Mrs. Cokburne, for I think she's a virtuoso like myself.' 'Dear Walter,' says aunt, 'what is a virtuoso?' 'Don't ye know? why, it's one who wishes and will know everything?' Now, sir, you will think this a very silly story. Pray, what age do you suppose this boy to be? Name it now, before I tell you. Why, 12 or 14? — no such thing. He is not quite six years old. He has a lame leg for which he was a year at Bath, and has acquired the perfect English accent which he has not lost since he came, and he reads like a Garrick. You will alow this an uncommon exotick? You will also alow this to be a pretty long letter. You owe it to lazyness and to a certain tiredness that grows dayly of that frivolous company that makes me yawn. I begin to like my own company best of any . . .

48. Robert Burns in Edinburgh

To the Reverend Dr Donald Douglas   *Edinburgh 30 December 1786*

. . . The town is at present agog with the ploughman poet, who receives adulation with native dignity, and is the very figure of his profession — strong and coarse — but has a most enthusiastick heart of LOVE. He has seen dutchess Gordon and all the gay world. His favrite for looks and manners is Bess Burnet — no bad judge indeed . . .

49. The ball

1771

. . . On Wednesday I gave a ball. How do ye think I contrived to stretch out this house to hold twenty-two people, and had nine couples always dancing? Yet this is true: It is also true that we had a table covered with divers eatables all the time, and that everybody eat when they were hungry and drank when they were dry, but nobody ever sat down. I think my house, like my purse, is just the widow's cruse.

I must tell you my party of dancers. Captain Bob Dalrymple was King of the Ball, as it was his bespeaking. Tell Lady Balcarres that, as a nephew she will delight in him: he is my first favourite. Well, for men, there was Bob and Hew, young men both; Peter Inglis, a Mr Bruce, a lawyer; then Jock Swinton and Jock Turnbull. Then, for women, there were Tibbie Hall, my two nieces, Agnes Keith, Christy Pringle, Babie Carnegie, Christy Anderson, Jeanie Rutherford. Mrs Mure and Violy Pringle came and danced a reel, and went off. Now for our dance. Our fiddler sat where the cupboard is and they danced in both rooms; the table was stuffed into the window, and we had plenty of room. It made the bairns all vastly happy. Next day I went to the Assembly with all these misses . . .

Tobias Smollett (1721-71)

The novelist Tobias Smollett left Scotland when he was about 20 and spent most of his life out of it, in the West Indies with the navy, in London and finally in Italy. His strong Scottish partiality however is evident in his most popular novel, Humphrey Clinker, *and in this letter to Alexander Carlyle, (Letter 51), the reference to 'Hume' is to John Home who made many unsuccessful attempts to have his plays staged in London before he finally succeeded with his* Douglas *in 1757.*

50. Exile in London

To Alexander Carlyle   *Chelsea 1 March 1754*

Dear Carlyle,
I do not think I could enjoy Life with greater Relish in any part of the world than in Scotland among you and your Friends, and I often amuse my Imagination with schemes for attaining that Degree of Happiness, which, however, is altogether out of my Reach. I am heartily tired of this Land of Indifference and Phlegm where the finer Sensations of the Soul are not felt, and Felicity is held to consist in stupifying Port and overgrown Buttocks of Beef, where Genius is lost, Learning undervalued, and Taste altogether extinguished, and Ignorance prevails to such a degree that one of our Chelsea Club asked me if the weather was good when I crossed the Sea from Scotland, and another desired to know if there were not more Popes than one, in as much as he had heard people mention the Pope of Rome, an Expression which seemed to imply that there was a Pope of some other Place. I answered that there was a Pope of Troy, and another of Tartary, and he seemed perfectly well satisfied with the Information, which no Person present pretended to contradict.

The same Stolidity prevails among the audience of our Theatres so that I am not very sorry for the Dissapointment of Hume, whom I love exceedingly. Goody Criticism has been delirious a long time, but now she is quite lethargic, so that an Author who formerly went to hell in the thunder and whirlwind of a Riot is now negatively damned, and silently sinks into oblivion. The third night of Constantine did not pay the Expence of the House: think on that . . .

Alexander Carlyle (1722-1805)

For more than 50 years (1748 to 1805), Alexander Carlyle was minister of Inveresk, near Musselburgh. He was active in church politics in the Moderate interest and a familiar friend of most of the literati of the Scottish Enlightenment. His delightful Autobiography *is one of the best accounts of the social atmosphere of the time.*

In this letter to an old friend, John Macpherson (who succeeded Hastings as Governor of British India), Carlyle reports on the old age of the brilliant circle of his Moderate colleagues: Robertson, the historian; Blair, the Professor of rhetoric and arbiter of taste; Home, the author of Douglas; *and Adam Ferguson, one of the founders of modern sociology.*

51. The old age of the literati

To Sir John Macpherson 1796

. . . Now for an account of your old friends, which, if you saw Ferguson as he passed, which I think you did, I might spare.

To begin with Robertson, whom you shall see no more. In one word, he appeared more respectable when he was dying than ever he did even when living. He was calm and collected, and even placid, and even gay. My poor wife had a desire to see him and went on purpose, but when she saw him, from a window, leaning on his daughter, with his tottering frame, and directing the gardener how to dress some flower-beds, her sensibility threw her into a paroxysm of grief; she fled upstairs to Mrs. Russell and could not see him. His house, for three weeks before he died, was really an anticipation of heaven.

Dr. Blair is as well as possible. Preaching every Sunday with increasing applause, and frisking more with the whole world than ever he did in his youngest days, no symptom of frailty about him; and though he was huffed at not having an offer of the Principality, he is happy in being resorted to as the head of the university.

John Home is in very good health and spirits, and has had the comfort, for two or three winters, of having Major Home, his brother-in-law, a very sensible man, in the house with him, which makes him less dependent on stranger company, which, in advanced years, is not so easy to be found, nor endured when it is found.

With respect to myself, I have had many warnings within these three years, but, on the whole, as I have only fits of illness and no disease, I am sliding softly on to old age, without any remarkable infirmity or failure, and can, upon occasions, preach like a son of thunder (I wish I were the Bold Thunderer for a week or two against the vile levelling Jacobins, whom I abhor). My wife, your old friend, has been better than usual this winter, and is strong in metaphysics and ethics, and (can) almost repeat all Ferguson's last book of Lectures, which do him infinite honour. I say of that book, that if Reid is the Aristotle, Ferguson is the Plato of Scotch philosophers; and the Faculty of Arts of Edinburgh have adopted my phrase . . .

Adam Ferguson (1723-1816)

Ferguson, one of the central figures in the Scottish Enlightenment, was a native Gaelic speaker. His Essay on the History of Civil Society *(1767) was widely influential and it is one of the foundations of modern sociology. It was in his house that Scott met Burns (Letter 101).*

52. The character of the Highlander

(The original of this letter, which was once in Edinburgh University Library, has been misplaced. We do not know to whom it was addressed or when it was written).

. . . If I had not been in the Highlands of Scotland, I might be of their mind who think the inhabitants of Paris and Versailles the only polite people in the world. It is truly wonderful to see persons of every sex and age, who never travelled beyond the nearest mountain, possess themselves perfectly, perform acts of kindness with an aspect of dignity, and a perfect discernment of what is proper to oblige. This is seldom to be seen in our cities, or in our capital; but a person among the mountains, who thinks himself nobly born, considers courtesy as the test of his rank. He never saw a superior, and does not know what it is to be embarrassed. He has an ingenuous deference for those who have seen more of the world than himself; but never saw the neglect of others assumed as a mark of superiority . . .

Adam Smith (1723 – 90)

T.H. Buckle said of Adam Smith's masterpiece The Wealth of Nations *that it was 'probably the most important book which has ever been written, whether we consider the amount of original thought which it contains, or its practical influence'. It is the foundation of modern economic thought and an important influence as much on Marxists as on advocates of the free market system. Smith was typical of the literati of the Scottish Enlightenment in the width of his interests and in his close and amiable relations with his colleagues of all academic disciplines. He made a notable contribution also to moral and social psychology.*

53. Smith on Hume

To William Strahan   *Kirkaldy 9 November 1776*

Dear Sir,

It is with a real, though a very melancholy pleasure, that I sit down to give you some account of the behaviour of our late excellent friend, Mr. Hume, during his last illness.

Though in his own judgment his disease was mortal and incurable, yet he allowed himself to be prevailed upon, by the entreaty of his friends, to try what might be the effects of a long journey . . . Upon his return to Edinburgh, though he found himself much weaker, yet his cheerfulness never abated, and he continued to divert himself, as usual, with correcting his own works for a new edition, with reading books of amusement, with the conversation of his friends; and sometimes in the evening with a party at his favourite game of whist. His cheerfulness was so great, and his conversation and amusements ran so much in their usual strain, that notwithstanding all bad symptoms, many people could not believe he was dying. 'I shall tell your friend Colonel Edmonstoune,' said Dr Dundas to him one day, 'that I left you much better, and in a fair way of recovery.' 'Doctor,' said he, 'as I believe you would not choose to tell any thing but the truth, you had better tell him I am dying as fast as my enemies, if I have any, could wish, and as easily and cheerfully as my best friends could desire.' . . .

Thus died our most excellent, and never-to-be-forgotten friend; concerning whose philosophical opinions men will no doubt judge variously, every one approving or condemning them according as they happen to coincide, or disagree with his own; but concerning whose character and conduct there can scarce be a difference of opinion. His temper, indeed, seemed to be more happily balanced, if I may be allowed such an expression, than that perhaps of any other man I have ever known. Even in the lowest state of his fortune, his great and necessary frugality never hindered him from exercising, upon proper occasions, acts both of charity and generosity. It was a frugality founded not upon avarice, but upon the love of independency. The extreme gentleness of his nature never weakened either the firmness of his mind, or the steadiness of his resolutions. His constant pleasantry was the genuine effusion of good nature and good humour, tempered with delicacy and modesty, and without even the slightest tincture of malignity, so frequently the disagreeable source of what is called wit in other men. It never was the meaning of his raillery to mortify; and therefore, far from offending, it seldom failed to please and delight even those who were the objects of it. To his friends, who were frequently the objects of it, there was not perhaps any one of all his great and amiable qualities which contributed more to endear his conversation. And that gaiety of temper, so agreeable in society, but which is so often accompanied with frivolous and superficial qualities, was in him certainly attended with the most severe application, the most extensive learning, the greatest depth of thought, and a capacity in every respect the most comprehensive. Upon the whole, I have always considered him, both in his lifetime, and since his death, as approaching as nearly to the idea of a perfectly wise and virtuous man, as perhaps the nature of human frailty will admit.

    I am ever, Dear Sir,
        Most affectionately yours,

ADAM SMITH

54. Smith on himself

To Andreas Holt, Commissioner of the
Danish Board of Trade and Economy   *October 1780*

Dear Sir,
I am ashamed of having delayed so long to answer your very obliging letter; but I am occupied four days in every week at the Custom House; during which it is impossible to sit down seriously to any other business: during the other three days, too, I am liable to be frequently interrupted by the extraordinary duties of my office, as well as by my own private affairs and the common duties of society . . .

It is not worth while to take notice, even to you, of the innumerable squibs thrown out upon me in the newspapers. I have, however, upon the whole been much less abused than I had reason to expect, so that in this respect I think myself rather lucky than otherwise. A single, and, as I thought, a very harmless Sheet of paper, which I happened to write concerning the death of our late friend, Mr. Hume, brought upon me ten times more abuse than the very violent attack I had made upon the whole commercial system of Great Britain. So much for what relates to my Book . . .

Since I had the pleasure of seeing you, my own life has been extreamly uniform. Upon my return to Great Britain I retired to a small town in Scotland, the place of my nativity, where I continued to live for six years in great tranquility and almost in complete retirement. During this time I amused myself principally with writing my 'Enquiry concerning the Wealth of Nations,' in studying Botany (in which, however, I made no great progress) as well as some other sciences to which I had never given much attention before . . .

Wishing you every sort of happiness and prosperity, I have the honour to be with the highest respect and esteem, Dear Sir,

Your most affectionate, humble Servant.

ADAM SMITH

James Hutton (1726-97)

James Hutton, regarded as the founder of modern geology, was born in Edinburgh. Characteristically for a man of the Scottish Enlightenment, his interests were wide, including medicine, chemistry and agriculture as well as geology. He was ready to take advantage of any opportunity to advance scientific knowledge. While Captain James Cook was preparing to set out on his second expedition to the Antipodes in 1773, Joseph Banks, the naturalist of the first expedition, invited James Lind M.D. (1736-1812) to join the party. Lind told his friend, James Hutton, who promptly wrote with advice. Unfortunately it went for nothing, as Banks quarrelled with Cook over accommodation in the Resolution *and he and Lind withdrew.*

To James Lind   *Spring 1772*

Dear Doctor,

I hope this will find you setting about your glorious expedition with good health and spirits. I shall endeavour to set down by way of memorandum to you anything that may occur to me. It is your business to make a course of accurate observations of every subject; this will be expected of you, your knowledge and ingenuity qualifies you for such a business, to execute this you must begin with method and pursue it with unwearied steadiness . . .

You must consider that to us the curious observations of this country are very interesting, but it is the more common observations of a distant country that contribute to our instruction. Therefore never lose sight of the common observations to be made on such a country, which will afterwards, if full and accurate, come to be extremely useful in being compared with those of this or any other country. Is not this truly curious? — natural history in perfection . . .

The mineral observations consist both in a history both of soil or loose parts and of the solid parts or rocks and beds; the shortest and best way of doing this is to take samples more or less but not to neglect this however small the samples are; . . . N.B. a bag of gravel is a history to me, and, with the above will tell wondrous tales, in this manner I may yet be mineralogist to the expedition, almost to as good a purpose as if I had made the voyage. Would it not be curious to have a better natural history of New Zealand than that of any country extant, but to return — the country observations, besides those in common, include 1st figure and height of the land mountains and plains and precipices rivers lakes etc. etc. . . . I need say no more of this; only, mind, a bag of gravel is worth a bag of gold . . .

I inclose ship receipts for two boxes containing the diving machines. I flatter myself you shall have the utmost satisfaction in the use of them — pray exert yourself to get the machine down to the greatest depth; let no cord be spared, take enough to reach the bottom of hell and get us samples up from Tartarus. N.B. to prevent loss of line and machine, let it always be done from a boat that the line will make to ride; and have gradation of different sized lines, without great attention to every circumstance no success is to be expected . . .

In making experiments you will find one thing suggests another. Record all, but the regular course of observations is the anchor of our hope — Don't let the luxuries of the South Pole draw you off your post, or divert you from your duty as a Norlandus Bornus homo. When at the social board forget not the dainty tables of stone; mind everyone of them is wrote upon by gods own finger. I have known a duodecimo of this kind do more credit to the author than a quarto bible. I wish you all the most happy voyage and greater success. If you can spare the time let me hear from you. I am.

Yours   JAMES HUTTON

After Banks had withdrawn from Cook's expedition, he arranged a voyage to Iceland in August 1772.

56. 'Mediterranean Nature'

To Joseph Banks   *Winter 1772*

. . . I hope you will never set out to the northern frozen regions where you may be inveigled with land in unknown and inhospitable seas where a little delay alone may prove death. . . . In new countries . . . you neither know where to go and if you should there is nothing to be seen at least little of the Solum Sine veste and Dame Natures petticoat is not so easily lifted as that of the Princess Obrea* . . . notwithstanding that the mediterranean has been the beaten track of philosphers as well as fools I can't help thinking that more knowledge is to be reaped after them than may be gleaned in almost any other field . . . in the Mediterranean Nature seems to be lying on her back opening her arms and saying come hither sons of observation have you a desire that I cannot satisfy? — more distant and inaccessible countries may breed more desires than they will satisfy, the medit on the contrary may be capable of giving enjoyment superior to the desires. — I wish to see you follow your inclinations and compleat a work begun but if that should not take place, pray do not undertake an expedition which appears to me to end in feeding Russian bears. . . .

Robert Adam (1728 – 92)

Robert Adam, the greatest architect of his age, was in Rome from February 1755 to May 1757. Although he lived there in some style, he was not in Italy as a wealthy young man on the Grand Tour, but as a student of classical architecture. When he left Rome, he travelled through Venice to Spalatro in Dalmatia to make a record of the ruins of the palace of the Emperor Diocletian. He sent this account of his experiences in Venice to his sister, Peggy.

*Rumour had it that Banks had an affair with the Tahitian Princess, Obrea or Purea.

57. 'Water Gondolas and Voluptuousness'

To Peggy Adam   *Venice 6 July 1757*

My Dear Peggy,
. . . Friday the first of July I departed from Padua & at Midday I found myself sett down in these regions of Water Gondolas and Voluptuousness. I have found some few English Gentlemen here with whom I passed a good deal of my Time, having no acquaintance with the Italians. We generally went every other night to Lady Wentworth's House, who is now wife of our Resident Mr. Murray, but keeps the name of her former Husband. A good sensible and agreeable Woman. Mr. Smith the Consul has been at his Country House since my arrival here, about 10 miles from Venice by land and 5 by water. As these Gentlemen left Venice monday morning, I thought I could not do better than go Yesterday & pass some hours with Smith & his Lady at their Country Seat, accordingly yesterday morning by means of my Gondola and a Post chaise Master Donald & I arrived at the Consul's House, where I was received with open arms. Had a very handsome dinner & prodigiously entertained with as pretty a Collection of Pictures as I have ever seen. Not large pictures, but small ones of great masters & very finely preserved. In short my visit was taken as prodigiously kind. Mrs Smith is facetious, frank & of a sweet turn of behaviour. I had much pressing to stay there all night, but having my Gondola in waiting & my Youths expecting me home I could not accept this invitation.

Mr. Smith comes to Venice friday & is to come directly to my House. He is to obtain Allowance from the Republic for my digging at Spalatro & to procure me Letters for Governours etc when I go. I cannot help staring and being astonish'd with what warmth I am received by all & with what politeness I am treated, and how things turn out for me as if God was always puzzling his old noddle how to oblige me . . .

Now I think it time to mention my receipt of Jenny's Letter of the 9th of June. In which she mentions Jamie's behaviour on reading my Letter & the feeling way in which he express'd his joy on hearing of my success in getting my diplomas etc. Sympathy in crying goes farther than one would imagine, for had there not been people in the Room when I read Jenny's account of it, I should have burst out in the same way. But checking myself, bit my lip, crammed my Letter into my pocket & strutted up & down the Room for 20 minutes. This I think was but a natural way of accepting so sincere an instance of friendship. As soon as the Lump of feeling was gulp'd down, I drew forth my Letter a second time &

read to the end. And have since that time perused the same Epistle a Dozen of times, streach'd out at full length in Gondola, rowing through the Canals of Venice. Visiting here being perform'd on the broad of your Back in full Dress (a pretty sloathful way of doing business). And yet I find we Edinburgers easily come into all manner of fashions & that Laziness is not at all incongruous to our Natures . . .

John Ramsay of Ochtertyre (1736 – 1814)

John Ramsay succeeded as laird of Ochtertyre in 1748 when he was only 12. He was educated at the grammar school of Dalkeith and at Edinburgh University and then retired to his family estate. There he lived a life of elegant ease, like a classical Roman in his villa, looking after his estate, observing life, reading and writing notes on eighteenth-century Scotland which eventually filled 10 folio volumes. Burns visited him in 1787 and Scott in 1793. Most of his extensive correspondence has been lost. We do however have a series of long and frequent letters which Ramsay sent to Elizabeth, the wife of his cousin and heir, James Dundas, Clerk to the Signet, who lived in St Andrew's Square in Edinburgh.

Ramsay acquired a reputation as a letter writer in his own life-time and it is easy to see why. His letters have the natural flow of a good crack between friends and move easily over a wide range of his interests from politics and literature to scandal and family news.

All of the following extracts are from the letters to Elizabeth Dundas.

58. The Jacobites

1–2 February 1801

. . . It is needless to die for *fright* as Wright, minister of Larbert, did in consequence of seeing the highland army pass in 45. The man would have been wiser to have borne up and then he would have seen happier times. Sure I was afraid of them in those days and well do I remember a party of hussars who came one night and took arms, boots and horses, and of Glengyle's *requisitions under the pain of military execution*. It was perhaps one of the most innocent and orderly hosts ever seen, considering they had no discipline and not much pay. And though gloomy beyond expression it was the prelude to a happy period and a train of prosperity which was too great to be borne without intoxication. To show you, however, that

I do not altogether dispair of the public, and that I am not righteous over much, what suppose we make a party when these alarms shall be over past, to see a good play, Shakespeare's or a comedy of the old school, an entertainment I liked much and should prefer to midnight dances and morning suppers—and next Sunday make a party to hear a good sermon when it can be had—but when that shall happen, one cannot tell, nor is it proper to be too inquisitive at present about the future . . .

59. A country wedding

11–13 June 1802

. . . Having not been (except for a start) at a country wedding for twenty years it became me as an attentive spectator of manners to mark the changes. It is now the mode to marry privately, a day or two before the feast—no public bedding! no throwing the stocking! as in days of yore! all is privacy; love locks the door and keeps the key. I was too late to witness the arrival of the cavalcade which compared with former times was grand. The nymphs on their side saddles, the beaux in their boots and spurs, mounted on sightly horses were all properly arranged. No riding for the *brose*, one of the feats of former times! When I arrived I found the misses all as white as swans, and not very distinguishable from the Edinburgh ones, save they did not wear a man's shirt or aprons over all. They had moreover a greater proportion of linen about their necks than suits the fashion, though some of them were making approaches to it; and as one of the company expressed it, after the King's birthday, the fashions will travel west; and our country nymphs are very apt scholars. The men were less fine nearly in the same proportion with the Edinburgh bucks who scorn elegance of attire as vulgar and unbeseeming. Their heads too were uncovered very nearly in the ton, saving that they had not a tuft purposely set on end.

I was then introduced to the bride a decent sensible well looking woman of good people from Bandeath. We had a glass of port wine and then tea very good made by the bride's elder sister, who from her inordinate activity I denominated *Martha*; in the course of this we had to borrow or lend spoons to *steer* the cups. The swains and nymphs were intermixed and tho little was said, glances were interchanged, with a little *jogging* at times. We then adjourned to the barn, the tenants' drawing room, which was damp and darkish. While I continued there they had no country dances which sometimes breed schisms between the taught and the untaught.

Here too taste and delicacy are displayed in barns as much as in your balls. The complaint of Scotland tells us that in 1549 every dance began with *tua beiks and ane kiss* and so it was in my younger days; but thanks to the dancing schools, those academies of modesty and virtue in the country, it is exploded among our misses and masters. I did not think it proper to stay supper or the after dance which lasted till broad day, a thing the more necessary that the moon denied her light, and there were no lamps or flambeaux to guide the steps of the misses and their *joes*. I cannot therefore describe the progression of rural cooking since '82. Even then it was less nauseous than the *blacksboils* and the *birstled roasts* which almost turned ones stomach 20 or 30 years before. What marriages this one may give rise to I know not; but it is likely as many in proportion will follow as after the great Edinburgh ones. I must observe that this was what is called a private wedding; certain it is they had not their next neighbours not even a young batcheller tenant whom I wished to couple with the bride's younger sister, such is the progress of fastidious manners!! . . .

60. 'Mere Englishes'

5 October 1807

. . . Lady Christian does wisely in quitting the town for a season; the life of Dives (without the sin I confess) being too much for her years. It is astonishing how well she stood it. Two of *her* suppers would have *done* for me . . . You will probably see Mrs Drummond when settling Johnnie's household; for I do not imagine she goes *expressly* to hear Madame Catalini warble away in a celestial strain. A taste for Italian music is like a sixth sense, and is, I fear, a source of much hypocrisy in our hyperborean climate. Our sweet Scots melodies *married* to Allan Ramsay's verse, suit our northern *lugs* better. Such a Goth! says the dillitanti, or the would be so. Alas! for the season which threatens death disease etc, to appal the Diveses and the dilettanti, if the state of public affairs do not make any impression upon them . . . Were you at Catalini's concerts? Few of our modish Ladies can understand, much less relish a Scots song. A blessed, a classical reformation truly! That is not my affair. We are precisely in the state Edward wished when he courted us a little roughly to be 500 years ago, *mere Englishes*. Professed copying ever implies inferiority . . .

28 September 1809

. . . I understand Lord Balmutto is just returned from a visit to Lord Melville, whose *liberality* is great . . . I am exceedingly pleased with *his* better half, who, though past her bloom, is a pleasing Lady-looking well bred woman, without affectation or conceit, taking her share in the conversation, no easy matter among strangers or rather foreigners . . . If she cannot *help* speaking English, it sounds more naturally from her than from the *tonish* Edinburgh misses who are perhaps some steps *above* the standards. And were she to stay much longer in this country, she would acquire some knowledge of our *Doric* dialect which (I mean in books) is too much neglected by a fastidious generation, who forget that it is the language of pastoral poetry superior to anything ancient or modern. She was therefore gravelled at some of my *words* and stories, but very desirous of understanding them. *Mairbetaiken* and *Randy* required some circumlocution, and was almost too hard for Mrs Colonel Tytler who with her husband and daughter, were inmates of the family, he being on a cruize against the partridges, over whom it is poor to triumph, they being as defenceless as hares. Be that as it may, we had a very pleasing natural party. If our friends are deficient in aught, it is in *progeny*. George has only one son and James the same, a *chaffy-cheeked* spirited fellow of size. Miss was at Dunyra with her grandfather. Our entertainment was good but not over-loaded or overdressed and I have seldom seen a second course more honoured in the eating. Even I ate some fritters not to be particular; and though there were various wines, adhered to humble port with the addition of a glass of sweet wine which I liked . . .

James Watt (1736–1819)

Watt's invention of the condensing steam engine was the basis of the industrial revolution and the transformation of communications by steamship and railways. He made this discovery while he was working as mathematical instrument maker to the University of Glasgow, where his workshop, true to the spirit of the Scottish Enlightenment, became 'a kind of academy whither all the notabilities of Glasgow repaired, to discuss the nicest questions in art, science and literature'. It was at this time that Joseph Black, the discoverer of latent heat, and John Robison (Letter 64) became his close friends.

The following letter refers to a law case to which Hornblower laid claim to Watt's invention. It was, said Robison, not so much between Watt and Hornblower as between science and ignorance.

62. Watt's contribution to the steam engine

To John Robison

Heathfield, Birmingham
24 October 1796

My Dear Sir

Yesterday, only, I received your kind letter of the 15th. That I have not forgot you will appear from a letter I sent to you at Edinburgh, by Mr. William Withering which should be delivered to your home on Saturday last, to which I refer. I have been obliged to trouble many of my friends with these abominable law affairs but have hitherto, have only called those who lived near London, but now these scoundrels,—the Hornblowers and others have leagued against us we must call all who are willing to help us . . .

You will see from the papers sent you the objections and consequently the proper answers, I propose to send you my own general reply for your government, as soon as copy can be made—The point is to establish that I was the inventor that the invention was perfect as to the *saving steam and fuel* at the time of the patent 1769, and that the specification is sufficient to enable a Mechanick understanding Newcomens Engine to have constructed one with these properies.

I did not invent this method piece meal but all at once in a few hours in 1765 I believe. The first step was the idea from the elastic nature of steam of condensing in a seperate vessel, 2d the getting out the water by a long pipe and the air by a pump, 3d that the pump would extract the water also 4th that grease might be used in place of water to keep the piston tight, 5th that Steam might be employed to press upon the piston in place of air 6 to keep the Cylinder warm.

The next day I set about it. The boiler was ready, I took a large syringe of Tom Hamiltons 2 inches dia[mete]r and a foot long that was the Cylinder. I made two tin ends to it with a pipe to convey steam to both of them. I made a tin Condenser consisting of a pump about an inch dia[mete]r, and two small pipes about 10 inches long and ⅛ dia[mete]r immersed in a small round cistron, which I still have. I placed the Cyl[inde]r inverted tied a weight to the piston rod, blew out the air and condensed water through the piston rod, which was hollow, and when I judged the Cyl[inde]r filled with steam, I drew up the piston of the pumps and the weight immediately followed, to my great Joy, all this was done in a day or two after I had contrived it . . .

Your affectionate Friend

J. WATT

John Robison (1739-1805)

John Robison, while still a student at Glasgow, first suggested the steam engine as a subject for enquiry to James Watt. His own career took him to Quebec, Jamaica and St Petersburg before he became Professor of Natural Philosophy at Edinburgh. He was one of the leading scientific writers of his age and also an accomplished musician. Watt said of him that he was the man of 'clearest head and most science' that he had ever known.

As is evident from many of the letters in this anthology, the literati of the Scottish Enlightenment were bound together by strong ties of affection and mutual respect. We see this, for example, in the account of the death of his friend and colleague, Joseph Black, the most eminent chemist of his time in Europe.

63. 'Sir Isaac Newton of that Ilk'

To James Watt   *Edinburgh 3 May 1797*

My good Sir,

I don't know whether Mrs. Robison has told you how much she thinks of her own Judgement and Taste since she finds that her previous Stock of Silver and plated Goods comprehended the very articles that you thought most likely to be acceptable. I only know that your Authority is now frequently made use of against my opinions. I was in hopes of sending along with the returned Articles a specimen of Leith Glass Manufacture which my Wife boasted of at Mr. Rennies, but it is not yet ready — Your keepsake Standish is most welcome, but it will require some time's Service to put it on a par with the homely apparatus of my Study.

Mr. Boulton (to whom I request your kind remembrance of me) put a wish into my brain that you will perhaps think very extravagant. He told me that you had some Letters of Sir Isaac Newton's to Nicholas Facio — I dare say you don't altogether refuse your Sympathy to my superstitious veneration for every relick of that wonderful Man. I would give anything to have a Scrap, however insignificant of his writing, and if your Collection could admit of any pruning, a twig or two would be an inestimable present. I believe I told you that I had been on the hunt to find documents of his Scotch Extraction, and that he himself firmly believed that his Granfather was a younger Son of Sir — Newton of that Ilk in East Lothian, and wrote to the last Man of the family requesting information whether some of the younger Sons did not attend James VI When he succeeded to the Crown of England — I am still in hopes of finding that Letter. Should I be able to render this descent probable, I will lodge an account of my Labours in the University Library — Would not that be a proper deposit for your Collection of Letters.

And this brings another thing in to my head — Would not a description and even a good Model of your Engine be a becoming present from You to the Museum of the University of Glasgow — I know that it would be received with great Affection and Respect. — Think of this at your Leisure, as also of a new doctorat that I am scheming with some hopes of Success, if we can find a proper Name for it — Doctor of Arts — a Collegium or Corporation of Scientific Engineers, with three degrees of Bachelor Master and Doctor — not merely academical honours, of no more value than the offices of a Mason Lodge, but to have Civil Consequences — As a Man must have a diploma to entitle him to a consulting fee, so should an Engineer etc. etc. — I had more to say — but the Wright has come to close the Box — so farewell —

Your faithful Freind and Wellwisher

JOHN ROBISON

Mrs. Robison begs to be remembred to Mrs. Watt, and would have written just now but has been much occupyd by some strangers who are with us

64. The death of Joseph Black

To James Watt   *Edinburgh 11 December 1799*

My dear Sir

Colonel Burnet has devolved on me the mournful Task of informing You of the Loss of your dear freind Dr. Black, who died last Friday. Knowing how severely you must feel this long expected stroke, I should hardly have accepted of the unpleasant office, were it not in my power to tell you that his End was such as his most affectionate freind would wish; without a groan, and without warning. The Servant had set down his little dinner before him while he was busy with a Tinman about a pan for warming his Mess — Some time after, a Gentleman called — the Servant opened the door, and announced him the doctor sitting as usual, on the End of the Sopha, with his back to the door, and his legs lying along the Sopha. He made no answer, and John told the Gentleman that his Master was asleep, and desired him to call again — and then went down Stairs — but, recollecting that the doctor had scarcely had time to prepare and eat his little Mess, and that he never had observed him fall asleep at dinner before, he went up again, opened the door, and stepped forward till he could see his Masters face. He saw him with his Eyes shut, and having his Bason of Milk standing between his thighs, supported by his right hand — Thinking him asleep, and the Milk in no danger of spilling, he went back again, and shut the door — but as he was going down Stairs, his heart misgave him, and he returned, and came forward and called him by name pretty loud — got no answer — he then took hold of his hand, and felt all cold — in short, found, as he said, that his poor Master had given over living — the bason was not fully supported by its position, and was really kept up by Dr. Blacks hand.

What an enviable close of Life — to every Man — and to our dear freind, it was inestimable — You know that his mind was elegance itself — He sometimes hinted his uneasyness at the thought of becoming silly, or slovenly, or squalid — and even of the last Struggle of life — and could not bear the thought of any undecency of conduct or appearance — his wish was completely gratified — for life must have ceased without a pang — the Servant told me that for an hour there was not any change observable on his countenance — had skilful people been about him, that sweet countenance might have been preserved — when I saw him next morning the lips had been allowed to contract.

Dr. Black had been in remarkably good spirits ever since the beginning of Autumn, and was as busy as a Man hanging by his slender thread could be — He was scheming a new Laboratory, to be built by subscription, of which he was to be the Contriver and the Architect — and never was without some gentle occupation. — Elegance and propriety modelled every thought, and his every Sketch has a beauty which would be highly prized, if found at Herculaneum. *Quando ullum inveniemus parem?**

I think that You, my dear freind, and Mr Geddes of Leith, had the greatest share of Dr. Blacks esteem and affection. I am now proud of having had some of his attentions. You know well that he was both a sagacious and a delicate judge of character, and that Dr. Blacks favourable opinion[s] are an honour to any Man. I owe to him my first introduction to the notice and acquaintance of Men of Science and Worth, and his Countenance gave me more confidence in myself. — When I returned from London, at the account which I gave him of your triumph over Hornblower and Co[mpany] he was delighted, even to tears. He said 'it is very foolish, but I can't help it, when I hear of anything good to Jamy Watt'.

* When shall we find his like?

66

I think our excellent friend well away from a World that is no longer worth living in, and I envy his Situation, not tied to it by those whom he has brought into it, and must leave in it. We are posting as hard as we can to brutality and barbarism, and must, I think, soon shake hands w[i]t[h] confusion and calamity, I am decidedly of opinion that when Man ceases to respect himself as the subject of a moral government of the World, he will soon cease to think it beneath him to live like a brute, depending only on himself, and minding nothing but himself . . .

And now my dear Sir farewell — may the winter pass smoothly and all at your Fireside be hearty.

So prays,
    Your affectionate Friend and Serv[an]t

JOHN ROBISON

Please offer my best Compliments to
Mr. Boulton's Family

☆   ☆   ☆

James Boswell (1740-95)

Boswell was described by David Hume in a letter of 12 January 1766 as 'a young gentleman, very good-humoured, very agreeable, and very mad'. In his own lifetime, he published two notable books, his Life of Samuel Johnson *(1791), generally regarded as the greatest of all biographies, and his* Journal of a Tour to the Hebrides with Samuel Johnson *(1785). It was not until the present century that publication began of the full range of his Journals, perhaps the fullest and frankest self-portrait in any language.*

In a letter of 31 July 1764, Boswell said of himself: 'It is certain that I am not a great man, but I have an enthusiastic love of great men, and I derive a kind of glory from it'. His cultivation of Hume, Johnson and Rousseau are examples, but their response is a tribute to his own qualities.

He was married to Margaret Montgomerie (Letter 69).

65. Overture to Rousseau
(Original in French)

To Jean Jacques Rousseau   *Val de Travers 3 December 1764*

Sir,

I am a Scots gentleman of ancient family. Now you know my rank. I am twenty-four years old. Now you know my age. Sixteen months ago I left Great Britain a completely insular being, knowing hardly a word of French. I have been in Holland and in Germany, but not yet in France. You will therefore excuse my handling of the language. I am travelling with a genuine desire to improve myself. I have come here in the hope of seeing you.

I have heard, Sir, that you are very difficult, that you have refused the visits of several people of the first distinction. For that, Sir, I respect you the more. If you admitted all those who from vanity wished to be able to say, 'I have seen him,' your house would no longer be the retreat of exquisite genius or elevated piety, and I should not be striving so eagerly to be received into it.

I present myself, Sir, as a man of singular merit, as a man with a feeling heart, a lively but melancholy spirit. Ah, if all that I have suffered does not give me singular merit in the eyes of Monsieur Rousseau, why was I made as I am? Why did he write as he has written?

Do you ask if I have recommendations? Surely you do not need them? In the commerce of the world a recommendation is necessary in order to protect people who lack penetration from impostors. But you, Sir, who have made such deep study of human nature, can you be deceived in a character? I think of you thus: excepting for the incomprehensible essence of the soul, you have a perfect knowledge of all the principles of body and mind, of their movements, their sentiments; in short, of everything they can do, of everything they can acquire which truly affects man as man. And yet, Sir, I dare present myself before you. I dare to put myself to the test. In cities and in courts, where there are numerous companies, one can disguise one's self, one can sometimes dazzle the eyes of the greatest philosophers. But for my part, I put myself to the severest test. It is in the silence and the solitude of your sacred retreat that you shall judge of me, and think you in such circumstances I shall be able to dissimulate?

Your writings, Sir, have melted my heart, have elevated my soul have fired my imagination. Believe me, you will be glad to have seen me. You know what Scots pride is. Sir, I am coming to see you in order to make myself more worthy of a nation that has produced a Fletcher of Saltoun and a Lord Marischal. Forgive me, Sir, I feel myself moved. I cannot restrain myself. O dear Saint-Preux! Enlightened Mentor! Eloquent and amiable Rousseau! I have a presentiment that a truly noble friendship will be born today.

I learn with deep regret, Sir, that you are often indisposed. Perhaps you are so at present. But I beg you not to let that prevent you from receiving me. You will find in me a simplicity that will put you to no trouble, a cordiality that may help you forget your pains.

I have much to tell you. Though I am only a young man, I have experienced a variety of existence that will amaze you. I find myself in serious and delicate circumstances concerning which I eagerly hope to have the counsel of the author of the *Nouvelle Héloïse*. If you are the charitable man I believe you to be, you cannot hesitate to grant it to me. Open your door, then, Sir, to a man who dares to tell you that he deserves to enter it. Place your confidence in a stranger who is different. You will not regret it. But I beg you, be alone. In spite of all my enthusiasm, after having written to you in this fashion, I know not if I would not prefer never to see you than to see you for the first time in company. I await your reply with impatience.

Boswell

66. The misfortune of drink

To the Rev. William Temple   *Edinburgh 9 December 1768*

My dear Temple,
You are by this time well acquainted with my present situation. Many a different one have you known me in.

You must comfort me; for by the time I can have your answer, my spirits will be very low.

My present misfortune is occasioned by drinking. Since my return to Scotland I have given a great deal too much into that habit which still prevails in Scotland.

Perhaps the coldness of the Scots requires it. But my fiery blood is turned to madness by it. This will be a warning to me, and from henceforth I shall be a perfect man. At least I hope so. Adieu, my friend. Let us correspond once a fortnight. Write me fully. Tell me sincerely, Do I right to insist that my dear little woman shall stay? She was married very young. But she has three children. I hate to think of it. No matter. She is like a girl of eighteen. She has the finest black hair, she is paradisial in bed. Is it not right I should have a favourite to keep me happy? But, alas, I love her so much that I am in a kind of fever. This is unworthy of Paoli's friend. Lord Eglintoune once observed very justly that a man may be in love with an Italian woman of gallantry, because by the custom of the country she does not think she is doing wrong, — so may be called virtuous. But in this country a woman of gallantry is a woman without principle. There is too much truth in this. But I cannot apply it to my angel. By the by, she is now more affected by my bad conduct than she was at first. *Adieu encore.*

JAMES BOSWELL

67. With Johnson at Forres

To David Garrick   *Inverness 29 August 1773*

My dear Sir,
Here I am, and Mr. Samuel Johnson actually with me. We were a night at Fores, in coming to which, in the dusk of the evening, we passed over the bleak and blasted heath where Macbeth met the witches. Your old preceptor repeated, with much solemnity, the speech —

> How far is't called to Fores? What are these;
> So wither'd and so wild in their attire, &c.

This day we visited the ruins of Macbeth's castle at Inverness. I have had great romantick satisfaction in seeing Johnson upon the classical scenes of Shakspeare in Scotland; which I really looked upon as almost as improbable as that 'Birnam wood should come to Dunsinane'. Indeed, as I have always been accustomed to view him as a permanent London object, it would not be much more wonderful to me to see St. Paul's Church moving along where we now are. As yet we have travelled in post-chaises; but to-morrow we are to mount on horseback, and ascend into the mountains by Fort Augustus, and so on to the ferry, where we are to cross to Sky. We shall see that island fully, and then visit some more of the Hebrides; after which we are to land in Argyleshire, proceed by Glasgow to Auchinleck, repose there a competent time, and then return to Edinburgh, from whence the Rambler will depart for old England again, as soon as he finds it convenient. Hitherto we have had a very prosperous expedition. I flatter myself, *servetur ad imum qualis ab incepto processerit.** He is in excellent spirits, and I have a rich journal of his conversation. Look back, *Davy*, to Litchfield — run up through the time that has elapsed since you first knew Mr. Johnson — and enjoy with me his present extraordinary tour. I could not resist the impulse of writing to you from this place. The situation of the old castle corresponds exactly to Shakespeare's description. While we were there to-day, it happened oddly, that a raven perched upon one of the chimney-tops, and croaked. Then I in my turn repeated —

> The raven himself is hoarse,
> That croaks the fatal enterance of Duncan,
> Under my battlements.

I wish you had been with us. Think what enthusiastick happiness I shall have to see Mr. Samuel Johnson walking among the romantick rocks and woods of my ancestors at Auchinleck! Write to me at Edinburgh. You owe me his verses on great George and tuneful Cibber, and the bad verses which led him to make his fine ones on Philips the musician.

Keep your promise, and let me have them. I offer my very best compliments to Mrs. Garrick, and ever am,

Your warm admirer and friend,

JAMES BOSWELL

---

* Horace, *Ars Poetica*, l 126: May it keep on to the end in the same way as it began.

68. A complaint against the Lord Mayor

To the Printer of the Public Advertiser   *London 6 April 1779*

Sir,

I am by birth a *North Briton,* as a *Scotchman* must now be called, but like a great many of my countrymen love much to come to London. And why not, Sir? as since the union of the two kingdoms, which deprived us of all national dignity and all the advantages of a vice-court and of a parliament in our own district, London is now the metropolis of the whole island, the grand emporium of everything valuable, the strong centre of attraction for all of us, His Majesty's British subjects, from the Land's End to Caithness. Full of high notions of this GREAT CITY AND OF ITS CHIEF MAGISTRATE, THE LORD MAYOR, in the *abstract,* without respect of persons (as I am now old enough to know that the Mansion-house is successively inhabited by men of all characters, and that *there,* as at Baldock's mill,

> The grave and the gay, the clown and the beau,
> Without all distinction promiscuously go),

I went last night to the ball at the Mansion-house, and having feasted my eyes and my ears for some time, I desired to have a little negus to recruit my animal spirits. But what was my astonishment, Sir, when the waiters told me I could not have it; it was all gone, they had no more wine. Several ladies and gentlemen, I found, were in the same state of disappointment that I was. Upon which, Sir, I asked an English friend if this could possibly be countenanced by the Lord Mayor. I was informed he was a Mr. Alderman Plumbe, but that his penuriousness was excessive. I was determined however that he should not escape quite *impune,* if he had any *feeling,* and that I should be, if not a *thorn,* at least a *thistle* in his side. Accordingly, away I marched to find his *Lordship;* and pray, Sir, how d'ye think I found him occupied? Upon my honour (and I can bring fifty witnesses, with a city marshal at their head), I found him standing without his gown or chain, in a bag-wig and marone coat, with his back leaning against the staircase, telling the company not to go upstairs, in order that he might get rid of them. Up I went, though, in the first place to the Egyptian Hall, to see what was doing; and *there* was a number of ladies and gentlemen standing up for a country dance; but when they called for music, they were told the music were discharged by the Lord Mayor to play any more without fresh orders; and in a little time they moved off, amidst the hisses of the company, who I took it for granted would have instantly broke his lamps into shivers with a just indignation.

But to return to my negus, *his Lordship*, having come upstairs, stood despondent in one of the antechambers. I went to him, and with a low bow addressed him thus: 'My Lord Mayor, I ask pardon for giving your Lordship this trouble, but I beg your Lordship would order me a glass of negus. I am afraid your Lordship is ill used by some of your servants. I asked for negus, and they told me there was none.'

Now, Mr. Woodfall, upon the word of an honest man, which *you know* I am, I shall give you literally what passed, without the least exaggeration. His Lordship with awkward surprise and confusion said, 'Sir, I *wish* you had asked for it sooner.' I would not quit him. 'My Lord,' said I (putting the breasts of my coat in a buttoning attitude), 'I have got a little cold; if you'll let me have a single glass, I'll be obliged to you. Here, Sir' (calling one of his silver-laced attendants who approached us), 'if your Lordship will please give your orders to one of your servants —' 'Sir,' (replied THE LORD MAYOR OF LONDON), 'I have no command of the negus' — and slunk away.

Now, Sir, are not you Englishmen a set of pretty fellows? You talk with horror of an Edinburgh mob committing a few outrages, and you say not a word of a London mob the very week after breaking half the windows of your peaceable citizens. You talk of Scotch poverty, yet I will venture to say that at no public entertainment in the pettiest borough in Scotland would a gentleman have been refused a glass of negus. The Provost (or Mayor) of Little Lord Galloway's little borough of Whithorn would have lived on herrings and water for a week, rather than have his *toon* (town) so disgraced. At Edinburgh, *Walter Hamilton*, our worthy LORD PROVOST, would have ordered a DOUBLE BOTTLE, a SCOTCH PINT, a BONUM MAGNUM of excellent CLARET (which by the way, Harry, you would like very well to see) and would show that he 'has the command' of a generous cellar. But in the *Mansion-house of the City of London* a glass of negus is not to be had after one o'clock in the morning; and the Lord Mayor, with all the authority of his office, has not the command of a little wine and water and sugar. So wretchedly inhospitable a house as your Mansion-house last night I never was in. Let *Mr. Wilkes*, if he can spare time from his new employment of *Defender of the Faith*, (as he is always encroaching on *royal prerogative*,) defend *English* liberality if he can. Why, Sir, Whittington's cat must have starved had she been there. Though indeed I was not a *hungry* Scotchman; I wanted only a drop of *liquor*; and I went to the *fountain-head*. But, alas! it was quite *dry*; there was no *juice* in the *plum*. Yet this man, I am told, has amassed what you call a *plum* by *sweating* and *refining* gold. A *sweat*, and a hearty one too, he ought to have. But to *refine* him will be no easy task. For my own part, all that I can say is, that be his wealth ever so great, this PLUMBE of yours is in my opinion at present not worth a FIG.

TANTALUS

Margaret Montgomerie (1738-1789)

Margaret Montgomerie was a first cousin and childhood confidante of James Boswell (Letters 65-68) whom she married in November 1769. She was an ideal wife for Boswell because, as the following letter shows, she understood him very well and provided him with some necessary ballast. She was patient and tolerant, but fully capable of speaking her mind, as in her well-known comparison of Johnson's tour with Boswell to a bear leading a man. Her death in 1789 was a blow from which Boswell never quite recovered.

69. 'Resignation in everything'

To James Boswell   *Lainshaw 1 July 1769*

... I was very uneasy at your silence; fearful I had offended, or that want of health prevented you from writing. I own I am vastly too anxious, but I cannot help it; much I have endeavoured to be less so, but to no purpose.

I wish I had power to remove all uneasy thoughts from your mind — how happy would it make me! I would gladly recommend to you resignation to the Divine Will in everything, acknowledging that whatever He does is well and wisely ordered. I cannot see that, should what you suspect take place, it could hurt you. For God sake, do not therefore take any rash resolutions. You are warm, I know, but surely you will not allow any heat of passion to get the better of your good sense.

I will not allow the character you give of yourself to be just. If you are either sullen or discontented, it is your own fault. Naturally, you are quite the reverse. Allow your good principles once to get the better of bad habits, and you will be just as you could wish. Many times, though we are desirous to be cured of our faults, we are loath to part with them. Perhaps that may give you uneasiness without your being sensible of the cause; but persevere

74

in your good resolutions and you will find yourself quite a new man . . .

I shall perhaps write again in a post or two and put it in some other post office, as the Stewarton stamp may give rise to suspicions when so often making its appearance. Good night, God bless you. Remember me, if you think proper, to all with you, and believe me, my dear Jamie, your ever affectionate and obliged

M. MONTGOMERIE

* * *

Benjamin Forbes (fl. 1748)

In the seventeenth and eighteenth centuries, the Kirk Sessions regarded themselves as custodians of public and private morality. They were active in enquiring into the circumstances whenever an unmarried girl in the parish became pregnant, with a view to bringing both parents to repentance on the cutty stool. Dr Leah Leneman of Edinburgh University recently came across the following letter still attached to the records of the Kirk Session of Foveran near Aberdeen for the year 1748. The unfortunate Benjamin evidently went through every possible emotional reaction, but he seems to have been more afraid of his mother than of the Session.

70. 'If it be mine'

Margaret: I received a Note from you concerning your being with Child which I'm sorry for, however your best is to leave the Town and go up the Country among your Acquaintances, for my mother will be unsupportable if she find you out to be with Child in her service. Since you lay the Blame on me, I can't help it, but since you do, if you have a Boy you'll call his name Findlay. I'm just going to sail, so you'll best take my Advice and leave the Town. I am, your friend

BENJAMIN FORBES

P.S. If the Child be mine it's been gotten when asleep: however, when I return to the Country shall find the certainty of that, and take Care of it, if it be mine.

Hary Fergusson (1742-77)

Hary was the older brother of Robert Fergusson, the Edinburgh poet who in his short life captured incomparably in verse the spirit of the eighteenth-century city. Burns erected a tombstone to him in the Canongate Kirkyard, addressing him as 'My elder brother in misfortune, by far my elder brother in the muse'. No prose letter of Robert Fergusson appears to have survived, but in the following letter Hary not only refers to his brother's death but describes the beginning of the American Revolution. He seems subsequently to have obtained his discharge from the Tartar and supported the American cause.

71. The American Revolution

To his mother   Tartar *in Halifax Harbour*
6 May 1775

Dr Mother,

I received your letter of the 29th October last, containing the very disagreeable news of my brother's death, and acquainting me of Peggy's being married to one Mr. Alexander Duval who, you say, is in a very good way, but the particular branch of business he follows you forgot to mention. It is beyond the power of human invention to describe how I was affected by the loss of an only brother, who always had my interest at heart, and with whom I was yet in hopes to have spent many agreeable days. But that there is no certainty on this side the grave is a truth that we daily experience, and plainly proves that to repine is weakness in the highest degree. I earnestly desire you'll take care of all the papers and writings as he left for my perusal, for I shall be more pleas'd in being possess'd of them than riches, as the former may serve to perpetuate the memory which the latter can never do.

We are now actually at war with the Americans. A skirmish happen'd at a place ca . . . on the 18th ulto. betwixt the Provincials or rebels and . . . Majesty's . . . by . . . overpowered . . . after they had burnt two magazines of the enemies stores, obliged to retreat 15 or 18 miles through an incessant fire from behind the stone walls and branches on the roadside. No certain account of the loss on either side has as yet been published, but the rebels, it is said, have sustained treble the loss of the army. Both camps are so near that the sentries of each army can discourse together on their posts, and the rebels augment daily. Several places have lately been burnt by the army; and it is expected by this, that the town of Marblehead is reduced to ashes. No fresh provisions are to be had for any price in New England, and an entire stop is put to all trade. We are ordered here as a safeguard over the dockyard, where we do duty for fear of the disaffected attempting to set it on fire. Night before last, the New England people here set fire to a quantity of hay that was to have been purchased for the use of the troops at Boston, which obliges us to be more vigilant than formerly. I am glad that the money you received came so opportunely; whenever a remittance is made you shall not be forgot. My greatest desire is, to get home and settle for the remainder of my days, being, as I wrote you before, heartily tired of this way of life.

Remember me in the strongest manner to Mr. and Mrs. Inverarity and family, to Mr. and Mrs. Duval, and all acquaintances;

and do not forget to inform me what day of the month my brother expired on, and the disease.

I am, Dr Mother,

Your affectionate Son,

HARY FERGUSSON

Col. Alan Cameron of Erracht (1750-1828)

Colonel Cameron, who had fought in the American Civil War, raised the Cameron Highlanders, the 79th Regiment, in the 1790s and led them in the Peninsular campaign. In October 1804 Henry Thorpe, secretary to the Commander-in-Chief the Duke of York, wrote to Cameron to ask for his views on a proposal to abolish the kilt in the Highland regiments and substitute tartan trews. Cameron replied as follows:

72. In defence of the kilt

To Henry Thorpe Esq.   *Glasgow 27 October 1804*

Sir, — On my return hither some days ago from Stirling I received your letter of the 13th inst. (by General Calvert's orders) respecting the propriety of an alteration of the mode in clothing Highland regiments, in reply to which I beg to state, freely and fully, my sentiments upon that *subject*, without a particle of prejudice in either way, but merely founded on *facts* applicable to these corps — at least as far as I am *capable*, from thirty years' experience, twenty years of which have been upon *actual* service in all *climates*, with the description of men in question, which independent of being myself a Highlander, and well knowing all the convenience and inconvenience of our native garb in the field and otherwise, and perhaps, also, aware of the probable source and clashing motives from which the suggestion now under consideration originally arose. I have to observe, progressively, that in course of the late war several gentlemen proposed to raise Highland regiments — some for general service, but chiefly for home defence; but most of these corps were called upon from all quarters, and thereby adulterated by every description of men, that rendered them anything but real Highlanders, or even Scotchmen (which is not strictly synonymous); and the colonels themselves being generally unacquainted with the language and habits of Highlanders, while prejudiced in favour of, and accustomed to wear, breeches, consequently *adverse* to that free congenial circulation of that pure wholesome air (as an exhilarating native bracer) which has hitherto so peculiarly benefited the Highlander for *activity* and all the other necessary qualities of a soldier, whether for hardship upon scanty fare, *readiness in accoutring*, or making *forced marches*, — besides the exclusive advantage, when halted, of drenching his kilt in the *next brook*, as well as washing his limbs, and drying *both*, as it were, by constant *fanning*, without injury to either, but, on the contrary, feeling clean and comfortable; whilst the buffoon tartan pantaloon, with its fringed frippery (as some mongrel Highlanders would have it), sticking wet and dirty to the skin, is not very easily pulled off, and *less so* to get on again in case of alarm or any other hurry, and all this time absorbing both wet and dirt, followed by rheumatism and fevers, which alternately make great havoc in hot and cold climates; while it consists with knowledge, that the Highlander in his native garb always appeared more cleanly, and maintained better health in both climates, than those who wore even the thick cloth pantaloon Independent of these circumstances, I feel no hesitation in saying that the proposed alteration must have proceeded from a whimsical idea, more than from the real comfort of the Highland soldier, and a wish to lay aside that national martial garb, the very sight of which has, upon many occasions, struck the enemy with terror and confusion, and now metamorphose the Highlander from his real characteristic appearance and comfort in an odious incompatible dress, to which it will, in my opinion, be difficult to reconcile him, as a poignant grievance to and a galling reflection upon Highland corps, as levelling that martial distinction by which they have been hitherto *noticed and respected*, — and from my own experience, I feel well founded in saying that if anything was wanted to aid the rack-renting Highland landlord in destroying that source which has hitherto proved so fruitful in keeping up Highland corps, it will be that of abolishing their native garb, which His Royal Highness the Commander-in-Chief and the Adjutant-General may rest assured will prove a complete death-warrant to the recruiting service in that respect; but I sincerely hope his Royal Highness will never acquiesce in so painful and degrading an idea (come from whatever quarter it may) as to *stuff* us in a harlequin tartan pantaloon, which, composed of the usual quality that continues as at present worn, useful and becoming for twelve months, will not endure six weeks' fair wear as a pantaloon, and when patched makes a horrible appearance; besides that, the necessary quantity to serve decently throughout the year would become extremely expensive, but, above all, take away completely the appearance and conceit of a Highland soldier, in which case I would rather see him *stuffed* in breeches and abolish the distinction altogether. — I have the honour to be, sir, &c.,

Alan Cameron

The regimental historian adds the comment: 'This ridiculous proposal to abolish the kilt was then dropped.'

Lady Anne Barnard (1750-1825)

Better known as Lady Anne Lindsay for her poem Auld Robin Gray, *Anne Barnard was the wife of the first Secretary of Cape Colony. She was interested in the conversion of African tribes to Christianity. In a letter to Lord Melville, the British Secretary of State, to whom she wrote many witty letters, she describes her visit to the first Protestant mission station established in South Africa by George Schmidt, a Moravian missionary in 1737.*

73. Christian Hottentots

To Lord Melville   *Cape Town 18??*

... We set off again in our waggon, favoured with another charming day. Our object this morning was to see those humble missionaries who, sent by the Moravian Church about seven years ago, have made so great a progress in converting the Hottentots to Christianity... We travelled on over rough ground, and after about four hours arrived at the base of the Baviaan and Boscheman's Kloofs, where the settlement was... They asked us to step in to see the church; we found it about forty feet long and twenty broad; the pulpit was a platform raised only a few steps above the ground, and matted with some rushes, on which there were three chairs and a small table, on which was a Bible. I regretted very much that it was not Sunday — then I should have found the whole community, about three hundred Hottentots, assembled to Divine worship. The fathers said I should still see them, as at sunset every day, when business was over, there were prayers. Presently the church bell was a-ringing, and we begged leave to make part of the congregation.

I doubt much whether I should have entered St. Peter's at Rome with the triple crown, with a more devout impression of the Deity and His presence, than I felt in this little church of a few square feet, where the simple disciples of Christianity, dressed in the skins of animals, knew no purple or fine linen, no pride or hypocrisy. I felt as if I was creeping back seventeen hundred years, and heard from the rude and inspired lips of Evangelists the simple sacred words of wisdom and purity. The service began with a Presbyterian form of psalm; about one hundred and fifty Hottentots joined in the twenty-third psalm in a tone so sweet and loud, so chaste and true, that it was impossible to hear it without being surprised. The fathers, who were the sole music-masters, sang in their deep-toned bass along with them, and the harmony was excellent. This over, the miller took a portion of the Scripture and expounded it as he went along. The father's discourse was short, and the tone of his voice was even and natural, and when he used the words, as he often did, *myne lieve vriende*, 'my beloved friends,' I felt that he thought they were all his children.

Alexander MacDougall (1754-95)

Dr. Alexander MacDougall was a younger son of the 23rd Chief of the MacDougalls. He saw military service as a surgeon in India and died in Russia.

74. The campaign against Hyder Ally

To Patrick MacDougall

Camp near Marmelong, India
30 September 1780

... You see by the date of this letter that the Army is in the field. The campaign was open'd the beginning of Aug. under the command of Sir Hector Munro against Hyder Ally who entered the Congeveram with an immense army of 100,000 Horse, 40,000 infantry and 100 pieces of Canon ...

The enemy made a desperate Charge and cut through the line. Our Highlanders as usual, though their ammunition was almost expended, Charg'd through immense Columns of Horse with fix'd Bayonets. The other troops behaved with great Bravery but were at last overcome with numbers. In short the whole army under Baillie were all either kill'd, wounded or taken prisoners, the number killed is not yet known ... upon the whole nothing equal to it ever happened in this country.

When the General found the Misfortune to Baillie's Army confirmed he immediately contermarched back to Congeveram that same night where we had left all our provisions and Baggage, where we lay all night upon our arms after marching all day in the scorching heat without any provisions or refreshments of any kind. I myself was almost overcome with hunger and Fatigue yet was obliged to sit up all night dressing the wounded, in short you never saw such a butcher in the flesh market more compleatly bismeared with blood etc than I was at 3 o'clock in the morning without rest or food.

Daylight was not well come in when immense collums of the Enemy's horses appeared everywhere, in front, near and on both our Flanks. Our rear Guard would beyond a doubt have been cut off had not Lord MacLeod, who Commanded the right wing, sent them a timely reinforcement . . . Our Flanking parties were frequently beat back upon the line.

A Capt. George Campbell who Commanded a Battl. of Seapoys was shot through the loins. I cut out the Ball upon the field of Battle and he is now in a fair way of recovery. He is from Rosshire and an exceedingly good fellow . . .

We were from 3 o'clock in the morning of the 11th until 9 o'clock of the 12th constantly upon our feet, had been for 2 days I may say, without any food, constantly exposed to the intense heat of the sun and perpetually teased by the Enemy's horse, in which time we marched no less than 50 miles . . .

Surgeons in this country makes money in Proportion to the number of Europeans they have charge of . . . this reduces my revenue to one half, my Kings pay and profits always remains the same but it is so unconsiderable I never hardly count upon it, it does not by any means half pay my servants. But from Lord McLeod's being always my steady friend, indeed more in the style of a Father than anything else, I am still able in some measure to evade the loss I should other ways sustain by the Regt. being so much reduced. In short if I live and enjoy health and Lord McLeod and the regt. remains in this country, in 3 or 4 years I shall still, barring misfortunes, be able to render myself comfortable for life, at least it will assist. The lancet will not bleed a bit the worse of being assisted by the Gold Pagodas of the Carnatic.

Sir John Sinclair of Ulbster, Bart.
(1754 - 1835)

John Sinclair was the instigator and editor of one of the great achievements of the age of the Enlightenment, the Statistical Account of Scotland, *published in 21 volumes between 1791 and 1799, and the first attempt anywhere to describe the conditions of a country in detail and in all its aspects. Sinclair introduced the word 'statistics' into the language, but his usage was different from the modern practice. It applied, he wrote, to 'an inquiry into the state of a country, for the purpose of ascertaining the quantum of happiness enjoyed by its inhabitants, and the means of its future improvement'. The report was written by the ministers of the 938 parishes in response to a questionnaire which Sinclair sent to them with the approval of the General Assembly.*

75. The Statistical Account

To the Moderator of the General Assembly

> 133 George Street, Edinburgh
> 24 May 1825

Reverend Sir

I have already had the honour of presenting to the venerable assembly a copy of the statistical Account of Scotland, drawn up from the Communications of the Ministers of the several Parishes, and published in Twenty one volumes 8 vo. Though this work was completed in 1799 — though a period of above 25 years has since elapsed, — and though the same plan has often been attempted in other countries, it still remains *an unrivalled proof* of the general knowledge — the superior ability; — and the ardent public zeal of the Ministers of our National Church.

From the commencement of the Statistical Enquiry, it was my intention, (as stated in the advertisement to vol. 20), to lay before the public, *'an Analysis'* of the valuable information which it might contain. For some time past I have been occupied in drawing up that 'Analysis', the First Part of which being printed, I hasten to present it to the Assembly.

The Analysis, when completed, will be found to comprehend the substance of the valuable information transmitted to me by the Clergy, and as it will be condensed into one volume, octavo, that mass of useful knowledge which the Statistical Account contains, will be rendered much more accessible than it has hitherto been; and more likely to be known and justly appreciated, both at Home and Abroad. I have the satisfaction of adding that translations of the

Analysis into French and German have already commenced, under the auspices of some of the most distinguished characters on the Continent.

There was every reason to hope that such minute and extensive enquiries into the state of a country would throw much light on some important points in the science of Political Economy. In that expectation, the public will not, I trust, be disappointed. In that portion of the intended work which I have now the honour of presenting to the Assembly, the real state of a great political community has, for the First time, been analized; and all the various classes into which a society can be properly divided, are explained. Complete accuracy in a first attempt of that nature cannot be looked for; but the method is pointed out, by which greater perfection can be obtained; and thus the principles on which a great country may be successfully governed, will ultimately be fully ascertained and established.

The Clergy of Scotland will derive great satisfaction from having so essentially contributed by their labours, to the attainment of so important an object.

Permit me to add, that the very flattering manner in which the Assembly were pleased to recommend the original undertaking, by their unanimous vote of the 27th May 1793, was of the greatest advantage to me in carrying on the original work: and I am thence induced to hope that the Church still feels a warm interest in its farther progress and ultimate success.

Ann Grant (1755-1838)

Ann MacVicar, the daughter of a Highland officer, was born in Glasgow but brought up chiefly in America. In 1773 her father was stationed at Fort Augustus. There, in 1779, she married James Grant, the minister of Laggan. The people of the Highlands made a strong impression on her. She conveys the early impact in a letter she wrote from Oban, when she was eighteen, to Harriet Reid, a friend in Glasgow.

76. Highland old age

To Harriet Reid   *Oban 1773*

. . . This is certainly a fine country to grow old in. I could not spare a look to the young people, so much was I engrossed in contemplating their grandmothers.—Stately, erect and self-satisfied, without a trace of the langour or coldness of age, they march up the area [of the Kirk of Kilmore] with gaudy coloured plaids, fastened about their breasts with a silver brooch like the full moon in size and shape.

I was trying to account for the expression in the countenance of these cheerful ancients (many above fourscore) while the pastor, with vehement animation, was holding forth in the native tongue. Now here is the result: people who are forever consecrating the memory of the departed, and hold the virtues, nay the faults of their ancestors, in such blind veneration, see much to love and revere in their parents, that others never think of. They accumulate on these patriarchs all the virtues of their progenitors, and think the united splendour reflects a lustre on themselves. The old people, treated with unvaried tenderness and veneration, feel no diminution of their consequence, no chill in their affections. Strangers to neglect, they are also strangers to suspicion. The young readily give to old age that cordial, by which they hope to be supported when their own almond trees begin to blossom. But fine people do not seem ever to think they shall be old. Now, in their way, I should love my father not merely as such, but because he was the son of the wise and pious Donald, whose memory the whole parish of Craignish venerates, and the grandson of the gallant Archibald, who was the tallest man in the district; who could throw the putting stone farther than any Campbell living, and never held a Christmas without a deer of his own killing, four Fingalian greyhounds at his fireside, and sixteen kinsmen sharing his feast. Shall I not be proud of a father, the son of such fathers, of whose fame he is the living record? Now, what is my case is every other Highlander's; for we all contrive to be wonderfully happy in our ancestry; and by this means the sages here get a good deal of reverence and attention, not usually paid to the 'Struldbruggs' of other countries. Observe, moreover, that they serve for song books and circulating libraries; so faithfully do they preserve, and so accurately detail, 'the tales of the times of old', and the songs of the bards, that now strike the viewless harp on wandering clouds. All this, with their constant cheerfulness, makes them the delight of the *very young*, in the happy period of wonder and simplicity; and their finding themselves so, prevents their being peevish, or querulous. Ossian was never more mistaken than when he said, 'Age is dark and unlovely'; here it appears 'like the setting moon on the western wave', and we bless the brightness of its departure. . .

Robert Burns (1759 - 96)

In his Journal on 13 December 1813, Byron said that he had been reading 'a quantity of Burns's unpublished, and never to be published, Letters . . . What an antithetical mind—tenderness, roughness—delicacy, coarseness—sentiment, sensuality—soaring and grovelling, dirt and deity—all mixed up in that one compound of inspired clay!' DeLancey Ferguson, the editor of Burns's Letters, denied that there was any split in his personality; 'Like most first-rate minds, his was able to view life from more than one angle, . . . but the mind was integral . . . This is Burns as he was, with all his pride and passion, his "skinless sensibility" and his bawdry; above all with his Scots patriotism.'

77. 'Caledonia, and Caledonia's Bard'

To John Ballantine   *Edinburgh 14 January 1787*

. . . I went to a Mason-lodge yesternight where the Most Worshipful Grand Master Charters, and all the Grand lodge of Scotland visited.—The meeting was most numerous and elegant; all the different Lodges about town were present, in all their pomp.—The Grand Master who presided with great solemnity, and honor to himself as a Gentleman and Mason, among other general toasts gave, 'Caledonia, & Caledonia's Bard, brother B———,' which rung through the whole Assembly with multiplied honors and repeated acclamations.—As I had no idea such a thing would happen, I was downright thunderstruck, and, trembling in every nerve, made the best return in my power. — Just as I had finished, some of the Grand Officers said so loud as I could hear, with a most comforting accent, 'Very well indeed!' which set me something to rights again.

I have just now had a visit from my Landlady who is a staid, sober, piously-disposed, sculdudery-abhoring Widow, coming on her grand climacterick.—She is at present in sore tribulation respecting some 'Daughters of Belial' who are on the floor immediately above.—My Landlady who as I said is a flesh-disciplining, godly Matron, firmly believes that her husband is in Heaven; and having been very happy with him on earth, she vigorously and perseveringly practices some of the most distinguishing Christian virtues, such as, attending Church, railing against vice, &c. that she may be qualified to meet her dear quondam Bedfellow in that happy place where the Unclean & the ungodly shall never enter.—This, no doubt, requires some strong exertions of Self-denial, in a hale, well-kept Widow of forty five; and as our floors are low and ill-plaistered, we can easily distinguish our laughter-loving, night-rejoicing neighbors — when they are eating, when they are drinking, when they are singing, when they are &c., my worthy Landlady tosses sleepless & unquiet, 'looking for rest but finding none,' the whole night.—Just now she told me, though by the by she is sometimes dubious that I am, in her own phrase, 'but a rough an' roun' Christian' that 'We should not be uneasy and envious because the Wicked enjoy the good things of this life; for these base jades who, in her own words, lie up gandygoin with their filthy fellows, drinking the best of wines, and singing abominable songs, they shall one day lie in hell, weeping and wailing and gnashing their teeth over a cup of God's wrath!'

I have this day corrected my 152^d page.— My best good wishes to Mr Aiken.—

> I am ever, Dr Sir,
> your much indebted humble serv^t
> ROB^T BURNS

78. 'Landlowper-like stravaguin'

To Mr William Nicol *Carlisle 1st June 1787 — or*
Master of the High School Edinburgh *I believe the 39th o' May rather*

Kind, honest-hearted Willie,

I'm sitten down here, after seven and forty miles ridin, e'en as forjesket and forniaw'd as a forfoughten cock, to gie you some notion o' my landlowper-like stravaguin sin the sorrowfu' hour that I sheuk hands and parted wi' auld Reekie.—

My auld, ga'd Gleyde o' a meere has huchyall'd up hill and down brae, in Scotland and England, as teugh and birnie as a vera devil wi' me.— It's true, she's as poor's a Sang-maker and as hard's a kirk, and tipper-taipers when she taks the gate first like a Lady's gentlewoman in a minuwae, or a hen on a het girdle, but she's a yauld, poutherie Girran for a' that; and has a stomach like Willie Stalker's meere that wad hae digeested tumbler-wheels, for she'll whip me aff her five stimparts o' the best aits at a down-sittin and ne'er fash her thumb.—When ance her ringbanes and spavies, her crucks and cramps, are fairly soupl'd, she beets to, beets to, and ay the hindmost hour the tightest.—I could wager her price to a thretty pennies that, for twa or three wooks riding at fifty mile a day, the deil-sticket a five gallopers acqueesh Clyde and Whithorn could cast saut in her tail.—

I hae dander'd owre a' the kintra frae Dumbar to Selcraig, and hae forgather'd wi' monie a guid fallow, and monie a weel-far'd hizzie.—I met wi' twa dink quines in particlar, ane o' them a sonsie, fine fodgel lass, baith braw and bonie; the tither was a clean-shankit, straught, tight, weel-far'd winch, as blythe's a lintwhite on a flowerie thorn, and as sweet and modest's a new blawn plumrose in a hazle shaw.— They were baith bred to mainers by the beuk, and onie ane o' them has muckle smeddum and rumblegumtion as the half o' some Presbytries that you and I baith ken.— They play'd me sik a deevil o' a shavie that I daur say if my harigals were turn'd out, ye wad see twa nicks i' the heart o' me like the mark o' a kail-whittle in a castock.—

I was gaun to write you a lang pystle, but, Gude forgie me, I gat myself sae noutouriously bitchify'd the day after kail-time that I can hardly stoiter but and ben.—

My best respecks to the guidwife and a' our common friens, especiall M^r & Mrs Cruickshank and the honest Guidman o' Jock's Lodge.—

I'll be in Dumfries the morn gif the beast be to the fore and the branks bide hale.—

Gude be wi' you, Willie! Amen————

Rob^T Burns

79. 'The story of Wallace'
(From the autobiographical letter)

To John Moore   *Mauchline 2 August 1787*

. . . I was born a very poor man's son.—For the first six or seven years of my life, my father was gardiner to a worthy gentleman of small estate in the neighbourhood of Ayr.—Had my father continued in that situation, I must have marched off to be one of the underlings about a farm-house; but it was his dearest wish and prayer to have it in his power to keep his children under his own eye till they could discern between good and evil; so with the assistance of his generous Master my father ventured on a small farm in his estate.—At these years I was by no means a favorite with any body.—I was a good deal noted for a retentive memory, a stubborn, sturdy something in my disposition, and an enthusiastic, idiot piety.—I say idiot piety, because I was then but a child.—Though I cost the schoolmaster some thrashings, I made an excellent English scholar; and against the years of ten or eleven, I was absolutely a

Critic in substantives, verbs and particles.—In my infant and boyish days too, I owed much to an old Maid of my Mother's, remarkable for her ignorance, credulity and superstition.— She had, I suppose, the largest collection in the county of tales and songs concerning devils, ghosts, fairies, brownies, witches, warlocks, spunkies, kelpies, elf-candles, deadlights, wraiths, apparitions, cantraips, giants, inchanted towers, dragons and other trumpery.—This cultivated the latent seeds of Poesy; but had so strong an effect on my imagination, that to this hour, in my nocturnal rambles, I sometimes keep a sharp look-out in suspicious places; and though nobody can be more sceptical in these matters than I, yet it often takes an effort of Philosophy to shake off these idle terrors.—The earliest thing of Composition that I recollect taking pleasure in was, The vision of Mizra and a hymn of Addison's beginning — 'How are Thy servants blest, O Lord!' I particularly remember one half-stanza which was music to my boyish ear—

'For though in dreadful whirls we hung,
'High on the broken wave'—

I met with these pieces in Mas[s]on's English Collection, one of my school-books.—The two first books I ever read in private, and which gave me more pleasure than any two books I ever read again, were, the life of Hannibal and the history of Sir William Wallace.—Hannibal gave my young ideas such a turn that I used to strut in raptures up and down after the recruiting drum and bagpipe, and wish myself tall enough to be a soldier; while the story of Wallace poured a Scotish prejudice in my veins which will boil along there till the flood-gates of life shut in eternal rest.—Polemical divinity about this time was putting the country half-mad; and I, ambitious of shining in conversation parties on Sundays between sermons, funerals, &c. used in a few years more to puzzle Calvinism with so much heat and indiscretion that I raised a hue and cry of heresy against me which has not ceased to this hour. . .

My father's generous Master died; the farm proved a ruinous bargain; and, to clench the curse, we fell into the hands of a Factor who sat for the picture I have drawn of one in my Tale of two dogs.—My father was advanced in life when he married; I was the eldest of seven children; and he, worn out by early hardship, was unfit for labour.— My father's spirit was soon irritated, but not easily broken.—There was freedom in his lease in two years more, and to weather these two years we retrenched expences.—We lived very poorly; I was a dextrous Ploughman for my years; and the next eldest to me was a brother, who could drive the plough very well and helped me to thrash.—A Novel-Writer might perhaps have viewed these scenes with some satisfaction, but so did not I: my indignation yet boils at the recollection of the scoundrel tyrant's insolent, threatening epistles, which used to set us all in tears. —

This kind of life, the chearless gloom of a hermit with the unceasing moil of a galley-slave, brought me to my sixteenth year; a little before which period I first committed the sin of RHYME.—You know our country custom of coupling a man and woman together as Partners in the labors of Harvest.—In my fifteenth autumn, my Partner was a bewitching creature who just counted an autumn less.—My scarcity of English denies me the power of doing her justice in that language; but you know the Scotch idiom, She was a bonie, sweet, sonsie lass.—In short, she altogether unwittingly to herself, initiated me in a certain delicious Passion, which in spite of acid Disappointment, gin-horse Prudence and bookworm Philosophy, I hold to be the first of human joys, our dearest pleasure here below.—How she caught the contagion I can't say; you medical folks talk much of infection by breathing the same air, the touch, &c. but I never expressly told her that I loved her.—Indeed I did not well know myself, why I liked so much to loiter behind with her, when returning in the evening from our labors; why the tones of her voice made my heartstrings thrill like an Eolian harp; and particularly, why my pulse beat such a furious ratann when I looked and fingered over her hand, to pick out the nettle-stings and thistles.—Among her other love-inspiring qualifications, she sung sweetly; and 'twas her favorite reel to which I attempted giving an embodied vehicle in rhyme.—I was not so presumtive as to imagine that I could make verses like printed ones, composed by men who had Greek and Latin; but my girl sung a song which was said to be composed by a small country laird's son, on one of his father's maids, with whom he was in love; and I saw no reason why I might not rhyme as well as he, for excepting smearing sheep and casting peats, his father living in the moors, he had no more Scholarcraft than I had.—

Thus with me began Love and Poesy; which at times have been my only, and till within this last twelvemonth have been my highest enjoyment. . .

80. 'The old Scotch songs'

To Rev. John Skinner   *Edinburgh 25 October 1787*

Reverend and Venerable Sir,

Accept, in plain dull prose, my most sincere thanks for the best poetical compliment I ever received. I assure you, Sir, as a poet, you have conjured up an airy demon of vanity in my fancy, which the best abilities in your other capacity would be ill able to lay. I regret, and while I live I shall regret, that when I was in the north, I had not the pleasure of paying a younger brother's dutiful respect to the author of the best Scotch song ever Scotland saw—'Tullochgorum's my delight!' The world may think slightingly of the craft of song-making, if they please, but, as Job says—'O that mine adversary had written a book!'—let them try. There is a certain something in the old Scotch songs, a wild happiness of thought and expression, which peculiarly marks them, not only from English songs, but also from the modern efforts of song-wrights, in our native manner and language. The only remains of this enchantment, these spells of the imagination, rests with you. Our true brother, Ross of Lochlee, was likewise 'owre cannie'—a 'wild warlock'; but now he sings among the 'sons of the morning'.

There is a work going on in Edinburgh, just now, which claims your best assistance. An engraver in this town has set about collecting and publishing all the Scotch songs, with the music, that can be found. Songs in the English language, if by Scotsmen, are admitted, but the music must all be Scotch. Drs. Beattie and Blacklock are lending a hand, and the first musician in town presides over that department. I have been absolutely crazed about it, collecting old stanzas, and every information remaining respecting their origin, authors, &c., &c. . . .

I am, with the warmest sincerity, Sir
Your obliged humble servant,
[Robᵀ Burns]

81. 'My national prejudices'

To Mrs Dunlop   *Ellisland 10 April 1790*
. . . I have just now, my ever honored friend, enjoyed a very high luxury, in reading a paper of the Lounger.* You know my national prejudices. I have often read and admired the Spectator, Adventurer, Rambler, and World; but still with a certain regret, that they were so thoroughly and entirely English. Alas! have I often said to myself, what are all the boasted advantages which my country reaps from a certain Union, that can counterbalance the annihilation of

*A periodical published in Edinburgh; the others which Burns mentions were published in London.

her Independance, and even her very name! I often repeat that couplet of my favorite poet, Goldsmith—

> '——States of native liberty possest,
> Tho' very poor, may yet be very blest.'

Nothing can reconcile me to the common terms, 'English Ambassador, English court,' &c. And I am out of all patience to see that equivocal character, Hastings, impeached by 'the Commons of England.' Tell me, my friend, is this weak prejudice? I believe in my conscience such ideas as 'my country; her independance; her honor; the illustrious names that mark the history of my native land'; &c—I believe these, among your *men of the world,* men who in fact guide for the most part and govern our world *they* look on such ways of thinking as just so many modifications of wrongheadedness. They know the use of bawling out such terms, to rouse or lead THE RABBLE; but for their own private use, with almost all the *able statesmen* that ever existed, or now exist, when they talk of Right and Wrong, they only mean proper and improper; and their measure of conduct is, not what they *ought*, but what they *dare*. . .

82. 'Scots, wha hae. . . '

To George Thomson   *About 30 August 1793*

. . . You know that my pretensions to musical taste, are merely a few of Nature's instincts, untaught & untutored by Art,—For this reason, many musical compositions, particularly where much of the merit lies in Counterpoint, however they may transport & ravish the ears of you, Connoisseurs, affect my simple lug no otherwise than merely as melodious Din.—On the other hand, by way of amends, I am delighted with many little melodies, which the learned Musician despises as silly & insipid.—I do not know whether the old air, 'Hey tutti taitie', may rank among this number; but well I know that, with Fraser's Hautboy, it has often filled my eyes with tears.—There is a tradition, which I have met with in many places of Scotland, that it was Robert Bruce's March at the battle of Bannockburn.—This thought, in my yesternight's evening walk, warmed me to a pitch of enthusiasm on the theme of Liberty & Independance, which I threw into a kind of Scots Ode, fitted to the Air, that one might suppose to be the gallant ROYAL SCOT'S address to his heroic followers on that eventful morning.—

Robert Bruce's march to BANNOCKBURN—
To its ain tune—

Scots, wha hae wi' WALLACE bled
Scots, wham BRUCE has aften led,
Welcome to your gory bed,—
    Or to victorie.—

Now's the day, & now's the hour;
See the front o' battle lower;
See approach proud EDWARD'S power,
    Chains & Slaverie.—

Wha will be a traitor-knave?
Wha can fill a coward's grave?
Wha sae base as be a Slave?
    —Let him turn & flie:—

Wha for SCOTLAND'S king & law,
Freedom's sword will strongly draw,
FREE-MAN stand, or FREE-MAN fa',
    Let him follow me.—

By Oppression's woes & pains!
By your Sons in servile chains!
We will drain our dearest veins,
    But they *shall* be free!

Lay the proud Usurpers low!
Tyrants fall in every foe!
LIBERTY'S in every blow!
    Let us DO—or DIE!!!

So may God ever defend the cause of Truth and Liberty, as he did that day!—Amen!

RB

P.S. I shewed the air to Urbani, who was highly pleased with it, & begged me to make soft verses for it; but I had no idea of giving myself any trouble on the subject, till the accidental recollection of that glorious struggle for Freedom, associated with the glowing ideas of some other struggles of the same nature, *not quite so ancient*, roused my rhyming Mania.—Clarke's set of the tune, with his bass, you will find in the Museum; though I am afraid that the air is not what will entitle it to a place in your elegant selection.—However, I am so pleased with my verses, or more properly the Subject of my verses, that although Johnson has already given the tune a place, yet it shall appear again, set to this Song, in his next & last Volume.—

RB

83. Burns's last letter

My dear Sir,

Do, for Heaven's sake, send Mrs Armour here immediately. My wife is hourly expecting to be put to bed. Good God! what a situation for her to be in, poor girl, without a friend! I returned from sea-bathing quarters today, and my medical friends would almost persuade me that I am better; but I think and feel my strength is so gone that the disorder will prove fatal to me.

> Your Son-in-law,
> R.B.

☆　☆　☆

Lord Daer (1763-94)

Basil William Douglas, Lord Daer, was the eldest son of the fourth Earl of Selkirk and, like his father, a supporter of parliamentary reform. He was one of a number of Scots who were in correspondence with Charles Grey who, as Earl Grey and Prime Minister, eventually achieved the first Reform Act in 1832. The following is part of the famous letter in which Daer described the political situation in Scotland.

84. The cause of Scotland's misfortunes

To Charles Grey   *Edinburgh 17 January 1793*

. . . Scotland has long groaned under the chains of England and knows that its connection there has been the cause of its greatest misfortunes. Perhaps you may shrug your shoulders at this and call it Scot's prejudice, but it is time at moments like these when much may depend on suiting measures to the humour of the people, that you Englishmen should see this rather as it is or at least be aware of how we Scotsmen see it. We have existed a conquered province these two centuries. We trace our bondage from the Union of the Crown and find it little alleviated by the Union of the Kingdoms. What is it you say we have gained by the Union? Commerce, Manufactures, Agriculture. Without going deep into the principles of political economy or asking how our Government or any country can give these to any nation, it is evident in this case that the last Union gave us little assistance in these except removing a part of the obstacles which your greater power had posterior to the first union thrown around us. But if it did more what would that amount to, but to the common saying that we bartered our liberty and with it our morals for a little wealth? You say we have gained emancipation from feudal tyranny. I believe most deliberately that had no Union ever taken place we should in that respect have been more emancipated than we are. Left to ourselves we should probably have had a progression towards Liberty and not less than yours. Our grievances prior to the accession of the Stewarts to your throne were of a kind which even had that event not taken place, must before this time have been annihilated. Any share of human evil that might have awaited us we are ignorant of, whereas we feel what we have undergone. Even to the last of our separate parliaments they were always making laws for us and now and then one to remedy a grievance. And a people acquiring knowledge must have compelled a separate legislature to more of these. Since the parliaments were united scarcely four acts have been passed in as many score of years affecting Scots law or merely the incongruities which must arise betwixt old laws and modern manners . . .

We have suffered the misery which is perhaps inevitable to a lesser and remote country in a junction where the Governing powers are united but Nations are not united. In short, thinking we have been the worse of every connection hitherto with you, the Friends of Liberty in Scotland have almost universally been enemies to Union with England. Such is the fact, whether the reasons be good or bad . . .

William Lyon and George Lyon (fl. 1784)

Charles Cameron (c. 1740-1812), the Scottish architect, was employed by Catherine the Great, Empress of Russia, from about 1778 to create a complex of buildings in her park at Tsarskoe Selo, which was about 15 miles from St Petersburg. Cameron found himself handicapped in the work by the lack of skilled craftsmen, the Russians being accustomed to work with wood, not stone. As a consequence an advertisement appeared in the Edinburgh Evening Courant of 21 January 1784, under the name of the Empress of Russia, asking for highly competent masons, smiths and other craftsmen. 'The encouragement' went the advertisement, 'will be considerable'. On 3 May 1784 between 60 and 70 craftsmen, many with their wives and children, the full complement amounting to 140 persons, set sail from Leith. In July 1784 the brothers William and George Lyon, who had gone to Russia with their father, wrote home to their mother. The brothers paint an affectionate picture of their generous master, Charles Cameron, whose works, several in the Grecian style and the first of their kind in Russia, are admired there to this day.

85. Two Scottish craftsmen write home from Russia

To Mrs Lyon   *Zeskazelle 6 July 1784*

Dear Mother,
We are realy sencible of our long silence and likwise the uneasiness of mind which will rest on you till this come to your relief which most not be inputed to us as being neglectfull, as no opertunities

worth the trusting favoured us. We are obliged to wait the return of the ship which is much longer than we expected as we landed on May 23. The ship has layng here ever since till the above deat. Dear mother, we should thank God that we had so fine a passage and keeps our healths so weell and free of all accidents. We had the finest weather and the quickest passage that has been sailed this long time. Very few passangers in the ship escaped sickness but ourselves, my father especially who was remarked to be the only man among the passangers who stood the fatigue best. We was only about 12 days on sea . . .

Our first landing in Rusia was at Cronstade, a place where ships from all nations of the glob comes to tread, and when you come in vue of this place you would take it to be a very large wood. The ships all ly along side of one another and are lined out in streets for to let smal ships or boats pass throw. In this place we staid 3 days and Mr Cameron was sent for to Pettersburgh which is 15 miles from Cronstead. He cam on all heast him self and his wife, accompanied by Mr Forester. They were very glade to see us and gave us a grand treat at a teavron. From hence we set out for Pettersburg in a small ship, where we landed in 2 hours at the English taveron: there is but one in the town. Here we was ordred to stay till places or houses would be provided for us. Se we have been a fortnight in this taveron where we was ordred to want for nothing but call for what ever we wanted. This orders came from the Empress. We hade tea for b[r]eakfast, all kind of flesh, both rost and boild, for denner, and plainty of English strong ale, the same for supar. Here we had nothing to do but stroll about and vue the curiosities of the town, which is 6 miles square, 24 miles in circomference. This town is verry regular built, with kinals in every street. The Empress has 2 grand pallaces in the town, one of which is marrable, and a new marrable church which is building just now. I shall endavour to give you more larger and better description of the place and maners of the people in my next which will be in a month after this befor another letter can be sent, at least befor it arives at Edinburgh, as I mean to write by post. There is no posibily of geting any money raised at present as the Empres only pais 4 times in the year. Than she pais it in great sooms. It is out of Mr Cameron's own poket that we are subsisted till the end of the quarter . . .

Dear mother, we are your afectionate sons and with our dear father

WILLIAM LYON
GEORGE LYON

Mrs Calderwood of Polton (fl. 1786)

In 1735 Margaret Steuart of Coltness married Thomas Calderwood of Polton. Her brother Sir James Steuart of Coltness was forced to flee to the continent on account of his Jacobite sympathies. In 1756 the Calderwoods and their two sons set out to visit the Steuarts in Brussels. Mrs Calderwood gave her daughter, Anne, who had married James Durham of Largo, an account of the family's journeys on the continent, and later her impressions of London. The exact dating of the letters is uncertain because Mrs Calderwood finally combined them into a journal.

86. 'As for London . . .'

To Anne Durham   *Date unknown*

. . . As for London, everybody has either read of it, or seen it. The first sight of it did not strike me with anything grand or magnificent. It is not situated so as to show to advantage, and, indeed, I think the tile roofs have still a paltry look, and so has the brick houses; for a village it does well enough, as the character of a village is clean and neat; but there is something more substantiall and durable in our ideas of a great city than what brick and tile can answer.

You will think it very odd, that I was a fortnight in London, and saw none of the royall family, but I got no cloaths made till the day before I left it, though I gave them to the making the day after I came. I cannot say my curiosity was great: I found, as I approached the Court and the grandees, they sunk so miserably in my oppinion, and came so far short of the ideas I had conceived, that I was loath to lose the grand ideas I had of Kings, Princes, Ministers of state, Senators, etc., which I suppose I had gathered from romance in my youth. We used to laugh at the English for being so soon afraid when there was any danger in state affairs, but now I do excuse them. For we, at a distance, think the wisdom of our governours will prevent all these things; but those who know and see our ministers every day see there is no wisdom in them, and that they are a parcell of old, ignorant, senseles bodies, who mind nothing but eating and drinking, and rolling about in Hyde Park, and know no more of the country, or the situation of it, nor of the numbers, strength and circumstances of it, than they never had been in it: or how should they, when London, and twenty miles round it, is the extent ever they saw of it? . . .

There is no depending on news at London: there was a lye coined for every day I was there, and every one of them the English beleived, providing it was agreeable. And the Court is no better informed than the vulgar: for, providing there are two lyes raised in one day, a good one in the forenoon; then the Duke of Newcastle drinks Mr. Byng's health at dinner: out comes a defeat in the afternoon; he damns Mr. Byng for a scoundrell. Out goes one of the Princess's masters to Kew: he tells, Mr. Byng has defeat the French. The Prince of Wales hears it: then it comes, Who told you, Heny Peny? At last, it lands on the French dancing-master, who lays it on a Hanoverian officer, whose name he knew not. So the reports go abroad . . .

No body thinks of going further to air than Hyde Park, which is very pretty. But nothing but the greatest stupidity can suffer the same mile or two of ground every day in their lives, when, at the same time, it is no exercise nor air, for it is a gravell road, quite smothered with trees. The trees indeed are very pretty, being fine timber, and fine carpet-grass, with cows and deer going in it; but it is a small part of the Park in which coaches are allowed to go . . .

Any of the English folks I got acquainted with I liked very well. They seem to be good-natured and humane; but still there is a sort of ignorance about them with regard to the rest of the world, and that their conversation runs in a very narrow channell. They speak with a great relish of their publick places, and say, with a sort of flutter, that they shall to Vauxhall and Ranelagh, but do not seem to enjoy it when there. As for Vauxhall and Ranelagh, I wrote you my opinion of them before. The first I think but a vulgar sort of entertainment, and could not think myself in genteel company, whiles I heard a man calling,

'Take care of your watches and pockets.' . . .

General Sir John Malcolm (1769-1833)

John Malcolm was granted a commission in the army of the East India Company when he was only 13. He spent most of the rest of his life in India and he went on several diplomatic missions to Persia, of which he wrote a history. He has been described as 'simple, manly, generous and accessible' and as one of the most successful of British administrators in the East.

87. John Leyden

(see Letter 110)

To the Editor, the Bombay Courier   *September 1811*

. . . It is not easy to convey an idea of the method which Dr Leyden used in his studies, or to describe the unconquerable ardour with which these were pursued . . .

The temper of Dr Leyden was mild and generous, and he could bear, with perfect good humour, raillery on his foibles. When he arrived at Calcutta, in 1805, I was most solicitous regarding his reception in the society of the Indian capital. 'I entreat you, my dear friend, (I said to him the day he landed,) to be careful of the impression you make on entering this community; for God's sake learn a little English, and be silent upon literary subjects, except among literary men.' 'Learn English!' he exclaimed, 'no, never; it was trying to learn that language that spoilt my Scotch; and as to being silent, I will promise to hold my tongue, if you will make fools hold theirs.'. . .

His love of the place of his nativity was a passion in which he had always a pride, and which in India he cherished with the fondest enthusiasm. I once went to see him when he was very ill, and had been confined to his bed for many days; there were several gentlemen in the room; he inquired if I had any news; I told him I had a letter from Eskdale. 'And what are they about in the borders?' he asked. 'A curious circumstance,' I replied, 'is stated in my letter;' and I read him a passage which described the conduct of our volunteers on a fire being kindled by mistake at one of the beacons. This letter mentioned that the moment the blaze, which was the signal of invasion, was seen, the mountaineers hastened to their rendezvous, and those of Liddesdale swam the Liddel river to reach it. They were assembled (though several of their houses were at a distance of six and seven miles) in two hours, and at break of day the party marched into the town of Hawick (at a distance of twenty miles from the place of assembly) to the Border tune of *'Wha dar meddle wi' me.'* Leyden's countenance became animated as I proceeded with this detail, and at its close he sprung from his sick-bed, and, with strange melody, and still stranger gesticulations, sung aloud, *'Wha dar meddle wi' me, wha dar meddle wi' me.'* Several of those who witnessed this scene looked at him as one that was raving in the delirium of a fever.

James Hogg (1770-1835)
Margaret Hogg (1790-1870)

James Hogg had only a few months formal education and he was in his late teens before he taught himself to read and write and to play the fiddle. For most of his life he was a working farmer and hence the title, 'the Ettrick Shepherd', which John Wilson applied to him. How then did he come to write his songs and poetry, revealing highly sophisticated parody, and his stories and novels, including The Private Memoirs and Confessions of a Justified Sinner, *one of the most powerful and original novels in the language? Part of the answer is that he was highly educated in Border song and ballad, in the Bible and in the logically argued sermons of the Kirk. Hogg was one of the last living examples in the Lowlands of a man whose mind and imagination were stimulated mainly by an ancient oral tradition.*

James married Margaret Phillips, the daughter of a prosperous farmer in Dumfriesshire, in 1820. They had five children.

88. 'A living miscellany of old songs'

To Walter Scott   *Ettrick House 30 June 1802*

Dear Sir,—I have been perusing your Minstrelsy very diligently for a while past, and it being the first book I ever perused which was written by a person I had seen and conversed with, the consequence hath been to me a most sensible pleasure; for in fact it is the remarks and modern pieces that I have delighted most in, being as it were personally acquainted with many of the antient pieces formerly.

My mother is actually a living miscellany of old songs. I never believed that she had half so many until I came to a trial. There are none in your collection of which she hath not a part, and I should by this time have had a great number written for your amusement,—thinking them all of great antiquity and lost to posterity—had I not luckily lighted upon a collection of songs, in two volumes, published by I know not who, in which I recognised about half a score of my mother's best songs almost word for word. No doubt I was piqued, but it saved me much trouble, paper, and ink; for I am carefully avoiding everything which I have seen or heard of being in print, although I have no doubt that I shall err, being acquainted with almost no collections of that sort; but I am not afraid that you too will mistake. I am still at a loss with some. . .

Suspend your curiosity, Mr. Scott. You will see them when I see you, of which I am as impatient as you can be to see the songs for your life. But as I suppose you have no personal acquaintance in this parish, it would be presumption in me to expect that you will visit my cottage, but I will attend you in any part of the Forest if you will send me word. I am far from supposing that a person of your discernment—d—n it, I'll blot out that word, 'tis so like flattery—I say I don't think that you would despise a shepherd's 'humble cot an' hamely fare' as Burns hath it; yet though I would be extremely proud of the visit, hang me if I would know what I would do w'ye. I am surprised to find that the songs in your collection differ so widely from my mother's. . .

Many indeed are not aware of the manners of this place; it is but lately emerged from barbarity, and till this present age the poor illiterate people in these glens knew no other entertainment in the long winter nights than in repeating and listening to those feats of their ancestors which I believe to be handed down inviolate from father to son for many generations, although no doubt, had a copy been taken of them at the end of every fifty years, there must have been some difference which the repeaters would have insensibly have fallen into, merely by the change of terms in that period. I believe it is thus that many very antient songs have been modernised, which yet a connoisseur will bear visible marks of antiquity. The Maitlen [the Auld Maitland of the Border Minstrelsy], exclusive of its mode of description, is all composed of words which would, mostly every one, both spell and pronounce in the very same dialect that was spoken some centuries ago.

I formed a project of collecting all the tenors of the tunes to which these old songs were sung, and having them set to music. . ., but I find it impossible. I might compose kind of tunes to some of them, and adapt others, but can in no wise learn the original ones. I find it was only the subject-matter which the old people concerned themselves about; and any kind of tunes that they had, they always make one to serve a great many songs.

My uncle hath never had any tune whatsoever saving that which he saith his prayer to: and my mother's is quite gone, by reason of age and frailty, and they have had a strong struggle with the world ever since I was born, in all which time, having seldom or never repeated many of the songs, her memory of them is much impaired. My uncle, said I! He is, Mr. Scott, the most incorrigible man alive. I cannot help telling you this: he came one night professedly to see me and crack with me, as he said. Thinking this a fair opportunity I treated him with the best the house could afford, gave him a hearty glass, and to humour him, talked a little of religion. Thus I set him on, but good L—d, had you heard him, it was impossible to get him off again. In the course of his remarks he had occasion to cite Ralph

Erskine. Sundry times he'd run to the dale* where the books lay, get the sermons and read near every one of them from which he had a citation. What a deluge was poured on me of errors, sins, lusts, covenants broken, burned and buried, legal teachers, patronage, and what not! In short, my dram was lost to my purpose. The mentioning of a song put him in a passion ** . . .

Pardon, my dear Sir, the freedom I have taken in addressing you,—it is my nature, and I could not resist the impulse of writing to you any longer. Let me hear from you as soon as this comes to your hand, and tell me when you will be in Ettrick Forest, and suffer me to subscribe myself, Sir, your most humble and affectionate servant,

JAMES HOGG

89. 'A thing. . . of no consequence'

To John Aitken   *Edinburgh 20 December 1817*

My dear Aiken

I am vexed to see your mind so much ruffled and discomposed and that too about a thing which I regard as of no consequence. If you really imagine that the world regards you with less respect on that account or that either sex will undervalue you for such a circumstance You will ere long find yourself agreeably mistaken. The disrespect believe me is all in your own bosom and I certainly esteem you the more for such a feeling as it bespeaks a heart uncorrupted. I have myself stood with a red face on the Stool of Repentance where I perhaps got the highest compliment paid to me ever I got in my life as the minister began by saying 'he was sorry he had that day to rebuke a man who was more fit to be his teacher &c. &c.' I have two very lovely daughters who bear my name the one 11 the other 8 years of age the one I am sure is my own the other may be mine for any thing that I know to the contrary. The mothers are both married long ago to men much more respectable in life than ever I was the one of them to my own Cousin-German and even with their nearest relations I have never been for a day out of favour. The aunt of one of the young ladies ventured in full asembly of friends to propose marriage to me with her lovely niece. I said I

* Deal or wooden shelf   ** Hogg's relation was Will Laidlaw of Phawhope, of whom Scott wrote that 'one of our best reciters has turned religious in his later days, and finds out that old songs are unlawful.'

was sure she advised me well but really I could not get time. She said I had had plenty of time since Candlemass. 'O yes said I that's very true but then the weather was so wet I could not get through the water' at which they all burst out laughing, the girl herself among the rest and there was no more of the matter nor was there ever a frown on either side. If you now saw my Keatie at church with her hat and feather and green pelice you would think it the best turn ever I did in my life. I have a great mind that you shall have her for your wife as I am sure she will never find a kinder heart . . .

90. Hogg in London

In 1831 Hogg had a disagreement with his Edinburgh publisher, William Blackwood. Early in the following year he visited London for negotiations with a publisher and lingered there for several weeks. He was lionised by London society and there was talk of a knighthood, an idea which his wife firmly rejected.

James to Margaret   *London 10 January 1832*

. . . Notwithstanding of all the caressing I have met with, which is perfectly ridiculous, I hate London, and I do not think that either flattery or profit can ever make me love it. It is so boundless that I cannot for my life get out of it, nor can I find any place that I want . . . I never get home before three in the morning, and have been very much in the same sort of society. I have been with Lockhart, Jerdan, Captain Burns, Pringle, Cochrane, Murray . . . it is almost a miracle that I keep my health so well, considering the life I lead, for I am out at parties every night until far into the morning—great literary dinner—I am sure I have received in the last three days three hundred invitations to dinner, and I am afraid I have accepted too many of them—I positively will not come to London again without you—a London paper of this morning says that 'I had my wife and part of my beautiful family with me at church on Sunday', whereas it was only Mrs. Cochrane and Miss Cochrane who is the age of Jessie and Alex who is a year older than Maggie. Mrs. Cochrane is a very beautiful lady with black hair and eyes very like your Mamma's, but she is nor half so bonny to me. But she is very kind to your Papa, indeed so kind that she does not know what to do with me. . .

91. 'Warm drawers'

Margaret to James   *Altrive Lake 22 January 1832*

My dearest James

I was indeed disappointed at not getting a letter from you on Friday
however I hope it was only neglect & that you are in good health,
by this time you will I expect have got reconciled to London & to
the customs of the place, few people like it at first but I believe you
have but to stay a while & then get very fond of it, so I hope you
will leave before you get too fond of it. I need not tell you how
much we are all wearying for you back, if possible I weary more
now than at first, because I think you should be talking of coming
home, you must arrange your plans in London come home & put
them into execution as I don't suppose you can have time to collect
your thoughts, for composing it must be entirely out of the
question, endeavour to come at all your *scraps* (which cannot be had
here) that may be useful in the publication. I am indeed anxious to
have you home on your account I fear you are doing yourself out,
& leave before you are threadbare I do not exactly mean your coat,
but leave the Londoners something to guess at—by the bye the coat
is no joke either for you are apt to wear it too long but take care
don't do so, buy a good new one & whatever articles of dress you
may require by no means appear shabby—you went so hurriedly,
there was no time to prepare for so long a journey—I should rather
wear a worse gown than that you should appear in a shabby coat
you must get your stockings & other things mended by the person
who washes your clothes it is pitiful to think of you going about
with great holes in your stockings. I hope you have got warm
drawers & do by all means attend to your health you know I often
tell you, you abuse a good constitution, when I think of your late or
rather early hours I am perplexed about you I know you cannot
stand it. . .

92. 'Such flummery'

James to Margaret   *London 17 February 1832*

My ever dearest Marg^t

I have received your letter only within this hour and I cannot tell
you how much I was wearying for it nor how great satisfaction it
has given me. I think of nothing with any delight but of my return
home and all the delight I have in being here is the satisfaction that I

am doing all that I can for those who are nearest and dearest to me in the world . . . Blessed be God for his kindness in preserving you all in good health and may he continue to be your guide and director. I am for my own part exceedingly well indeed I never was better and although constantly in the public and generally in great companies I never spent a more sober winter season. The people here are all sober there being no deep drinking here as in Scotland. You will think it strange when I assure you that in this great overgrown metropolis for these last six weeks night nor day Sunday nor Saturday I have not seen one drunk person neither poor nor rich. My mode of living is this when invited I accept on condition that there is not to be a party 'O no there shall be no party just a few friends merely a family party' Well I go at 7 o'clock no fashionable dinner before that! By the time we get a few glasses of wine drunk the rapping at the door begins and continues without intermission for an hour and a half. Then we go up stairs and find both drawing rooms crammed as full as ever you saw sheep in a fold and there I am brought in and shown like any other wild beast all the ladies courtesying and fluttering and begging for one shake of my hand such flummery I never saw in this world. . . parties always last until two or three in the morning I am grown quite gray in the head shurly for want of sleep I get no sleep to speak of. It was a downright mistake of the reporters of the festival *I did not mount the table* to speak and though the weekly papers set the matter right it was then too late the news had run through all Britain and could not be recalled. But the truth is that when I rose to speak there was a lamp or chandalier, that covered my face entirely from the multitude on which there was a deafening shout of 'up up! mount mount!' On which Sir John said I would be obliged to mount the table I then drew back my chair half behind him and stood on it. In Allan Cunningham's paper the speech was reported nearly right in all the rest most absurdly. . .

I wonder you do not tell me one word about the house nor the fishing nor the stable nor the plowing nor the beasts nor the dung leading nor anything. Kindest respects to all our kind neighbours God bless them for their attentions to my dear Margt I send a kiss and a blessing to each of the children as usual and remain

Your ever affectionate husb^d

JAMES HOGG

93. A question of knighthood

James to Margaret   *London 10 March 1832*

... I got a public dinner from the great Walton Cotton-Club yesterday was made an honorary member and decorated with the order. You must consult your own heart whether you would like to be Lady Hogg or remain the Ettrick Shepherdess because you may now have the former title if you please. The Queen is it seems intent on it and I got a letter the other day from Lord Montagu requesting me not to see his Majesty until he and I consulted together as he understood there was some risk of being knighted which would run me into the expense of at least £300: of fees. For my part I despise it in our present circumstances and can see no good that it could do us. It might indeed introduce our family into the first ranks but then where is £300: to come from. In short I want you to dissuade me from it but I'll not look near his Majesty till I hear from you so write me directly. Dr Brewster was knighted yesterday. The cholera is raging and spreading terribly here now but do not say a word about that to James else it will kill him. How I am longing to have you all one by one in my arms again Bestow a benediction on every one of our dear dear children in their father's name and kiss each of them for me.

Your very affectionate husband
JAMES HOGG

94. 'No such titles'

Margaret to James   *Altrive Lake 15 March 1832*

My ever dearest James
From my heart I can say I like no such titles & if you value your own comfort & my peace of mind you will at once, if offered you, refuse it, it is an honor you may be proud to refuse but not to accept I think a title to a poor man is a load scarcely bearable. I daresay there are many men born with one on their back who would be thankful if they could to get rid of it, Her Majesty must be entirely ignorant of your circumstances if the thing has *really* ever been thought of. So I hope if you are to have an interview with their Majesties, you will in your own short pithy way express your gratitude for the honor they intended to confer upon you assuring them you know they wish you well but from prudent reasons you must decline the offer, did I possess five thousand a year I should

wish to be unencumbered with a title I want no more than to be the wife of plain James Hogg, we ought to consult the happiness of our family & such a thing I should look upon in every respect would be to them in all probability great misery. I could say a thousand against it, did I consider it at all necessary but not doubting for a moment your seeing the impropriety of it shall say little more only I must say should you come back with such a burden on your back you will return infinitely poorer than when you left me suppose you were to add hundreds to your income. . .

Margaret enclosed this letter from their son, James, then aged 11:

My dear Papa
I have not been well since you left us but I think I shall get well when you come home now dear Pappa come this month-your affet son

JAS HOGG

95. 'My beloved Margaret'

James to Margaret   *London 23 March 1832*

My beloved Margt,
Your last has fairly upset my resolution of remaining here any longer my dear boy's health being far dearer to me than either honour or riches of course I shall neither see the King nor Queen. I called on the Duke of Buccleuch yesterday but find that he will not arrive here before the 28th so I shall not see him either but I will call again on Lord Montague. I dine again with the Highland Society to night and shall meet with many of the first nobles of the land this being their great anniversary. I leave London to morrow evening and sail for Edinr on Sabbath morning in the United Kingdom steamship which never takes above fifty-two hours at farthest in a trip, so that I shall be in Edinr in all probability on Tuesday the 27th where at Mr Watson's I shall be happy to meet with you and Mary and Harriet or if you cannot possibly get away you might send Peggy with her. I will buy her a new hat and any thing she needs there. If you do not meet me I will make as little stay in Edinr as possible but haste home. I am positively worried with kindness so that I do not know what to do first and I positively will not come to London again without you. I am in excellent good health and

Your ever affectionate husband

JAMES HOGG

Sir Walter Scott (1771-1832)

In Byron's phrase, Scott was 'undoubtedly the Monarch of Parnassus'. He was the most successful writer of his day, with an influence that was world-wide and long-lasting and which affected not only literature but music and painting and attitudes towards the writing of history and the past generally. He was also, as it were, the uncrowned king of Scotland, to whom people looked naturally for leadership. Somehow among all his diverse activities, he also found time to carry on a very lively correspondence. His letters fill 12 volumes in the Grierson edition and that is far from complete.

96. Ossian

To Anna Seward   *Ashestiel September 1806*

. . . As for the great dispute I should be no Scottish man if I had not very attentively considered it at some period of my studies & indeed I have gone to some length in my researches for I have beside me translations of some twenty or thirty of the unquestioned originals of Ossians poems. After making every allowance for the disadvantages of a literal translation & the possible debasement which those *now* collected may have suffered in the great & violent change which the Highlands have undergone since the researches of Macpherson I am compelled to admit that incalculably the greater part of the English Ossian must be ascribed to Macpherson himself and that his whole introductions notes &c &c is an absolute tissue of forgeries . . .

The Highland Society have lately set about investigating, or rather, I should say collecting materials to defend the authenticity of Ossian. Those researches have only proved that there were no real originals using that word as is commonly understood to be found for them. The oldest tale they have found seems to be that of Darthula but it is perfectly different both in diction & story from that of Macpherson—it is, however, a beautiful specimen of Celtic poetry & shews that it contains much which is worthy of preservation—indeed how should it be otherwise when we know that till about fifty years ago the Highlands contained a race of hereditary poets. Is it possible to think that perhaps among many hundreds who for such a course of centuries have founded their reputation & rank on practising the art of poetry in a country where the scenery & manners gave such effect & interest & imagery to their productions, there should not have been some who have attained excellence? In searching out those genuine records of the Celtic Muse & preserving them from oblivion with all the curious information which they must doubtless contain I humbly think our Highland antiquaries would merit better of their country than confining their researches to the fantastic pursuit of a chimera . . .

Believe me, I shall not be within many miles of Lichfield without paying my personal respects to you; and yet I should not do it in prudence, because I am afraid you have formed a higher opinion of me than I deserve: you would expect to see a person who had dedicated himself much to literary pursuits, and you would find me a rattle-sculled half-lawyer, half-sportsman, through whose head a regiment of horse has been exercising since he was five years old; half-educated—half-crazy, as his friends sometimes tell him; half everything, but *entirely* Miss Seward's much obliged, affectionate, and faithful servant,

WALTER SCOTT

97. 'A valiant Jacobite'

To Robert Surtees   *17 December 1806*

. . . You flatter me very much by pointing out to my attention the feuds of 1715 and '45. The truth is that the subject has often and deeply interested me from my earliest youth. My great-grandfather was *out*, as the phrase goes, in Dundee's wars and in 1715, and had nearly the honour to be hanged for his pains, had it not been for the interest of Duchess Anne of Buccleuch and Monmouth, to whom I have attempted *longo intervallo* to pay a debt of gratitude. But besides this, my father, although a Borderer, transacted business for many Highland lairds, and particularly for one old man called Stuart of Invernahyle, who had been out both in 1715 and '45, and whose tales were the absolute delight of my childhood. I believe there never was a man who united the ardour of a soldier and tale-teller—a man of talk as they call it in Gaelic—in such an excellent degree, and he was as fond of telling as I was of hearing. I became a valiant Jacobite at the age of 10 years, and ever since reason and reading came to my assistance I have never quite got rid of the impression which the gallantry of Prince Charles made on my imagination. Certainly I will not renounce the idea of doing something to preserve these stories, and the memory of times and manners which, though existing as it were yesterday, have so strangely vanished from our eyes. Whether this will be best done by collecting the old tales, or by modernising them as subjects of legendary poetry, I have never very seriously considered, but your kind encouragement confirms me in the resolution that something I must do and that speedily . . .

98. The bloodhound, Maida

To Joanna Baillie   *Abbotsford early April 1816*

. . . I have added a most romantic inmate to my family—a large bloodhound, allowed to be the finest dog of the kind in Scotland, perfectly gentle, affectionate, and good-natured, and the darling of all the children. I had him in a present from Glengarry, who has refused the breed to people of the very first rank. He is between the deer-greyhound and mastiff, with a shaggy mane like a lion, and always sits beside me at dinner, his head, as high as the back of my chair. Yet it will gratify you to know that a favourite cat keeps him in the greatest possible order and insists upon all rights of precedence, and scratches with impunity the nose of an animal who would make no bones of a wolf, and pulls down a red deer without fear or difficulty. I heard my friend set up some most piteous howls, and I assure you the noise was no joke, all occasioned by his fear of passing puss, who had stationed himself on the stairs . . .

99. 'Malachi'

In a letter to James Ballantyne in February 1826, Scott said: 'I am certainly serious in Malachi if seriousness will do good. I will sleep quieter in my grave for having so fair an opportunity of speaking my mind.' He was referring to the series of letters which he sent, under the name of 'Malachi Malagrowther', to the Edinburgh Weekly Journal. *Their immediate purpose was to defend the Scottish bank notes, but he took the opportunity to make a powerful case for the right and need of Scotland to manage her own affairs. The following is an extract from the second of these letters.*

To the Editor of the
Edinburgh Weekly Journal   *28 February 1826*

. . . There has been in England a gradual and progressive system of assuming the management of affairs entirely and exclusively proper to Scotland, as if we were totally unworthy of having the management of our own concerns. All must centre in London. We could not have a Caledonian Canal, but the Commissioners must be Englishmen, and meet in London;—a most useful canal they would have made of it, had not the lucky introduction of steam-boats—*Deus ex machina*—come just in time to redeem them from having made the most expensive and most useless of the kind ever heard of since Noah floated his ark! We could not be intrusted with the charge of erecting our own kirks, (churches in the Highlands,) or of making our roads and bridges in the same wild districts, but these labours must be conducted under the tender care of men who knew nothing of our country, its wants and its capabilities, but who, nevertheless, sitting in their office in London, were to decide, without appeal, upon the conduct of the roads in Lochaber!—Good Heaven, sir! to what are we fallen?—or rather, what are we esteemed by the English? Wretched drivellers, incapable of understanding our own affairs; or greedy peculators, unfit to be trusted? On what ground are we considered either as the one or the other?

But I may perhaps be answered, that these operations are carried on by grants of public money; and that, therefore, the English—undoubtedly the only disinterested and public-spirited and trust-worthy persons in the universe—must be empowered exclusively to look after its application. Public money forsooth!!! I should like to know whose pocket it comes out of. Scotland, I have always heard, contributes FOUR MILLIONS to the public revenue. I should like to know, before we are twitted with grants of public money, how much of that money is dedicated to Scottish purposes—how much applied to the general uses of the empire—and if the balance should be found to a great amount on the side of Scotland, as I suspect it will, I should like still farther to know how the English are entitled to assume the direction and disposal of any pittance which may be permitted, out of the produce of our own burthens, to revert to the peculiar use of the nation from which it has been derived? If England was giving us alms, she would have a right to look after the administration of them, lest they should be misapplied or embezzled. If she is only consenting to afford us a small share of the revenue derived from our own kingdom, we have some title, methinks, to be consulted in the management, nay, intrusted with it . . .

Lord Melville, a member of the government, who had been at the High School of Edinburgh with Scott, objected to Malachi *in a letter to Sir Robert Dundas. This was shown to Scott and other influential people to indicate the government's displeasure. The following is part of Scott's reply.*

100. 'My Scottish feelings'

To Sir Robert Dundas of Dunira   *18 March 1826*

My dear Sir Robert,—I had your letter to-day, and am much interested and affected by its contents. Whatever Lord Melville's sentiments have been towards me, I could never have lost remembrance of the very early friend with whom I carried my satchel to school, and whose regard I had always considered as one of the happiest circumstances of my life. I remain of the same opinion respecting the Letters, which have occasioned so much more notice than they would have deserved, had there not been a very general feeling in this country, and among Lord Melville's best friends too, authorizing some public remonstrances of the kind from some one like myself, who had nothing to win or to lose—or rather, who hazarded losing a great deal in the good opinion of friends whom he was accustomed not to value only, but to reverence . . .

Differing so much as we do on this head, and holding my own opinion as I would do a point of religious faith, I am sure I ought to feel the more indebted to Lord Melville's kindness and generosity for suffering our difference to be no breach in our ancient friendship. I shall always feel his sentiments in this respect as the deepest obligation I owe him; for, perhaps, there are some passages in Malachi's epistles that I ought to have moderated. But I desired to make a strong impression, and speak out, not on the Currency Question alone, but on the treatment of Scotland generally, the opinion which, I venture to say, has been long entertained by Lord Melville's best friends, though who that had anything to hope or fear would [not] have hesitated to state it? So much for my Scottish feelings—prejudices, if you will; but which were born, and will die with me. For those I entertain towards Lord Melville personally, I can only say that I have lost much in my life; but the esteem of an old friend is that I should regret the most; and I repeat I feel most sensibly the generosity and kindness so much belonging to his nature, which can forgive that which has probably been most offensive to him. People may say I have been rash and inconsiderate; they cannot say I have been either selfish or malevolent—I have shunned all the sort of popularity attending the discussion; nay, have refused to distribute the obnoxious letters in a popular form, though urged from various quarters.

Adieu! God Bless you, my dear Sir Robert! You may send the whole or any part of this letter if you think proper; I should not wish him to think that I was sulky about the continuance of his friendship—I am yours most truly,

WALTER SCOTT

101. Scott's meeting with Burns

To J. G. Lockhart   *1827*

. . . As for Burns, I may truly say, *Virgilium vidi tantum**. I was a lad of fifteen in 1786-7, when he came first to Edinburgh, but had sense and feeling enough to be much interested in his poetry, and would have given the world to know him; but I had very little acquaintance with any literary people, and still less with the gentry of the west country, the two sets that he most frequented. Mr. Thomas Grierson was at that time a clerk of my father's. He knew Burns, and promised to ask him to his lodgings to dinner, but had no opportunity to keep his word, otherwise I might have seen more of this distinguished man. As it was, I saw him one day at the late venerable Professor Ferguson's, where there were several gentlemen of literary reputation, among whom I remember the celebrated Mr. Dugald Stewart. Of course we youngsters sate silent, looked and listened. The only thing I remember which was remarkable in Burns' manner, was the effect produced upon him by a print of Bunbury's, representing a soldier lying dead on the snow, his dog sitting in misery on the one side, on the other his widow, with a child in her arms. These lines were written beneath,—

> 'Cold on Canadian hills, or Minden's plain,
> Perhaps that parent wept her soldier slain:
> Bent o'er her babe, her eye dissolved in dew,
> The big drops, mingling with the milk he drew,
> Gave the sad presage of his future years,
> The child of misery baptized in tears.'

Burns seemed much affected by the print, or rather the ideas which it suggested to his mind. He actually shed tears. He asked whose the lines were, and it chanced that nobody but myself remembered that they occur in a half-forgotten poem of Langhorne's, called by the unpromising title of 'The Justice of the Peace'. I whispered my

---

* I have seen a man like Virgil himself.

114

information to a friend present, who mentioned it to Burns, who rewarded me with a look and a word, which, though of mere civility, I then received, and still recollect, with very great pleasure.

His person was strong and robust: his manners rustic, not clownish; a sort of dignified plainness and simplicity, which received part of its effect perhaps from one's knowledge of his extraordinary talents. His features are represented in Mr. Nasmyth's picture, but to me it conveys the idea that they are diminished as if seen in perspective. I think his countenance was more massive than it looks in any of the portraits. I would have taken the poet, had I not known what he was, for a very sagacious country farmer of the old Scotch school — *i.e.* none of your modern agriculturists, who keep labourers for their drudgery, but the *douce gudeman* who held his own plough. There was a strong expression of sense and shrewdness in all his lineaments; the eye alone, I think, indicated the poetical character and temperament. It was large, and of a dark cast, and glowed (I say literally *glowed*) when he spoke with feeling or interest. I never saw such another eye in a human head, though I have seen the most distinguished men in my time. His conversation expressed perfect self-confidence, without the slightest presumption. Among the men who were the most learned of their time and country, he expressed himself with perfect firmness, but without the least intrusive forwardness; and when he differed in opinion, he did not hesitate to express it firmly, yet at the same time with modesty. I do not remember any part of his conversation distinctly enough to be quoted, nor did I ever see him again, except in the street, where he did not recognise me, as I could not expect he should. He was much caressed in Edinburgh, but (considering what literary emoluments have been since his day) the efforts made for his relief were extremely trifling.

I remember on this occasion I mention, I thought Burns' acquaintance with English poetry was rather limited, and also, that having twenty times the abilities of Allan Ramsay and of Ferguson, he talked of them with too much humility as his models; there was doubtless national predilection in his estimate . . .

Scott sent the letter above to Lockhart when he was writing a biography of Burns. The following is part of a long letter which Scott sent to Croker to help with his edition of Boswell's Johnson. Lord Auchinleck was Boswell's father.

To J.W. Croker   *30 January 1829*

. . . Old Lord Auchinleck was an able lawyer, a good scholar, after the manner of Scotland, and highly valued his own advantages as a man of good estate and ancient family, and moreover, he was a strict Presbyterian and Whig of the old Scottish cast, videlicet a friend to the Revolution and the Protestant line. This did not prevent his being a terribly proud aristocrat, and great was the contempt he entertained and expressed for his son James for the nature of his friendships, and the character of the personages of whom he was *engoué* one after another. 'There's nae hope for Jamie, man,' he said to a friend; 'Jamie is gaen clean gyte. What do you think, man? He's done wi' Paoli; he's off wi' the land-louping scoundrel of a Corsican; and whase tail do you think he has pinned himself to now, man?' — here the old judge summoned up a sneer of most sovereign contempt — 'a *dominie*, man — an auld dominie. He keepit a schule, and caa'd it an academy!'. . .

At Glasgow Johnson had a meeting with Smith, which terminated strangely. John Millar used to report that Smith, obviously much discomposed, came into a party who were playing at cards. The Doctor's appearance suspended the amusement, for as all knew he was to meet Johnson that evening, every one was curious to hear what had passed. Adam Smith, whose temper seemed much ruffled, answered only at first, 'He is a brute! he is a brute!' Upon closer examination it appeared that Dr. Johnson no sooner saw Smith than he brought forward a charge against him for something in his famous letter on the death of Hume.* Smith said he had vindicated the truth of the statement. 'And what did the Doctor say?' was the universal query: 'Why, he said — he said —' said Smith, with the deepest impression of resentment, 'he said— "*You lie!*"' 'And what did you reply?' 'I said, "You are a son of a b———h!"' On such terms did these two great moralists meet and part, and such was the classic dialogue betwixt them. . . .

* Letter 53

☆   ☆   ☆

Mungo Park (1771-1806)

Mungo Park was born in a small cottage at Foulshiels, near Selkirk. Despite his disadvantages he qualified as a physician. His fame as an explorer rests on his two journeys to Africa: from Senegal to the Niger and from Gambia to the Niger, which journey ended tragically with Park drowning in the river while under attack by natives. Thomas Carlyle referred to Park as 'one of the most unpretending, and at the same time valuable specimens of humanity'.

103. An explorer's love-letter

To Ailie Park   *London 12 March 1801*

My lovely Ailie, nothing gives me more pleasure than to write to you, and the reason why I delayed it a day last time was to get some money to send to you. You say you are wishing to spend a note upon yourself. My sweet Ailie, you may be sure I approve of it. What is mine is yours, and I receive much pleasure from your goodness in consulting me about such a trifle. I wish I had thousands to give you, but I know that my Ailie will be contented with what we have, and we shall live in the hope of seeing better days. I long very much to be with you, my love, and I was in great hopes of having things settled before now, but Sir Joseph (Banks) is ill, and I can do nothing till he recovers.

I am happy to know you will go to New South Wales with me, my sweet wife. You are everything that I could desire; and wherever we go, you may be sure of one thing, that I shall always love you. Whenever I have fixed on this or any other situation, I shall write to you. In the meantime, let nobody know till things are settled, as there is much between the cup and the lip.

My lovely Ailie, you are constantly in my thoughts. I am tired of this place, but cannot lose the present opportunity of doing something for our advantage. When that is accomplished I shall not lose one moment. My darling, when we meet I shall be the happiest man on earth. Write soon, for I count the days till I hear from you, my lovely Ailie.

Park's intention to go to Australia was frustrated.

Robert Stevenson (1772-1850)

Robert Stevenson was the grandfather of R. L. Stevenson (q.v.) and the first of five generations of the family who were great engineers and lighthouse builders. In the words of Craig Mair, 'almost every beacon and lighthouse built in Scotland and the Isle of Man was designed and built by a Stevenson, and many inventions in the world advancement of lighthouses were produced by them. Nowadays there is hardly a light anywhere in the world which does not incorporate some aspect of their work.' The Bell Rock lighthouse, built between 1807 and 1811 on a dangerous reef in the Firth of Forth, submerged at every high tide, was one of Robert Stevenson's first achievements. This letter gives some idea of the difficulties.

104. The Bell Rock lighthouse

To John Rennie
          On board the Bell Rock Floating Light
                   2 September 1807

. . . Your letters of the 27 inst have this moment been forwarded me by a boat which from the state of the wind and tide must make but little delay, and at present this vessel rolls so unmercifully that in order to write you I have my chair firmly lashed and my legs round the feet of the table. . .

I have been on board this vessel about three weeks, and I really think it will be necessary for me to remain still about the same time, when I have every appearance of getting the beams of the wooden house fixed—which will in all respects be of the utmost consequence—for we have been most fortunate with regard to tides and weather hitherto and if we can get over the Boating as much, it would in all respects answer our purpose.

I have just returned from the Rock—in all we count 31—I have the Smeaton, a small ship which in complement to your old acquaintance I renamed.—She is made fast to a Buoy not far from the Rock, as this vessel cannot stow Boats to take the number of people. It happened this morning when we were on the rock that she drifted, and is now many miles to leeward.—By the greatest good fortune the boat that brought your letter was at the rock and took the Smeaton complement of workmen on board;—but the wind having got up suddenly we were two hours of pulling one mile and some of the men in one of the boats were so exhausted that a life line was passed astern here and the boat pulled along side. I was in that boat myself. . .

I have made shift to write but I wish you may can read. We are clearing away at the foundation as to try my method of landing. I had last night six large blocks landed with the greatest facility.— These will answer for filling up some holes in the Rock, but I do not think we shall get anything in that way done this season and I have a forge in the Rock for sharpening the tools without which we could not have done half the work. It is only necessary to remove the bellows every tide. . .

Lord Jeffrey (1773-1850)

Francis Jeffrey edited the Edinburgh Review *from its first appearance in 1802 until 1829. During that time he was probably the most influential literary critic in the English-speaking world, even if some of his judgements now seem untenable. An advocate by profession and a Whig in politics, he became Lord Advocate and Member of Parliament for Edinburgh and much involved in the politics of parliamentary reform.*

105. A walking tour

To George J. Bell   *Montrose 26 August 1799*

Dear Bell—Here we are, only at Montrose yet, you see; and it is only by wondrous exertions that we have got so far. We stopped for two days at Perth, hoping for places in the mail, and then set forward on foot in despair. We have trudged it now for fifty miles, and came here this morning very weary, sweaty, and filthy. Our baggage, which was to have left Perth the same day that we did, has not yet made its appearance, and we have received the comfortable information that it is often a week before there is room in the mail to bring such a parcel forward. In this forlorn situation we have done what we could. We have made clean the outside of the platter, shaved and washed our faces, turned our neckcloths, brushed our pantaloons, and anointed our hair with honey water, and so we have been perambulating the city, and have accepted an invitation from Mr. Wm. Baillie, writer in Edinburgh. . .

Bob lugs along with him, in his bosom, and his breeches, and one way or another, a volume of Petrarch, a Northern Tour, and a volume of Cicero; so we have occupation enough when we choose not to talk, and have succeeded wonderfully in making sonnets and sapphics upon all the oddities we have met with; Montrose is a good, gay-looking place. It was furiously gay indeed yesterday, being the last day of the races, and a mercy it was we did not come, weary and way-worn (as we once intended), into it in the evening, for there was not a corner into which they could have stowed us. We shall be in Aberdeen to-morrow, I think, or Monday at the latest, and shall go out of it, if possible, on Thursday. . .

106. 'All my recollections are Scottish'

To Lord Murray   *Liverpool 20 August 1813*

. . . I have been dining out every day for this last week with Unitarians, and Whigs, and Americans, and brokers, and bankers, and small fanciers of pictures and paints, and the Quaker aristocracy, and the fashionable vulgar, of the place. But I do not like Liverpool much better, and could not live here with any comfort. Indeed I believe I could not live anywhere out of Scotland. All my recollections are Scottish, and consequently all my imaginations; and though I thank God that I have as few fixed opinions as any man of my standing, yet all the elements out of which they are made have a certain national cast also. In short, I will not live anywhere else if I can help it; nor die either; and all old Esky's* eloquence would have been thrown away in an attempt to persuade me that *banishment furth the kingdom* might be patiently endured. . .

107. The poverty of Robert Burns

To William Empson   *Craigcrook 11 November 1837*

. . . In the last week I have read all *Burns'* life and works—not without many tears, for the life especially. What touches me most is the pitiable poverty in which that gifted being (and his noble-minded father) passed his early days—the painful frugality to which their innocence was doomed, and the thought, how small a share of the useless luxuries in which *we* (such comparatively poor creatures) indulge, would have sufficed to shed joy and cheerfulness

---

* Lord Eskgrove, a Judge, who consoled a friend he was obliged to banish, by assuring him, that there really were places in the world, such as England for example, where a man, though out of Scotland, might live with some little comfort.

in their dwellings, and perhaps to have saved that glorious spirit from the trials and temptations under which he fell so prematurely. Oh my dear Empson, there must be something *terribly* wrong in the present arrangements of the universe, when those things can happen, and be thought natural. I could lie down in the dirt, and cry and grovel there, I think, for a century, to save such a soul as Burns from the suffering and the contamination and the *degradation* which these same arrangements imposed upon him; and I fancy that, if I could but have known him, in my present state of wealth and influence, I might have saved, and reclaimed, and preserved him, even to the present day. He would not have been so old as my brother judge Lord Glenlee, or Lord Lynedoch, or a dozen others that one meets daily in society. And what a creature, not only in genius, but in the nobleness of character; potentially at least, if right models had been put *gently* before him. But we must not dwell on it. You south Saxons cannot value him rightly, and miss half the pathos, and more than half the sweetness. There is no such mistake as that your chief miss is in the *humour* or the shrewd sense. It is in far higher and more delicate elements—God help you! We shall be up to the whole, I trust, in another world. When I think of *his* position, I have no feeling for the *ideal* poverty of your Wordsworths and Coleridges, comfortable, flattered, very spoiled, capricious, idle beings, fantastically discontented because they cannot make an easy tour to Italy, and buy casts and cameos; and what poor, peddling, whining drivellers in comparison with him! But I will have no uncharity. They too should have been richer. . .

Thomas Scott (1774-1823)

Thomas, the younger brother of Sir Walter Scott, spent some time as an army officer in Canada. These are two of his letters about his experiences there.

108. A Mohawk chief

To Walter Scott   *15 July 1815*

   . . . I am here at present for a few days on leave, as my time was short, the roads scarcely passable. I ran the risk of finding the ice open, and proceeded in a canoe with my father and two of my red brethren down the St. Lawrence. We had a prosperous voyage, and paddled ninety miles from sunrise to sunset—shooting all the rapids in a style that would surprise any person unacquainted with the dexterity of the Indians. This favour I acquired from my situation amongst my tribe, being a Mohawk chief and warrior by adoption, under the name of Assarapa. In truth, my intercourse with the Indians was the only thing from which I received any pleasure at Cornwall. Their settlement at St. Ridac and on the islands was nearly opposite to Cornwall, and I preferred the manners of the native Indians to the insipid conversation of our own officers. . .

109. A literary Red Indian

To Walter Scott (No date)

. . . Yesterday morning Captain Norton, the chief of the Five Nations, left. I had the pleasure to be his intimate acquaintance, and he is a man who makes you almost wish to be an Indian chief. What do you think of a man speaking the language of about twelve Indian nations, English, French, German, and Spanish, all well, being in possession of all modern literature—having read with delight your *Lady of the Lake*, and translated the same, together with the Scriptures, into Mohawk—having written a history of the five nations, and a journal of his own travels, now in London ready for publication, and being at the same time an Indian chief, living as they do and following all their fashions. For, brother, you ask doth he paint himself, scalp, etc. etc.? I answer yea, he doth; and with the most polished manner of civilised life, he would not disdain to partake of the blood of his enemy at the banquet of sacrifice. Yet I admire and love the man, and would cheerfully give fifty guineas that you could see him for one half-hour. He is afraid that the *Edinburgh Review* will be hard on his book. I promised to write to you to have it reviewed in the *Quarterly*. It surely is a strange circumstance that an Indian Chief should produce a literary child. . .

John Leyden (1775-1811)

John Leyden, one of the most extraordinary of all lads o pairts, was described by John Buchan as 'a curious blend of the polymath and the Border reiver'. In spite of his poverty, he went through virtually all classes of all faculties of the

University of Edinburgh. He had an insatiable curiosity about languages and learned to speak more than 30 of them. His knowledge of early Scottish literature was extensive and he helped Scott with his collection of Border ballads. Looking for new linguistic worlds to conquèr, he acquired the necessary additional learning in a space of six months to qualify for an appointment as a surgeon in India. There he rapidly learnt several Indian and Malayan languages and was the first to analyse the relationships between them. He died during the invasion of Batavia in 1811 of a fever caught by spending several hours in a dank cellar voraciously reading the manuscripts that were stored in it. Robert Southey commented: 'So Batavia has cost us John Leyden's life which was worth more than ten Batavias'. See also Letter 87.

110. 'I have not been idle'

To James Ballantyne   *Puloo Penang 24 October 1805*

. . . I was appointed medical assistant to the Mysore Survey, and at the same time directed to carry out inquiries concerning the natural history of the country, and the manners and languages, &c., of the natives of Mysore. This, you would imagine, was the very situation I wished for; and so it would had I previously had time to acquire the country languages. But I had them now to acquire after severe marches and countermarches in the heat of the sun, night-marches and day-marches, and amid the disgusting details of a field hospital, the duties of which were considerably arduous. However, I wrought incessantly and steadily, and without being discouraged by any kind of difficulty, till my health absolutely gave way, and when I could keep the field no longer, I wrought on my couch, as I generally do still, though I am much better than I have been. As I had the assistance of no intelligent European, I was obliged long to grope my way; but I have now acquired a pretty correct idea of India in all its departments, which increases in geometrical progression as I advance in the languages. The languages that have attracted my attention since my arrival have been Arabic, Persic, Hindostani, Mahratta, Tamal, Telinga, Canara, Sanscrit, Malayalam, Malay, and Armenian. You will be ready to ask, where the devil I picked up these hard names, but I assure you it is infinitely more difficult to pick up the languages themselves; several of which include dialects as different from each other as French or Italian from Spanish or Portuguese; and in all these I flatter myself, I have made considerable progress. What would you say, were I to add the Maldivian and Mapella languages to these? Besides I have deciphered the inscriptions of Mavalipoorani, which were written in an ancient Canara character, which had hitherto defied all attempts at understanding it, and also several *Lada Lippi* inscriptions, which is an ancient Tamal dialect and character, in addition to the Jewish tablets of Cochin, which were in the ancient Malayalam, generally termed Malabar. I enter into these details merely to show you that I have not been idle, and that my time has neither been dissipated, nor devoid of plan, though that plan is not sufficiently unfolded. . . .

John Galt (1779-1839)

Galt was a prolific novelist who enlarged the scope of the novel in several directions. Most of his novels, including the best, such as Annals of the Parish, The Provost *and* The Entail, *deal very convincingly with life around Irvine and Greenock where he grew up. He also travelled widely and sought a role in commerce and public affairs. For two years he was responsible for the settlement of a large area of Ontario in Canada, where he founded the city of Guelph. His enthusiasm and his social conscience alarmed his Directors in London and they replaced him without even the bleak courtesy of a formal dismissal. The following letter was addressed to David Moir, a doctor in Musselburgh and one of Galt's colleagues on* Blackwood's Magazine.

111. The foundation of Guelph

To David Moir   *Guelph, U.C. 1 August 1827*

. . . The town thrives amazingly. Upwards of a hundred and sixty building lots are engaged, and houses rising as fast as materials can be prepared. The approach to it, on one side, is probably the finest avenue in the world, being upwards of seven miles in length. It is an opening through the forest two hundred feet in width, with a lofty wall of about a hundred and thirty feet high on each side. I almost regret that the progress of improvement will soon deform it with many breaches. By the way, in clearing for a quarry we discovered a neat formed niche in the rock, with a vase like an Etruscan in it, filled with dust and ashes—unfortunately it was broken by one of the workmen.

When I had got my city fairly a-going I then went to Lake Huron, crossing Lake Simco with singing boatmen—a race fast disappearing. The passage of that lake is exceedingly beautiful, but not picturesque. We met in the twilight of the dawn with a canoe full of Indian children, piloted by a negro. They were gliding over the glassy water between us and the waning, like imps and their leader, as silent and solemn as spirits. I embarked at Portangushire on Lake Huron, in a gun-vessel fitted out for the voyage; and off Cabot's-head I had a fine view, for upwards of four hours, of that rare and visionary reflection of the land in the water, of which no one has given any satisfactory explanation. There were three distinct landscapes or reflections of the scene, visible so plainly that you could not tell which was the real but by the position only. The voyage itself was comfortless and uninteresting, save for its object. We left the gun-boat at Detroit, and came down Lake Erie in a steam-boat to Buffalo, where there is a hotel that beats the Waterloo tontine or the Regent bridge of Edinburgh (as the Yankees would say) to immortal smash. By the way, the Americans were very civil to us at Detroit. When we entered the theatre one of the players recognized me, and the orchestra forthwith were instructed to play a Scotch air; and between the play and farce the officers who were of the party were honoured with Rule Britannia and God save the King. This was more remarkable as it was on the 5th July, the evening immediately after their grand festival of the Independence. In fact, the king is very popular among them, and you will often meet with his and Canning's portrait in the bars of the roadside taverns.

I am much pleased with the Canadian summer as it shines forth in this province. It is warmer certainly than in England, or rather there are more consecutive warm days than we experience in England; but in other respects the sensible heat is not greater. Of literature or learned men I can say nothing. I have not had a book in my hand, save an old magazine, for the last six weeks; but I am laying the foundation of an academy, the Company having allowed me to reserve one half of the money arising from the sale of the land in the town for that purpose, by which I have already upwards of two thousand dollars in store. I have got a school already opened in a shed—three taverns filled with boarders—a khan after the Turkish fashion, which accommodates eighteen families. I am about to begin a church, having received £100 from the Bishop to begin with. We have a regular mail-coach twice a-week, a post-office, and they speak already of getting up a newspaper and a bank agent; all this since the 23d April, at which time the site of the market-place was in the centre of the wood, some miles from any habitation.—Give my best respects to all friends, and believe me, ever yours, most truly,

JOHN GALT

Lord Cockburn (1779-1854)

Henry Thomas Cockburn was an advocate and ultimately a law lord and Solicitor-General. He was a Whig, a close friend of Francis Jeffrey (q.v.), a contributor to the Edinburgh Review, *and active in the cause of parliamentary reform. His concern for the preservation of Edinburgh is reflected in the name of the Cockburn Association, the principal Edinburgh amenity society. It has been said that everybody who lives in Edinburgh should read his* Memorials of his Time *at least once a year. He is one of the most entertaining of letter writers, irreverent, high spirited and ironic; but very few of his letters have so far been published.*

112. Cocky

To Sir Thomas Dick-Lauder   *Friday (1833 or 1834)*

My dear Sir Thomas,—It will be a great delight to us to receive Mr. and Miss Smith into our pastoral paternity. Indeed a Findhorn face to me is the face of a friend.

I hope that Mr. Smith is aware that whatever Mr. Cockburn was, His Majesty's Solicitor General is a decorous person—arrayed in solemn black—with a demure visage—an official ear—an evasive voice—suspicious palate—ascetic blood—and flinty heart. There is a fellow very like him, who traverses the Pentlands in a dirty grey jacket, white hat, with a long pole. That's not the Sol. Gen. That's Cocky—a frivolous dog; Mr. Smith may use all freedom with him.—Ever,

H.C.

113. Breakfast at Habbies How

To Miss Cockburn   *Bonaly*
(in London)   *Sunday 11 August 1833*

My dearest Jane,—Tell Dr. Warren that if he has any patients who can't walk, he should send them to a Habbies How breakfast, where not walking is impossible. We had one yesterday in the grandest style, of which the only want as occurred to me a thousand times was your absence, and the kind friends under whose roof you are.

There were only 3 Lauders and 3 Craigs asked, but applications became thick in the course of the week and at last we amounted to

23. The day was absolutely perfect, but not altogether cloudless or breezeless. Graham, and Graham Maitland and Frank went in the cart—the good old rural way of going, and the only respectable one. Your mother and I and wifie went in the Droskie.

Near the Hunters Tryst we fell in with Sir Thomas Lauder and a very excellent Findhorn friend of his called Smith in his gig, and my Lady with Miss Smith and the three daughters in their carriage, and John and George Lauder on a pony each; and thus the two gigs, the one carriage, and the two outriders made a very handsome procession, past Woodhouselee, and flaring up the peaceful glen. Near Logan House we joined the cart, with Lawrence on 'Jessie,' James on a hired beast and his inseparable, Alex. Wight, on another.

After going on a little William Craig and two sisters appeared in a chaise, and Archibald Davidson on a pony. We had a very agreeable stroll in detached parties up the quiet, sunny, turfy glen till we reached the scene of the more animal part of the proceedings. Here Professor James Pillans appeared, having walked alone from Edinburgh.

Then began the lighting the fire—the setting the table—the building seats, the unpacking the stores—the sighing for its not being ready—the children climbing up and sliding down etc.; till at last our hermit fare was ready; then what clattering—what scrambling—what roaring—what upsetting of seats . . . Graham, and Charlotte Lauder secretly removed a small stone from Mr. Smith's seat and tumbled him back nearly into the burn.

For my part, I sat on a stone retired, and reasoned high of Patie and of Ramsay. My soul was with the Gentle Shepherd*. But I trust that I kept my temper sufficiently not to let them see how I despised their low tastes. Their food (Oh! to think of food in such a place) consisted of rolls, butter, honey, marmalade, jelly, eggs, cold veal pie, tongue (no want of that) broiled salmon hot (Oh! Oh! hot salmon under the ray of an August morning sun in a pastoral, classical valley) tea, coffee, chocolate—closed on the part of the male, and a few of the female, brutes by a dram—an absolute dram—God bless me—of Whisky!! . . .

Adieu, my dearest Jane.—Ever,

H. COCKBURN

---

* The pastoral comedy by Allan Ramsay (q.v.). It is set in this part of the Pentland Hills.

114. Thomas Chalmers
(See Letter 116)

To Mrs Rutherford   *Bonaly 1 June 1847*

My Dear Mrs Rutherford,
We are struck, & saddened, by this unexpected death of
Chalmers.—Who was a greater living Scotchman? Who has
Scotland to boast of, as a Churchman, & on matters connected with
the policy of religion, beyond him, since the Reformation?—with
his enthusiasm & eloquence, if he had lived in Knox's days, it may
be doubted whether even Knox would have been owned by history
as the leader. Everyone else, even the Academic Robertson,—would
have withered in his furnace. And his walks have been so
varied.—Not confined to the common place, technical, salvation of
souls, he has enriched & enobled this pursuit by striking discussions
on every kindred moral·& political subject; & often leaves us to ask
whether his pen or his tongue be the most powerful. He never
wasted himself on little objects, nor tried to reach his ends in a little
way; but aimed high, & sought no conquests but those that reason
& enthusiasm, operating on the minds of masses, could atchieve.
That concentration of the mind on the object of present interest,
which zeal always implies, sometimes made him forget what was
due to other men & matters, & has exposed him to the only
doubt,—that of inconsistancy,—to which he has ever been
supposed to be liable. But this partiality of vehemence never made
him long, or seriously, unjust. And thro'out a life of ardent practical
conflict, he was uniformly simple, affectionate, & true. He was of
incalculable use,—both from what he did, & what he prevented
being done. His name was a tower. His voice a thunderbolt. Many
of his opponents will now rail, & many of his own party chatter,
who were dumb before him. How thankful I am that I was often
within the flames of his eloquent enthusiasm; & that I was familiar
with the honest smile, & the quaint, picturesque, oddities, of this
most loveable original.—He seems to have passed away almost as
gently as Dr Black, for death had not made him even fall down on
his bed, or relaxed his clasped hands from the apparent attitude of
prayer. It is pleasant to think of his pecularities, & his worth. The
homage that he himself would prefer, is that,—very largely
given,—that proceeds from the hovels & the vennels.
    Our ranks are thinning. I clouded myself today on my way out,
sitting behind that faithful Geordie, by considering how the loss of
two or three more would wreck me; & recalling the days in
which,—all at the gaiety of the bar, & not one of us dreaming of
office,—we closed a gay & not inglorious, week, amidst the bowls,

the claret, the talk, the boyishness of Craigcrook.—But these visions are all nonsense.—They are not for practical man. The only wise conclusion, is, let those who remain cling closer. . .

Therefore I give you up to the lowness of your avocations. And I,—proceed to dinner. Young neeps,—gooseberry fool,—cold punch—genuine grass-cow cream,—& other innocent ruralities,— such as sheeps head & marrow bones. Would that Providence would be placed to take somebody I could name, to itself; so that lad Andrew Rutherford and I might once more have a few, easy, self-poped days e'er our pilgrimage be done.

The gong rings. Now for the marrow.

Ever   H COCKBURN

115. The Royal Scottish Academy

To Mrs Andrew Rutherford   *Bonaly 31 August 1850*

. . . Think of Phiffys felicity yesterday! At one Oclock Albert laid the foundation of his Galleries, & at 4 The Queen went over his Hospital, *speaking very much to the architect himself*—& admiring everything. It was his great day. And delighted, modest, & amiable, he was;—in spite of all the laughter, & bad jokes, & parodies, that I could exhaust myself in pouring out on him. Her Majesty was charmed by the *scite* of the Hospital; but, poor royal creature,—she had never heard of the Pentland Hills!—on which she gazed with especial admiration. Think of a crowned head never having heard of the Pentland Hills! But her admiration shows that the head was not unworthy of the crown.

She had beautiful weather. When she arrived, she went slowly, in an open carriage, past Parsons Green, to the Abbey; with, it is supposed, 100,000 cheering people on Arthur Seat. Yesterday morning she went round The Drive, & walked from Loch Sappy to the *Top of the Hill;* under a splendid, calm, sun,—& with not 100 people on the hill to disturb her. I suppose she is the only soverign who has been there since the days of Arthur himself; & when were his days?—

The Founding was beautiful. The Orators were His Reverence Principal Lee, who prayed a good prayer,—only the sun blinded him, & was not heard 5 yards off;—Davie Bole, the handsomest & youngest man there,—& Albert, whose address,—whosoever composed it, was excellent, & excellently spoken. All we—I mean of the Board of Trustees & Co were introduced to him in the

129

Gallery of the Royal Institution, thro which he walked. He particularly admired my shoes.—Every body was in some sort of uniform, or decent private dress; except 3 noble Lords,—who chose to show their superiority, & their familiarity with royalty, by appearing as scurvy as possible. These were Roseberry,—a scruff; who always pretends to be ill when he is required to pay out a penny; Bucchan,—who used to remind us by his elegance & sprightliness of the aerial Henry Erskine,—but always a fool,—now a broken down beggar; & Belhaven, who gets £2,000 a year for upholding the Kirk by dressing himself up 10 days yearly,—yet yesterday had positively robbed a scarecrow for his dirty raggs.

After this ceremony Her Majesty went, in an open carriage, thro' both new & old towns,—& again round the drive. Even the severe Dumphy says that the Apartments in Holyrood are magnificent.

She is off this morning; & in 7 hours hears the murmur, & sees the liquid crystal, of the Dee.

The Foundation stone is the great event. It greatly adorns Edin^r,—& saves it from a fatal danger, which nothing except the ornamental appropriation of the ground could have averted; it marks, & promotes, the progress of Art; it gives the Artists a dignity, & a permanency, of station, which nothing but a connection with Government could have given; & it refines & elevates the local taste, & the local objects. I hope the Artists will show, by their works, that they deserve it. Paton, I hear, is pretty far on with a beautiful conception.

Sir John Watson Gordon, their President, was the most picturesque gentleman in the ceremony. A full suit of black velvet,—lace frills & ruffles; silver buckles,—& a very handsome gold medal hung from his neck. He was exactly an English nobleman, 250 years ago, going forth to get his head taken off.—What can I say more?

When do you mean to come back? I have no idea that Rutherford needs you; & I am so afraid of the Autumnal strangers exhausting him, that I would rather he was with you. Anyhow, take care of yourself. There are fewer pearls on the string now than when we first knew it. Let none that remain drop off unnecessarily.

Miss Elphinstone is dead;—mercifully—for she could never have moved. We are all wellish.—Tho' Joe disturbs us, with her back & her weakness.—I asked little Charlotte t'other day, if she had a spine? To which she said 'No, but I've a spade.'—A much better thing certainly.

H Cockburn

The Disruption and Science

There is an unexpected association between religion and science in the men of the Disruption, but the width of their interests was perhaps a natural outcome of the Scottish Enlightenment.

Thomas Chalmers (1780-1847)

Of all Scottish churchmen of the mid-nineteenth century Thomas Chalmers had the most influence on the affairs of the church and the people. He began his career as an assistant to the Professor of Mathematics at St Andrews University, but about 1810 felt himself called to be the advocate of an evangelical religion with a social message. His practical Christianity drew immense crowds to hear him preach in the Tron Kirk in Glasgow, while his theological abilities earned him the Chair of Divinity at Edinburgh University in 1828. He entered with zeal into the debate on the church relationship with the State, protesting the need for the church to free itself from secular interference. When, almost inevitably, the Disruption came in 1843, the strongest lead to define the character of the new Free Church came from Thomas Chalmers (see Letter 114).

116. On the necessity for an independent Scottish Church

To the Rev. Mr Bruce   *10 April 1828*

My Dear Sir,—In the present state of our Church controversy, the first and nearest concern is the integrity of our jurisdiction.

After the treatment we have received both from Government and Parliament, as well as the Court below, the time seems now to be fully come when we should put forth a Claim of Rights, with a statement of what we hold to be our duty, along with our determination to adhere to it.

I hold it a great advantage, that in the preparation of such a document, we can set ourselves forth in the light of a suffering and aggrieved party—not as claimants, but as complainers; that is, not as seeking for ourselves any new powers, but as protesting against an invasion made upon our old liberties, and which have been ours in undisturbed possession for many generations. . . Have we no access to the people but *via* London? They are at our own door; and might not we in daily and immediate converse with them, make it clear as day that it is for their cause the Church is now perilling all which belongs to her in the world?. . . above all let the people be made to see, that, in defence of their Christian liberties, the ministers are putting to hazard if not their lives at least their livelihoods. . .

Let the Government take their choice. Let all who have a patriotic regard for the country's peace and welfare, set the alternative before them. Let every man who values the blessings of an efficient Church decide the question for himself. . .

I ever am, my dear Sir, yours most cordially,

THOMAS CHALMERS

Sir David Brewster (1781-1868)

Sir David Brewster in his range of talents and interests epitomised the Scottish Enlightenment. At the age of ten he invented a telescope. At eleven he was a student at Edinburgh University. While continuing his scientific experiments, he studied for the ministry and became a minister in the Church of Scotland. Following his submission of papers including Some Properties of Light *(1813) and* The Polarisation of Light *(1814) he was elected a Fellow of the Royal Society. In 1837 he became Principal of the colleges of St Mary's and St Leonard's at St. Andrews University and finally in 1859 Principal of Edinburgh University.*

His combined interests in optics and religion made him the catalyst of the great photographic achievement of David Octavius Hill and Robert Adamson. When in 1843 The Disruption occurred, which Lord Cockburn saw as 'one of the rarest occurrences in moral history,' Brewster saw the possibility of photographing, by means of the new invention, the calotype, members of the newly created Free Church, from which Hill would paint a portrait of their first Assembly. First he required the goodwill of the inventor of the process, the English scientist, Fox Talbot.

117. The calotype and the Free Church of Scotland

To William Henry Fox Talbot   *St. Leonard's College*
                                                 3 July 1843

. . . You may probably have heard . . . of the great moral event in Scotland of 500 ministers quitting their manses and glebes and stipends for Conscience sake and forming a Free Church unshackled by secular interferences. A grand historical picture is undertaken by a first rate artist to represent the first General

Assembly of the Free Church. I got hold of the artist—showed him the Calotype and the eminent advantage he might derive from it in getting likenesses of all the principal characters before they dispersed to their respective homes. He was at first incredulous, but went to Mr Adamson, and arranged with him preliminaries for getting all the necessary portraits.

They have succeeded beyond their most sanguine expectations. They have taken, on a small scale, groups of 25 persons in the same picture all placed in attitudes which the painter desired, and very large pictures besides have been taken of each individual to assist the painter in the completion of his picture.

Mr D. O. Hill the painter is in the act of entering into partnership with Mr Adamson and proposes to apply the Calotype to many other general purposes of a very popular kind . . . I think you will find that we have, in Scotland, found out the value of your invention, not before yourself, but before those to whom you have given the privilege of using it. I have seen one of the groups of 25 persons with our distinguised Moderator Dr Chalmers sitting in the heart of them, and I have never seen anything finer. . . .

David Octavius Hill (1802-70)

The good fortune of early portrait photography in Scotland was that its first practitioners were men of outstanding ability in the two areas germane to its practice. D. O. Hill, R.S.A., Secretary to the Royal Scottish Academy, a portrait painter (as well as a painter of landscapes), carried over characteristics of the tradition of Wilkie and Raeburn into the new art of the calotype. The aesthetic achievement could not have been realised without the practical science of his partner, Robert Adamson, who had available the researches into optics and the camera of Sir David Brewster and Dr John Adamson at St Andrews University. In the letter to David Roberts, R.A., H.R.S.A., Hill shows he is well aware of where he stands in the partnership, and also how the new art in the wrong hands could be trivialised.

118. 'Calotypes'

To David Roberts   *Inverleith Place, Edinburgh*
                                                          12 March 1845

. . . I cannot fail to be more than gratified by the intelligence I received from you this morning as to the manner in which the portfolio of our Calotypes had been received by yourself, by Stanfield, and the distinguished guests of Lord Northampton. Your flattering opinions have been shared by Etty, Allan, Leitch and many artists and a few who know what art is, and these I have used as a warm blanket, to restore me to my natural heat, after a few cold bucketings of ignorant criticism, which my desire to foster and improve this hand maiden of Fine Art, has exposed me to. Most welcome therefore and highly prized by me are Stanfield's and your own cordial approval of our labour. Accept of my gratitude both of you . . .

The Art is the invention of Mr Fox Talbot who is the sole patentee: his patent extends in England only. About three years ago this said process was chemically and artistically speaking a very miserable affair. Dr Adamson of St Andrews—brother of my friend R. Adamson whose manipulation produced the pictures now with you, took up Mr Talbot's process as an amateur. You are aware how jealous some scientific men are, as to their rights in the paternity of inventions or improvements, therefore I say *entre nous* that I believe Dr Adamson & his brother to be the fathers of many of these parts of the process which make it a valuable and practical art. I believe also from all I have seen that Robert Adamson is the most successful manipulator the art has yet seen, and his steady industry and knowledge of chemistry, is such that both from him and his brother much new improvements may yet be expected . . .

James Nasmyth (1808-90)

James Nasmyth was the son of Alexander Nasmyth, Honorary R.S.A., the landscape artist and portrait painter, whose most notable subject was Robert Burns (1787). Nasmyth senior's four sons and seven daughters all painted, but James's fame rests on his invention of the steam hammer. His long, rambling letter to D.O. Hill reflects his ranging interests and also the good-humoured character of the man. His publications include The Moon.

119. Photography, steam hammers and the moon

To David Octavius Hill   *Fire Side, Patricroft 1847*

. . . I am happy to say trade in my line is in a most flourishing condition we are literally crammed full of orders and driving a rattling trade in Steam Hammers, Pile Drivers and Locofocos without numbers: never was such a time for us, and with every prospect of continuing as long as I need . . .

I have upwards of 600 chaps at work knocking the work out in fine style and sending it flying all over the world . . . My Pile Drivers . . . Two have been sent out to Egypt and are now at work damming up the Nile at Cairo. two go out to Russia immediately the Baltic opens . . .

The moon and I are still on the most intimate terms and she answers me many many authentic questions I put to her very face through my tube thus . . . I use the Newtonian construction it is by far the most handy simple and perfect you look in at the side of the tube which is far more handy nor looking thus. I hope I shall have the happiness to show you the wonders of the moon's surface some of these fine afternoons its really a fine sight when the moon is about the age as above.? The telescope is a constant source of the highest pleasure to me and enables me to have vast treats when the day's work is over at ½ past 8 in the evening when I come home for the night and weather permits—Everyone must have some hobby to divert himself with so telescope making and moon investigating is mine so far . . .

Calotype appears to be making good progress . . . I wish I had time and knowledge to practise so fascinating an art as it is. There is to me a charm quite inexpressible in those bits of nature clipt out of the pages of time. There is so much of the actual precision of the great 'I am' in them. The knowledge and feeling that every minute particular has its actual counterpart in positive reality causing one to regard them with deep deep interest . . .

☆   ☆   ☆

Susan Edmonstone Ferrier (1782-1854)

Susan Ferrier had family connections with the legal and literary worlds of Edinburgh and through them with the Highlands. Her father, for instance, was the legal agent of the Duke of Argyll and later a colleague of Sir Walter Scott as Clerk to the Court of Session. She was therefore well placed to write her three novels based on close observation of both Edinburgh and Highland society, Marriage *(1818),* The Inheritance *(1824) and* Destiny *(1831).*

120. 'An old empty throne'

To Mrs Connell   *Edinburgh 1822*

. . . Mrs. John has been out, but is still far from well. I saw her yesterday in the drawing-room, but she said she is still *rheumy* and her pulse at 120. General Graham has been confined to bed for a fortnight from the same cause, and Mrs. Riddell's fever was a rheumatic one, but last time I heard of her she was recovering. To add to *their* misfortunes their house has been broken into and all their bits of plate and linen taken away; so much for the miseries of human life, which seem to be all that I hear of at present, though happily exempt from experiencing them, as my father is in his usual robust health and I feel stronger than I have done for some months. Our greatest distress is how to dispose of our apples, but that seems also an *epidemic*, and one which I dare say you have felt very severely. The town is in a state of deathlike repose after its late excitement, but as most of my friends happen to be in it I find it particularly agreeable. I went with the Fletchers one day to see Holyrood, and we thought black, burning shame of ourselves for having been such gowks as to go and look at a bare room and an old empty throne. The *presence chamber* is just decent and no more, so you lost nothing there. . . The weather is very broken and the trees getting a wintry aspect, but I have still a fine show of flowers, and I feel no inclination to leave them, so am not sorry to look forward to another month at Morningside. . .

Sir David Wilkie (1785-1841)

Wilkie was on friendly terms with both Scott and Galt and there is a close association between his paintings and their novels. All three were concerned to record Scottish social life and character which was under attack from external assimilation.

Wilkie's reference to The Antiquary *in this letter is to chapter XXXI where Scott describes a scene as one 'which our Wilkie alone could have painted with that exquisite feeling of nature that characterises his enchanting productions'. Wilkie pleads with Scott not to kill himself with overwork in his efforts to clear his debts.*

121. 'Do spare yourself'

To Sir Walter Scott
7 Terrace, Kensington,
London January 1829

Dear Sir Walter.—I pass over all those disastrous events that have arrived to us both since our last, as you justly call it, melancholy parting, to assure you how delighted I shall be if I can, in the most inconsiderable degree, assist in the illustration of the great work which we all hope may lighten or remove that load of troubles by which your noble spirit is at this time beset, considering it as only repaying a debt of obligation which you yourself have laid upon me when, with an unseen hand in the *Antiquary*, you took me up, and claimed me, the humble painter of domestic sorrow, as your countryman. . .

In my late travels, I found all eyes turned towards you and your labours with deep anxiety and interest. Connected with this is an apprehension which is general, but which I, though a humble individual, feel strongly, in particular from dear-bought experience. It is that you will, in your gigantic efforts, overwork yourself. I claim the privilege with you, Sir, of repectfully offering an admonition on this head: miraculous as your powers are, do spare yourself as much as possible. I, when first in trouble, found unceasing labour my only resource, and the lassitude that has never since left me was the consequence. I hear repeated good accounts of your health from Mrs. Lockhart, but the wearied faculties sometimes do not betray their exhaustion till it is too late.

Excuse this liberty from a Sufferer who is anxious only to guard those powers he so ardently admires.—Your very obliged and very faithful Servant,

DAVID WILKIE

Lord Byron (1788-1824)

Byron, whose mother was a Gordon of Gight, spent most of his first ten years in Aberdeen, where he attended the Grammar School. He left Scotland in 1798 when he succeeded to the title, but he never lost his Scottish feelings and attitudes. As he said in Don Juan (X, 17 and 19):

> *'But I am half a Scot by birth, and bred*
> *A whole one, and my heart flies to my head,—...*
> *I "scotch'd not kill'd" the Scotchman in my blood,*
> *And love the land of "mountain and of flood".'*

His letters, of which nearly 3,000 survive, would establish his reputation as a writer even if he had never written a line of verse. Elizabeth Longford has described him as 'the most enjoyable letter-writer in the world'.

122. Swimming the Hellespont

To Henry Drury   *Salsette frigate. May 3d 1810*
                              in the Dardanelles off Abydos

My dear Drury,—When I left England nearly a year ago you requested me to write to you.—I will do so.—I have crossed Portugal, traversed the South of Spain, visited Sardinia, Sicily, Malta, and thence passed into Turkey where I am still wandering. . .

This morning I *swam* from *Sestos* to *Abydos*, the immediate distance is not above a mile but the current renders it hazardous, so much so, that I doubt whether Leander's conjugal powers must not have been exhausted in his passage to Paradise.—I attempted it a week ago and failed owing to the North wind and the wonderful rapidity of the tide, though I have been from my childhood a strong swimmer, but this morning being calmer I succeeded and crossed the 'broad Hellespont' in an hour and ten minutes.—Well, my dear Sir, I have left my home and seen part of Africa & Asia and a tolerable portion of Europe.—I have been with Generals, and Admirals, Princes and Pachas, Governors and Ungovernables, but I have not time or paper to expatiate. I wish to let you know that I live with a friendly remembrance of you and a hope to meet you again, and if I do this as shortly as possible, attribute it to any-thing but forgetfulness.—Greece ancient and modern you know too well to require description. Albania indeed I have seen more of than any Englishman (but a Mr. Leake) for it is a country rarely visited from the savage character of the natives, though abounding in more natural beauties than the classical regions of Greece, which however are still eminently beautiful, particularly Delphi, and Cape Colonna in Attica. . .

The only vestige of Troy, or her destroyers, are the barrows supposed to contain the carcases of Achilles, Antilochus, Ajax &c. but Mt. Ida is still in high feather, though the Shepherds are nowadays not much like Ganymede.—But why should I say more of these things? are they not written in the *Boke* of Gell? and has not Hobby got a journal? I keep none as I have renounced scribbling.—I see not much difference between ourselves & the Turks, save that we have foreskins and they none, that they have long dresses and we short, and that we talk much and they little.—In England the vices in fashion are whoring & drinking, in Turkey, Sodomy & smoking, we prefer a girl and a bottle, they a pipe and pathic.—They are sensible people, Ali Pacha told me he was sure I was a man of rank because I had *small ears* and hands and *curling hair*. —By the bye, I speak the Romaic or Modern Greek tolerably, it does not differ from the ancient dialects so much as you would conceive, but the pronunciation is diametrically opposite, of verse except in rhyme they have no idea.—I like the Greeks, who are plausible rascals, with all the Turkish vices without their courage.—However some are brave and all are beautiful, very much resembling the busts of Alcibiades, the women not quite so handsome.—I can swear in Turkish, but except one horrible oath, and '*pimp*' and 'bread' and 'water' I have got no great vocabulary in that language.—They are extremely polite to strangers of any rank properly protected, and as I have got 2 servants and two soldiers we get on with great eclât. We have been occasionally in danger of thieves & once of shipwreck but always escaped.—At Malta I fell in love with a married woman and challenged an aid du camp of Genl. Oakes (a rude fellow who grinned at something, I never rightly knew what,) but he explained and apologised, and the lady embarked for Cadiz, & so I escaped murder and adultery . . .

Now, you will ask, what shall I do next? and I answer I do not know. . . I am like the jolly miller caring for nobody and not cared for. All countries are much the same in my eyes, I smoke and stare at mountains, and twirl my mustachios very independently, I miss no comforts, and the Musquitoes that rack the morbid frame of Hobhouse, have luckily for me little effect on mine because I live more temperately.—I omitted Ephesus in my Catalogue, which I visited during my sojourn at Smyrna,—but the temple has almost perished, and St. Paul need not trouble himself to epistolize the present brood of Ephesians who have converted a large church built entirely of marble into a mosque, and I dont know that the edifice looks the worse for it.—My paper is full and my ink ebbing, Good Afternoon!—If you address to me at Malta, the letter will be forwarded wherever I may be.—Hobhouse greets you, he pines for his poetry, at least some tidings of it.—I almost forgot to tell you that I am dying for love of three Greek Girls at Athens, sisters, two of whom have promised to accompany me to England, I lived in the same house, Teresa, Mariana, and Kattinka, are the names of these divinities all of them under 15.—your ταπεινοτατοσ δουλοσ *

BYRON

123. Byron to Scott

To Sir Walter Scott   *Pisa 12 January 1822*

. . . I owe to you far more than the usual obligation for the courtesies of literature and common friendship—for you went out of your way in 1817—to do me a service when it required not merely kindness—but courage to do so;—to have been seconded by you in such a manner would have been a proud memorial at any time—but at such a time—when 'all the World and his Wife' (or rather *mine)* as the proverb goes—were trying to trample upon me was something still higher to my Self esteem. I allude to the Quarterly rev[iew] of the 3d. Canto of C[hild]e H[arol]d which Murray told me was written by you—and indeed I should have known it without his information—as there could not be *two* who *could* and *would* have done this at the time.—Had it been a common criticism—however eloquent or panegyrical—I should have felt pleased undoubtedly and grateful—but not to the extent which the extraordinary Good-heartedness of the whole proceeding—must induce in any mind capable of such sensations.—The very *tardiness* of this acknowledgement will at least show that I have not forgotten the obligation—[and] I can assure you that my Sense of it has been out at compound interest during the delay . . .

You disclaim 'Jealousies' but I would ask as Boswell did of Johnson 'Of *whom could* you be jealous'—of none of the living certainly—and (taking all and all into consideration)—of which of the dead?—I don't like to bore you about the Scotch novels (as they call them though two of them are wholly English—and the rest half so) but nothing can or could ever persuade me since I was the first ten minutes in your company that you are *not* the Man.—To me those novels have so much of 'Auld lang syne' (I was bred a canny Scot till ten years old) that I never move without them—and when I removed from Ravenna to Pisa the other day—and sent on my

*most humble servant

library before—they were the only books that I kept by me—although I already knew them by heart. . .

yrs. ever most affectly

BYRON

Jay 27th, 1822 . . .

P.S.—Why don't you take a turn in Italy—you would find yourself as well-known and as welcome as in the Highlands among the natives.—As for the English you would be with them as in London—and I need not add that *I* would be delighted to see you again—which is far more than I shall ever feel or say for England or (with a few exceptions 'of kith—kin—and allies') any thing that it contains.—But my 'heart warms to the Tartan' or to any thing of Scotland which reminds me of Aberdeen and other parts not so far from the Highlands as that town—(about Invercauld & Braemar where I was sent to drink Goat's *Fey* in 1795-6. . . Pray present my respects to Lady Scott—who may perhaps recollect having seen me in town in 1815.

I see that one of your Supporters (for like Sir Hildebrand I am fond of Gwillim) is a *Mermaid*—it is my *Crest* too—and with precisely the same curl of tail.—There's concatenation for you! I am building a little cutter at Genoa to go a cruising in the summer—I know *you* like the sea too.

124. Byron on Scott

To Henri Beyle (Stendhal)   *Genoa 29 May 1823*

. . . Of your works I have seen only 'Rome', etc., the Lives of Haydn and Mozart, and the *brochure* on Racine and Shakespeare. The 'Histoire de la Peinture' I have not yet the good fortune to possess.

There is one part of your observations in the pamphlet which I shall venture to remark upon;—it regards Walter Scott. You say that 'his character is little worthy of enthusiasm,' at the same time that you mention his productions in the manner they deserve. I have known Walter Scott long and well, and in occasional situations which call forth the *real* character—and I can assure you that his character *is* worthy of admiration—that of all men he is the most *open,* the most *honourable*, the most *amiable*. With his politics I have nothing to do: they differ from mine, which renders it difficult for me to speak of them. But he is *perfectly sincere* in them; and Sincerity may be humble, but she cannot be servile. I pray you, therefore, to correct or soften that passage. You may, perhaps, attribute this officiousness of mine to a false affectation of *candour*, as I happen to be a writer also. Attribute it to what motive you please, but *believe* the *truth*. I say that Walter Scott is as nearly a thorough good man as man can be, because I *know* it by experience to be the case. . .

your ever obliged and obedt. humble Servt.

NOEL BYRON

★ ★ ★

Thomas Carlyle (1795–1881)
Jane Welsh Carlyle (1801–66)

Contemporaries had no doubt of Thomas Carlyle's genius as a prophet and sage who faced up to the moral problems of the new industrial age. His departure to London in 1834 is something of a symbolic date because it marks the end of the great period of Edinburgh's intellectual leadership. If it is now difficult for us to come to terms with much of his writing, His Reminiscences *and his voluminous letters are highly accessible and illuminating of his thought and times.*

Thomas Carlyle married Jane Welsh in 1826. She wrote nothing for publication but her letters reveal a lively literary talent.

125. The 'nonsensical' suitor

Jane to Eliza Stodart   *Haddington 8 March 1823*

Well! my beloved Cousin, here I am once more at the bottom of the pit of dullness, hemmed in all round, straining my eyeballs, and stretching my neck to no purpose. Was ever Starling in a more desperate plight? but I *will 'get out'*—by the wife of Job I *will*. Here is no sojourn for me! I must dwell in the open world, live amid life; but *here* is no life, no motion, no variety. It is the dimest, deadest spot (I verily believe) in the Creators universe: to look round in it, one might imagine that time had made a stand: the shopkeepers are to be seen standing at the doors of their shops, in the very same postures in which they have stood there ever since I was born; '*the thing that hath been is that also which shall be*'; everything is *the same*, every thing is stupid; the very air one breathes is impregnated with stupidity. Alas my native place! the Goddess of dullness has strewed it with all her poppies!

But it is my native place still! and after all there is much in it that I love. I love the bleaching-green, where I used to caper, and roll, and tumble, and make gowan necklaces, and chains of dandelion stalks, in the days of my '*wee existence*'; and the schoolhouse where I carried away prizes, and signalized myself not more for the quickness of my parts, than for the valour of my arm, above all the boys of the community; and the mill-dam too where I performed feats of agility which it was easier to extol than to imitate, and which gained me at the time the reputation of a sticket callant (un garçon assasiné) which I believe I have maintained with credit up to the

143

present hour; and above all I feel an affection for a field by the side of the river, where corn is growing now, and where a hayrick once stood—you remember it? For my part I shall never forget that summer's day; but cherish it *'within the secret cell of the heart'* as long as I live—the sky was so bright, the air so balmy, the whole universe so beautiful! I was happy then! all my little world lay glittering in tinsel at my feet! but years have passed over it since; and storm after storm has stript it of much of its finery—Allons ma chere!—let us talk of the *'goosish'* man, my quondam lover.

He came; arrived at the George Inn, at eleven o'clock at night, twelve hours after he received my answer to his letter; slept there *'more soundly'*, according to his own statement, *'than was to have been expected, all the circumstances of the case considered'*; and in the morning sent a few nonsensical lines to announce his nonsensical arrival. Mother and I received him more politely 'than was to have been expected, all the circumstances of the case considered'; and we proceeded to walk, and play at battledoor; and talk inanities, about new novels, and new belles, and what had gone on at a splendid party, the night before, where he had been (he told us) for half an hour *with his arm under his hat*; and there he corrected himself, and said, *with his head under his arm*! it was of very little consequence where his head was; it is not much worth; but the Lord defend me from visitors so equiped, when I come to give parties! Before dinner he retired to his Inn, and vapoured back, in the course of an hour of so, in all the pride of two waistcoats (one of figured velvet, another of sky-blue satin) gossamer silk stockings and morocco leather slippers—*'these little things are great to little men'*—I should not like to pay his Tailor's bill however—Craigenputtock could not stand it. Next morning he took himself away, leaving us more impressed with the idea of his imbecillity than ever. In a day or two after his return to town, there came a huge parcel from him, containing a letter for Mother, expressed with a still greater command of absurdity than any of the preceeding ones, and a quantity of music for me; (*pour parenthèse*, I shall send you a sheet of it, having another copy of *'Home sweet home'* beside) and in two days more another letter, and another supply of music. Hitherto there had been nothing of *hope*, nothing more of love or marriage; but now my Gentleman presumed to flatter himself, in the expansion of the folly of his heart, that I *might possibly change my mind*. Ass! I change my mind indeed! and for him! Upon my word, to be an imbécille as he is, he has a monstrous stock of modest assurance! However I very speedily relieved him of any doubts which he might have upon the matter. I told him *'ce que j'ai fait je le ferais encore'* in so many words as must (I think) have brought him to his senses—if he has any. He has since written to

Mother begging of her to deprecate my displeasure—there the transaction rests and peace be with it!

I have neither heard nor seen anything of '*Doctor Fieff*'—The Lord be praised! He not only wasted a very unreasonable proportion of my time; but his *fuffs* and explosions were very hurtful to my nervous system.

Talking of nerves, we got a horrible fright in church on Saturday. An old Lady dropt down in the adjoining seat and was carried out as dead. Mother screamed out 'Oh' so stoutly, that Mr Gordon was obliged to stop in his prayer, and sit down: She seems destined to make a distinguished figure in all church hub bubs. Witness the scene of the repenting stool! The old Lady has got better—

What of *Wull*? is he coming out soon? a visit from any man with brains in his head would really be an act of mercy to us here.

There is a long letter for you! now will you write to me soon? I cannot recollect your excuse without some feeling of displeasure. '*You cannot write letters that I will care about*' surely this compliment to my understanding (if it was meant as such) is at the expense of my heart. It is not for the sake of grammar or rhetorick (I should think) that friends, like you and I, write to one another. When your letters cease to interest me, credit me, I will not ask them My Mother has quite got rid of her cold. It was as bad as need be after we came home. For myself I am quite well, still suffering a little from the *maladie des adieux*; but that is all. Both of us unite in kindest love to your Uncle and yourself. *Will* you kiss him for me?

Ever most affectionately yours

Jane Baillie Welsh

126. 'Alas poor Byron!'

Thomas to Jane   *Mainhill 19 May 1824*

... Poor Byron! Alas poor Byron! The news of his death came down upon my heart like a mass of lead; and yet, the thought of it sends a painful twinge thro' all my being, as if I had lost a Brother! O God! That so many sons of mud and clay should fill up their base existence to its utmost bound, and this, the noblest spirit in Europe, should sink before half his course was run! Late so full of fire and generous passion, and proud purposes, and now forever dumb and cold! Poor Byron! And but a young man; still struggling among the perplexities, and sorrows and aberrations of a mind not arrived at maturity or settled in its proper place in life. Had he been spared to the age of three score and ten, what might he not have done, what might he not have been! But we shall hear his voice no more: I dreamed of seeing him and knowing him; but the curtain of everlasting night has hid him from our eyes. We shall go to him, he shall not return to us.—Adieu, my dear Jane! There is a blank in your heart and a blank in mine, since this man passed away. Let us stand the closer by each other!

I am yours forever,

TH. CARLYLE

127. 'Why don't you write?'

Jane to Thomas   *Haddington 20 May 1824*

In the name of Heaven why don't you write to me? I have waited day after day in the utmost impatience; and hope deferred has not only made my heart sick, but is like to drive me out of my judgement.

For Godsake write the instant this reaches you, if you have not done it before. I shall learn no lesson, settle no occupation, till I have your Letter. Wretch! You cannot conceive what anxiety I am in about you. One moment I imagine you ill or in trouble of some sort; the next tired of me; the next something else as bad. In short there is no end to my imaginings.

I do not think that in the whole course of our correspondence so long an interval has ever elapsed before: never but when we quarrelled—and this time there is no quarrel! To add to my perplexities, there have I had a Letter from that stupendous Ass the Orator, telling me such nonsensical things; and among the rest, that he is full of joy because Thomas Carlyle is to be with him this month! Can he mean you? This month! and twenty days of it already past and gone! The man must have been delirious when he wrote such an impossible story. You can never, never mean to be in London this month! You promised to be here before you went, in words that it would be impiety to doubt. I have looked forward to your coming for weeks. You cannot dream of disappointing me!

What I would give to be assured this moment that excessive occupation is the sole cause of your present neglectfulness: that 'devils' are dunning you for the rest of your book, and that you are merely giving yourself all to *Meister* just now that you may the sooner be all for me. Is it not hard? This is the only comfortable conjecture I can form to explain your silence; and yet I can never believe in it for more than a minute at a time. Were I but certain that all is really well, what a Devil of a rage I would be in with you! Write, write.—I will tell you about my *visit to London*, then; I have no heart for it now. What an idiot I was ever to think that man so estimable! But I am done with his Preachership now and forever.

And Byron is dead! I was told it all at once in a roomful of people. My God, if they had said that the sun or the moon had gone out of the heavens, it could not have struck me with the idea of a more awful and dreary blank in the creation than the words, 'Byron is dead!' I have felt quite cold and dejected ever since: all my thoughts have been fearful and dismal. I wish you was come.

Yours forever affectionately,

JANE WELSH

128. Thomas proposes

Thomas to Jane   *Hoddam Hill 26 February 1826*

. . .O Jane, Jane! your half-jesting enumeration of your wooers does any thing but make me laugh. A thousand and a thousand times have I thought the same thing in deepest earnest. That you have the power of making many good matches is no secret to me; nay it would be a piece of news for me to learn that I am not the very *worst* you ever thought of. And you add with the same tearful smile: 'Alas! we are married already.' Let me now cut off the interjection, and say simply what is true that we are *not* married already; and do you hereb[y] receive farther my distinct and deliberate declaration that it depends on yourself, and shall [al]ways depend on yourself whether ever we be married or not. God knows I do not say this in a vulgar spirit of defiance; which in our present relation were coarse and cruel; but I say it in the spirit of disinterested affection for you, and of fear for the reproaches of my own conscience should your fair destiny be marred by me, and you wounded in the house of your friends. Can you believe it with the good nature which I declare it deserves? It would absolutely give me satisfaction to know that you thought yourself entirely free of all ties to me, but those, such as they might be, of your own still-renewed election. It is reasonable and right that you should be concerned for your future establishment: Look round with calm eyes on the persons you mention or may hereafter so mention; and if there is any one among them whose wife you had rather be—I do not mean whom you love better than me—but whose wife, *all*

147

things considered, you had rather be than mine, then *I* call upon you, I your brother and husband and friend thro' every fortune, to accept that man and leave me to my destiny. But if on the contrary my heart and my hand with the barren and perplexed destiny which promises to attend them shall after all appear the *best* that this poor world can offer you, then take me and be content with me, and do not vex yourself with struggling to alter what is unalterable; to make a man who is poor and sick suddenly become rich and healthy. You tell me that you often weep when you think what is to become of us. It is unwise in you to weep: if you are reconciled to be *my* wife (not the wife of an ideal *me*, but the simple actual prosaic *me*), there is nothing frightful in the future. I look into it now with more and more confidence and composure. Alas! Jane you do not know me: it is not the poor, unknown, rejected Thomas Carlyle that you know, but the prospective rich known and admired. I am reconciled to my fate as it stands or promises to stand ere long: I have pronounced the word *unpraised* in all its cases and numbers; and find nothing terrific in it, even when it means *unmonied*, and by the mass of his Majesty's subjects · *neglected* or even partially *contemned*. I thank Heaven I have other objects in my eye than either *their* pudding or their breath. This comes of the circumstance that my Apprenticeship is ending, and yours still going on. O Jane! Jane! I could weep too; for I love you in my deepest heart. . .

T. CARLYLE

129. Jane accepts

Jane to Thomas   *Haddington 4 March 1826*

. . . But surely, surely Mr Carlyle, you must know me better, than to have supposed it possible I should ever make a new choice! To say nothing of the sentiments I entertain towards *you*, which would make a marriage with another worse than death; is there no spark of honour, think you, in this heart, that I should not blush at the bare idea of such shame? Give myself to another, after having given myself with such unreservedness to you! Take another to my arms, with your image on my heart, your kisses on my lips! Oh be honest, and say you knew this would never be,—knew I could never sink so low! Let me not have room to suppose, that possessing your love, I am unfortunate enough to be without your respect! For how light must my open fondness have seemed; if you doubted of its being sanctified by a marriage-vow—a vow spoken, indeed, before no Minister, but before a presence, surely as awful, God and my Conscience—And yet, it is so unlike *you*, the sworn enemy of cant, to make high-sounding offers, in the firm confidence of their being rejected! and unless I lay this to your charge in the present instance how can I help concluding that there is some virtue in me, which you have yet to learn?—for it is in no jesting, or yet 'half-jesting' manner that you tell me my hand is free—'If there be any other—*you do not mean whom I love more*—but whose wife all things considered I would rather be; you call upon me as my Husband—(as my Husband!) to accept that man.' Were these words really Thomas Carlyle's, and addressed to *me*? Ah! ich kenne dich nicht mehr!* Dearest! Dearest! it will take many caresses to atone for these words! . . .

You say you are 'the very worst *match* I ever thought of'; that 'it is reasonable and right I should be concerned for my future *establishment*' and that I do not know you as 'the poor, unknown, rejected Thomas Carlyle; but as 'the prospe[c]tive rich, known, and admired'—Alas! my brother, you were wont to call me 'generous,' 'devoted,' 'noble-minded': how comes it you address me now as a vulgar creature whose first object is *'a good settlement'*? Such sayings from another would have found with me no gentle hearing; and probably called forth an indignant exposition of my mind: but when the man I have loved with a love so pure from all worldliness,—for whom I am ready to sacrifice every thing on earth but my sense of right,—when *he* talks to me of matches, and establishments, and riches and honours, it is the thrust of a Brother which it would be ignominy to resist. . .

One thing more; and I am done. Look cross at me, reproach me, even whip me if you have the heart; your next kiss will make amends for all: but if you love me, cease I beseech you to make me offers of freedom; for this is an outrage which I find it not easy to forgive. If made with any idea that it is in the nature of things I should take you at your word; they do a wrong to my love, my truth, my modesty, that is, to my whole character as a Woman; if not, they are a mocking better spared; since you know my answer must be still: 'permit me O Shinvarig, to wear out my days in prison, for its walls are to me more pleasing than the most splendid palace!'—but ohe jam satis!** Farewell my Beloved! I am still yours
JANE BAILLIE WELSH

It may not be amiss to mention that I am recovering strength—Write without loss of time if you can write as my own

***

* Goethe, *Faust* l.2720: 'I know you no more.'

** One of Martial's epigrams ends with a poem containing these words: 'Ohe jam satis est! Ohe, Libelle' (Hold, it is enough now! Hold, little book!).

kind Husband; but if not delay a day or two till I have got my nerves a little braced in the open air. I have by no means told you 'all I know' but my paper is already overfull.

130. Messages from Edinburgh

Jane to Eliza Stodart   *Craigenputtoch 28 July 1828*

'My dear dear Angel Bessy'!!!

What a world of trouble is in these words announced to you! In fact my tea is done, and my coffee is done, and my sugar white and brown; and without a fresh supply of these articles my Husband would soon be done also: it might be got at Dumfries—but bad; and so I have bethought myself of your kind offer to do my commissions as of old, and find it come more natural for me to employ *you* in this way than another.

To proceed then, at once, to business; that so I may afterwards proceed with freedom to more grateful topics; will you order for me at Polland's in North Hanover Street (nearly opposite Miss Grey's) two stones of brown sugar at 8d and one stone—*very* brown at 6d½; as also a small loaf of white at 12d—with five pounds of ground rice. Then Angel Bess you must not go home by the Mound but rather along the Bridges that you may step into the new tea establishment in Waterloo place and get me four pounds of tea at five and fourpence per pound—two pounds at seven shillings—and two pounds of ground coffee at two shillings—this the Cockneys must be instructed to wrap up in strong paper and carry to Pollands addressed to Mrs Carlyle Craigen &c &c. And you will have the goodness to tell Polland before hand, that such a parcel will be sent to him to forward along with his sugar—and that he must pack the whole nicely up in a box and send it to the first Dumfries carrier addressed to me to the care of Mr Aitken Academy Street Dumfries. Now one thing more thou Archangel Bessy you will pay these things (somewhere about 4 pounds as I calculate) in the trembling hope of being repaid by the earliest opportunity. And unless it goes hard with me I will take good care that you are not disappointed. The truth is I have no five pound note to send you and four small ones would make rather a bulky letter. And here you may draw your breath as I do mine; for I have nothing farther to trouble you with except on recollection half a pound of Dickson's mustard; not even a long-winded Apology for the trouble already given.

By this writing you will know that I have survived my

astonishing change—and the talk about tea &c will show you that I even look hopefully into life. Indeed Craigenputtoch is no such frightful place as the people call it: till lately indeed our existence here has been made black with smoke; and confusion unspeakable was nearly turning our heads. But we are beginning to get a settlement made at last; and see a distinct prospect of being more than tolerably comfortable. The solitude is not so irksome as one might think. if we are cut off from good society, we are also delivered from bad; the roads are less pleasant to walk on than the pavement of Princes Street but we have horses to ride; and instead of shopping and making calls I have bread to bake and chickens to hatch. I read, and work & talk with my Husband and never weary.

I ride over to Templand occasionally; and my Mother and Agnes Ferguson were here last week. They seemed content with the aspect of things—but my Mother is so confined at home now! She cannot be absent one night, and *that* home, I fear is no peaceful place for *her*. I am sadly vexed about her she is looking so ill and so unhappy.

You will write and tell me how all is going on at 22 and in Edinburgh generally. dear Edinburgh I was very happy there; and shall always love it; and hope to see it again often and often before I die—Will you give my kind regards to Mr Simpson when you see him and tell him I was wellpleased to hear of his success. Remember us also to Mr Aitken and most affectionately to your Uncle.

Do you know of any good Habit maker in Edinburgh (not very expensive)? I have got fine cloth for a habit and am almost afraid to risk the making of it in Dumfries. Perhaps you could make inquiry for me and let me know the charge, and whether a habit could be made from a pattern gown or pelisse.

Grace Macdonald is turning out a most excellent servant and seems the carefullest *honestest* creature living. She broke her arm soon after we came hither but it is now almost quite strong again. I never miss a drop of *'broth'*. And my linens are all entire.

My best wishes for Maggy and her new child and *'I hope Mr Dudgeon is quite well.'* Letters from Germany and all parts of the earth reach us here just as before. It is so strange to see Craigenputtoch written in Goethe's hand—But my paper is done. Every Truly your friend.

J W Carlyle

Thomas to John Bradfute   *5 Great Cheyne Row, Chelsea, London*
29 July 1834

My Dear Sir,

It is surely the duty of some of us to give special notice at George's Square that Craigenputtoch is desolate, and London sending up the smoke of a new hearth: no doubt, you know it already, but one so well-disposed towards us should know it from ourselves. Nevertheless, my wife, I perceive, is too lazy; so I take the duty in my own hand.

If you remember Battersea Bridge, and Don Saltero's Coffee-house (celebrated in the *Tatler*) with the ancient row of red-brick mansions, clad with ivy and jasmine, shaded by high old lime-trees, along the bank of the River, you have Cheyne *Walk*, and are within a cat's-leap of Cheyne *Row* (at right-angles to the *Walk*, and otherwise a miniature copy of it), wherein my new workshop, still and clear almost as the Craigenputtoch one, I now write to you. We like our old House extremely; have got it all set in order, out even to the little Garden and the vine and walnut-tree; have a Servant of the best quality, and shall begin by and by to feel once more at home. We have both fair health too; Jane especially is much better than before: the change, so needful under every point of view, is happily *effected*, turn out how it may.

As for Literature and Book-publishing, the more I look at it hitherto, the more confused it looks. Alas, of quite bottomless confusion! Meanwhile, it would seem, Book-sellers can actually print Books now, the Author writing them gratis; which is a great improvement compared with former experiences of mine. Not seeking to decipher farther, what is indeed undecipherable, chaotic, fearful hateful as a madman's Dream, I stand by this so comfortable fact; and am actually busy: at all awful hours, getting ready a new Book; of which (if I be spared alive some months) I hope to show you a copy, and ask your favourable judgement. It is about the French Revolution (but this is a *secret*), and requires immense preparation.—What is to follow after that will follow.

There is nothing passing here but changes of Ministry and other such daily occurences; of which the less one speaks it is perhaps the more charitable. Poor Coleridge, as you may have seen, died on Friday last: he had been sick and decaying for years; was well waited on, and one may hope prepared to die. Carriages in long files, as I hear, were rushing all round Highgate where the old man lay near to die. Foolish Carriages! Not one of them would roll near him (except to splash him with their mud) while he lived; had it not been for the noble-mindedness of Gilman the Highgate Apothecary, he might have died twenty years ago in a hospital or in a ditch. To complete the Farce-Tragedy they have only to bury him in Westminster-Abbey.

There is now no other Author here of a better than perfectly commonplace character; too many, one grieves to say, are of a worse, of a dishonest and even palpably blackguard character. 'My soul come not into *their* secrets, mine honour be not united to *them*!' We have also seen several 'celebrated women' of the literary sort; but felt small longing to see more of them. The world indeed is wide enough for all, and each can and shall wish heartily well to all, and faithfully act accordingly: meanwhile if poor Mrs Featherbrain Irrational All-for-glory and Company are walking in the western quarter, we shall do it all the better by keeping ourselves in the eastern.—But, in fine, there is a fraction of Worth and Wisdom here in London such as I have found nowhere else: let us use this, enjoy it, and be right thankful for it.

I get hardly any news from Edinburgh, well as I love and shall always love that old stone Town. It is hard, but clear and strong, in spirit as in outward form; built on rocks, looking out upon the everlasting sea . . .

(remainder badly damaged)

132. The lost manuscript

Thomas to John Carlyle   *5 Great Cheyne Row, Chelsea, London 23 July 1835*

. . . Mill had borrowed that first volume of my poor *French Revolution* (pieces of it more than *once*) that he might have it all before him, and write down some observations on it, which perhaps I might print as Notes. I was busy meanwhile with Volume Second; toiling along like a *Nigger*, but with the heart of a free Roman: indeed I know not how it was, I had not felt so clear and independent, sure of myself and of my task for many long years. Well, one night about three weeks ago, we sat at tea, and Mill's short rap was heard at the door. Jane rose to welcome him; but he stood there unresponsive, pale, the very picture of despair; said, half articulately gasping, that she must go down and speak to 'Mrs Taylor' (his platonic inamorata); with whom Jane fancied he must have at length *run off*, and so was come before setting out for the Devil, to take solemn leave of us. Happily, no;—and yet unhappily!

After some considerable additional gasping, I learned from Mill this fact: that my poor Manuscript, all except some four tattered leaves, was *annihilated!* He had left it out (too carelessly); it had been taken for wastepaper: and so five months of as tough labour as I could remember of, were as good as vanished, gone like a whiff of smoke.—There never in my life had come upon me any other *accident* of much moment; but this I could not but feel to be a sore one. The thing was *lost,* and perhaps worse; for I had not only forgotten all the structure of it, but the spirit it was written with was past; only the general impression seemed to remain, and the recollection that I was on the whole well satisfied with that, and could now hardly hope to equal it. Mill whom I had to comfort and speak peace to remained injudiciously enough till almost midnight, and my poor Dame and I had to sit talking of indifferent matters; and could not till then get our lament freely uttered. *She* was very good to me; and the thing did not beat us. I felt in general that I was as a little Schoolboy, who had laboriously written out his *Copy* as he could, and was shewing it not without satisfaction to the Master: but lo! the Master had suddenly torn it, saying: 'No, boy, thou' must go and write it *better*.' What could I do but sorrowing go and try to obey. That night was a hard one; something from time to time tying me tight as it were all round the region of the heart, and strange dreams haunting me: however, I was not without good thoughts too that came like healing life into me; and I got it somewhat reasonably crushed down, not abolished, yet subjected to me with the resolution and prophecy of abolishing. Next morning accordingly I wrote to Fraser (who had *advertised* the Book as 'preparing for publication') that it was all gone back; that he must not *speak of it* to any one (till it was made good again); finally that he must send me some *better paper,* and also a *Biographie Universelle,* for I was determined to risk ten pounds more upon it. Poor Fraser was very assiduous: I got Bookshelves put up (for the whole House was *flowing* with Books), where the *Biographie* (not Fraser's, however, who was countermanded, but Mill's), with much else stands all ready, much readier than before: and so, having first finished out the Piece I was actually upon, I began *again* at the beginning. Early the day after tomorrow (after a hard and quite novel kind of battle) I count on having the First Chapter on paper a second time, no worse than it was, tho' considerably different. The bitterness of the business is past therefore; and you must conceive me toiling along in that new way for many weeks to come. . .

☆ ☆ ☆

Hugh Miller (1802-56)

Hugh Miller, a sailor's son, was born in Cromarty. A stone-mason by trade his speculative mind turned naturally to geology, the main product of which were two books, The Old Red Sandstone *(1841) and* The Testimony of the Rocks *(1857). The latter reveals his strong religious interest, which led him to become Editor of the* Witness, *a newspaper which was the organ of the Free Church. The intensity of his scientific and religious interests, at a time of dispute as to the origins of man, may have been a factor in Miller's suicide in 1856. His descriptive prose shows nothing of these tensions but offers fluent, affectionate observations on nature and man, as may be seen in his letter to a friend. It is a long letter. The extract begins as the party approaches Loch Maree.*

133. Journey to Loch Maree

To a Friend

. . . We then began to descend into the deep narrow glen or ravine, through which there runs a little brattling streamlet, the first we saw falling towards the Atlantic. The hills rise to a great height on either hand, bare, rocky, stripped into long furrows, mottled over with *debris* and huge fragments of stone, and nearly destitute of even heather. The day had become clear and pleasant, but the voice of a bird was not to be heard in this dismal place, nor sheep nor goat to be seen among the cliffs. I wish my favourite John Bunyan had passed a night in it at the season when the heath-fires of the shepherds are flaming on the heights above,—were it but to enable him to impart more tangibility to the hills which border the dark valley of the shadow of death. Through the gloomy vista of the ravine a little paradise seemed opening before us,—a paradise like that which Mirza contemplated from the heights of Bagdad, of smooth water and green islands. 'There,' said my comrade, 'is Loch Marie;—we have to sail over it for about fourteen miles, as there is no path on which we could bring the cart with the baggage; but the horse and his master must push onward on foot.' Emerging from the ravine our road ran through a little moory plain, bordered with hills which seemed to have at one time formed the shores of the lake. A few patches of corn and potatoes, that, surrounded by the brown heath, reminded me of openings in the dark sky, together with half a dozen miserable-looking cottages, a little larger than ant-hills, though not quite so regularly formed, showed us that this part of the country had its inhabitants.

We found out and bargained with the boatman, left the carter and his horse to make the best of their way by land, and were soon sweeping over the surface of the lake. . .

At the lower end of the lake we encountered a large boat full of people. A piper stood in the bows, and the wild notes of his bagpipe, softened by distance and multiplied by the echoes of the mountains, formed a music that suited well with the character of the scene. 'It is a wedding party,' said my comrade; 'they are going to that white house which you see at the foot of the hill. I wish you understood Gaelic:—the boatmen are telling me strange stories of the loch that I know would delight you. Do you see that little green island, that lies off about half a mile to the right? The boldest Highlander in the country would hesitate to land there an hour after sunset. It is said to be haunted by wraiths and fairies, and every variety of land and water spirit. Directly in the middle of it there is a little lake, in the lake an island, and on the island a tree beneath which the Queen of the Fairies holds her court. What would you not give to see her?' Night came on before we got landed; and we lost sight of the lake while yet sailing over it. Is it not strange that with all its beauty it should be so little known?. . .

Marjorie Fleming (1803-11)

Marjorie Fleming was given posthumous fame by Dr John Brown (see Letter 137) who published an essay about her in which he quotes her sayings, poems and letters. These portray an engaging child, precocious and yet innocent. She describes her religious persuasion, 'I am a Prisbeteran at Kirkaldy. . . my native town'. She wrote sonnets, one to a monkey, which begins:

> 'O lively, O most charming pug
> Thy graceful air, and heavenly mug;'

Thanks to Marjorie's sister Isabella the letters and journals of Pet Marjorie were preserved. The first letter she wrote, before she was six, was to Isabella.

134. The first letter

To Isabella Fleming   *Kirkaldy 1808*

My Dear Isa,—I now sit down to answer all your kind and beloved letters which you were so good as to write to me. This is the first time I ever wrote a letter in my Life. There are a great many Girls in the Square and they cry just like a pig when we are under the painful necessity of putting it to Death. Miss Potune a Lady of my acquaintance praises me dreadfully. I repeated something out of Dean Swift, and she said I was fit for the stage, and you may think I was primmed up with majestick Pride, but upon my word I felt myselfe turn a little birsay—birsay is a word which is a word that William composed which is as you may suppose a little enraged. This horrid fat simpliton says that my Aunt is beautifull which is intirely impossible for that is not her nature.

135. 'The longings of a child'

To Mrs Fleming   *Kirkcaldy September 1811*

My Dear Little Mama,—I was truly happy to hear that you were all well. We are surrounded with measles at present on every side, for the Herons got it, and Isabella Heron was near Death's Door, and one night her father lifted her out of bed, and she fell down as they thought lifeless. Mr. Heron said, 'That lassie's deed noo'—'I'm no deed yet.' She then threw up a big worm nine inches and a half long. I have begun dancing, but am not very fond of it, for the boys strikes and mocks me.—I have been another night at the dancing; I like it better. I will write to you as often as I can; but I am afraid not every week. *I long for you with the longings of a child to embrace you—to fold you in my arms. I respect you with all the respect due to a mother. You don't know how I love you. So I shall remain, your loving child*

M. FLEMING

John Stuart Blackie (1809-1895)

Professor of Greek at Edinburgh, a well known figure in the life of the town and a regular contributor to Blackwood's Magazine, *Blackie was also a tireless campaigner for Scottish causes, including Gaelic and its literature. He helped to achieve the foundation of the Chair of Celtic at Edinburgh.*

To Mr. Blackie   *9 Douglas Cresent, Edinburgh*
                                                        15 February 1895

My Dear Sir,—Accept my best thanks for your last instalment of
the History of the Scottish People. I am a strong advocate for the
Union of the three Kingdoms of the Empire, but this Union should
be a genuine Union of the three people; each with its own head—a
Scottish Parliament to meet in Edinburgh, an Irish Parliament in
Dublin, an English Parliament in London and a British Parliament
there as well. This would be a *bonâ fide* Union, a brotherly Union,
not a swallowing up of the smaller by the one great member, by a
monstrous centralisation which is the destroyer of all variety: and
variety is the wealth of the moral as well as of the physical
world.—Ever yours,

                                                        J. S. BLACKIE

Dr John Brown (1810-82)

Dr John Brown is probably best remembered for his story Rab and his Friends.
*This Edinburgh doctor was described by one of his goddaughters as 'a warm
man', and it was his ready appreciation of the good in people and in dogs that
drew him to set down his impressions of contemporary Victorians without
respect for their station in life. He had a tendency to be sentimental about
children, but he had the ability to draw vivid impressions from exact
observation. There is a reality in his descriptions, as may be felt in the letter he
wrote to Sir George Reid, President of the Royal Scottish Academy, about his
etching of the Banffshire naturalist, Thomas Edward (q.v.).*

137. Two portraits — Thomas Edward and The Macnab

To Sir George Reid   *23 Rutland Street, Edinburgh*
                                                        November 1876

My Dear George Reid—It is good, *very*, in you to give me this quite
glorious etching. I have seen nothing so to the quick for long. What
a nose! buttressed like Ben Cruachan, and what nostrils! What an
apparatus for smell! what frontal sinuses! what power of

observation! and the broad high skull and the fearless unkempt hair, the wonderful look of a lifetime of loving and keen faculty, of shrewd simplicity and worth. It will astonish Murray and the world, and if Smiles does his work half as well, you will all be immortal. It is from your portrait, of course, and if so, why is your name not at it? Nothing now interests me but sleep and forgetfulness, but I confess to a longing to see this book. I was sorry I missed your call. You *must* see the Raeburns,—quite wonderful for honest, living, delightful work, manly and womanly, all of them, and all in their best moods. 'The Macnab' simply the perfection of the *Hee*land chieftain and ruffian, and snuffer, and ebriosus. But there is a want; I don't know what to call it, but it is what Sir Joshua and Gainsborough have—an ethereal something. I suppose we should call it the ideal. He, Sir Henry, gives the idea, the thing seen, of the man; he hardly reaches to the ideal—the unseen and imagined, and yet true. . . But you will judge for yourself. . . .

Charles Reeves (fl. 1824)

Charles Reeves, a surveyor, was responsible for assessing where postal carriers were required and the appropriate method of transport. The postal servicing of the Western Highlands was difficult on account of the terrain and the weather. In certain cases Reeves advocated a Ride, in others the service should 'be provided by footrunners', which he recommended to the Secretary of the Post Office in Scotland for 'the whole of Glencoe & the mountain of "Rest and be Thankful"', probably the most difficult and laborious stage in the Kingdom'.

138. The good postman

To Augustus Godby Esq.
Secretary of the Post Office in Scotland   *Edinburgh 1 May 1824*

Sir,
Connected with my report of this date on the subject of the West Highland posts I beg to state that the Postmaster of Arrochar has signified his intention of resigning.

As this office only produces £50-0-8 gross Revenue, and the amount of the Edinburgh Correspondence is only £7.8.10, I propose to make it a Sub Office on Luss, and reduce the Salary from £10 to £5 per Ann., thus diminishing the business along this line, precluding the necessity of a stop, and affording equal Accommodation to the Country.

As a saving of £5 per Ann. will thus be effected, I am induced to bring forward a case for the humane consideration of the Postmaster General, which has been sometime lying by, and repeatedly pressed by Mr Downie M.P. for Appin, and the other Residents of that part of the Highlands.

The Runner between Bonaw and Appin, a distance of 12 miles, has to cross two ferries, frequently dangerous, and to walk the rest of the distance through Glansalloch (or the dirty glen) the wildest path in the Highlands — so much so, that although the other road is 6 miles round and liable to great delay from the breadth of the ferries (which are crossed by the Runner at the narrowest part) I scarcely met with any Highland gentlemen who had ever been through it, the path being along a stream swelling over it on a fall of rain, which is here abundant.

(I can attest the difficulty of this path from personal inspection, having traversed it during a slight storm).

The Runner performs this stage *during the night;* and the difficulties he has to encounter during winter must be very great.

His pay is 9s. a week only, the same as is paid for a similar stage along the high road.

The present individual, his father *and Mother,* have performed this Journey with the Mails for above 25 years with zeal and astonishing regularity, and if the Postmaster General should be pleased to devote the sum of £5 to be reduced from the Salary of the Office at Arrochar to encrease the pay of the stage, I think it would be received as a mark of recognition of long and faithful performance of a most laborious duty, and have a good effect in the Service in general.

I am, Sir,
  Your obedient Servant,

CHAS. F. REEVES

Robert Dick (1811-66)

Robert Dick, a journeyman baker, found work in Leith, Glasgow and Greenock, none of which environments suited his interests in nature. He travelled to Caithness, where his father was supervisor of Excise, and set up a small bakery in Thurso, where he stayed until his death 36 years later. His first serious study was entomology. His enthusiasm for the subject and for any discovery, botanical or geological, was conveyed in letters, many addressed to Hugh Miller. With difficulty he was persuaded to write a paper on the discovery of Holy Grass on the bank of Thurso river.

His sister wrote from Haddington to tell him that she was low in spirits. Robert Dick replied.

139. 'Cheer up, my bonnie sister'

To his sister   *Thurso*

Cheer up, cheer up, my bonnie sister, and I will tell you a story. One fine summer evening, not long ago, your brother set out for the far-away hills. He had been there before. The sun's heat was strong when he set out (it was then August), but on he went, past bothies, and houses, and milestones, until he was 'o'er the muir amang the heather.' Then past burns and lochs, up a hill and over a hill, through a bog and through a mire, until the sun set, and still he was toiling on, with a long, long moor before him.

Have you ever been all alone on a dreary moor, when the shadows of the coming darkness are settling down, and the cold clammy fog goes creeping up the hill before you? It is hard work and very uncanny walking to pick your steps, as there is no proper light to guide you. For you must remember that moors are not bowling-greens or finely-smoothed lawns. They may be flowery paths, it is true, but very rough ones, full of man-traps, jags, and holes, into which, if you once get, you may with difficulty wade your way out again.

But on I went,—hop, step, and, jump,—now up, now down, huffing and puffing, with my heart rapping against my breast like the clapper of a mill. Then everything around looked so queer and so quiet, with the mist growing so thick that it was difficult to distinguish one hill from another. Had I not been intimately acquainted with every knowe and hillock of the country through which I was travelling, I never could have got through it. But, cheer up! never lose heart! There's the little loch at last, and there's the hill! Ay, but your work's not done yet. You must climb the hill, for what you seek is only upon its very top. . .

But I have no time to say out my say. Only this, sister, only this: never lose heart in the thickest mists you should ever get into; but take heart, for assuredly the sun will rise again, and roll them up and away, to be seen no more.

To Hugh Miller   *Thurso*

. . . 'But what got ye?' I hear you say. 'What got ye?' Well, I will tell you every word about it; and, believe me, unless I had the opportunity of telling it to you, I would never have gone a footstep in search of auld warld shells.

Well! on arriving at the eastern side of Dunnet cliffs, I made direct for a precipitous cliff at least 150 feet high; where, some years ago, I sat on a big boulder of sandstone, making my breakfast on cold rolls and cheese. In the present instance, I wound along the foot of these breakneck rocks, which, unless the tide had been out, I would not have been able to do,—for the tide comes close in under the cliff . . .

Then I went on to the cottage built beside the small, neat landing-place on the sea shore at Brough Haven . . . A very little to the west of this cottage there is a small burn. The burn has cut its way through the boulder clay. I went into the ravine and stood looking around me. No sight could give me so much pleasure and surprise. I found on walking along the little rill that there was a tiny cascade about eight or nine feet deep, down which the mossy water leapt dashing over a perpendicular wall of real, blue, stony, boulder clay! . . .

There are moments when a real heartfelt pleasure amply repays us poor mortals for years of sorrow. And such a moment was mine now. There I stood with evidences of Old World convulsions and changes environed round about me on every side. And yet there was a living cascade, merrily piping away the sunny hours at my feet, the crystal drops bedecking my clay-soiled boots. Columbus had never cast anchor here. No philosopher had ever entered this paradise. It was all a new world. To me for the moment it was The World. And I triumphed in the felt conviction that a humble individual like myself had, under Providence, 'done the State some service;' for the evidence that it brings to bear on geological science is not to be gainsaid.

Sir James Young Simpson (1811-70)

Simpson, the son of a baker in Bathgate, became Professor of Midwifery in the University of Edinburgh in 1840. He began to look for a substance which could be used as an anaesthetic by the simple, if alarming, method of trying the effect of various chemicals on himself and his friends. In this way, as he describes in the following letter, he discovered the properties of chloroform in November 1847. In the postscript he uses biblical arguments to answer in kind those who were already challenging the morality of anaesthetics in childbirth on the grounds that it was interference with the will of God. Simpson persisted and finally established the respectability of anaesthetics by administering chloroform to Queen Victoria at the birth of Prince Leopold in 1853.

141. Chloroform

To Mr Waldie   *Edinburgh 14 November 1847*

My Dear Sir,— I send you the first of the enclosed papers which I have myself sent off. My wife sent two yesterday—one, I think, to Dr. Petrie. I am sure you will be delighted to see part of the good results of our hasty conversation. I think I will get hold yet of some greater things in the same way.

I had the chloroform for several days in the house before trying it, as, after seeing it such a heavy unvolatile-like liquid, I despaired of it, and went on dreaming about others.

The first night we took it Dr. Duncan, Dr. Keith and I all tried it simultaneously, and were all 'under the table' in a minute or two.

I write in great haste, as I wish to scribble off several letters.

Be so good as say what you think may be the ultimate selling price of an ounce of it? Duncan and Flockhart charge 3s for the ounce.

There has been great demand for the pamphlet yesterday at the booksellers' here.—Yours very truly,

J. Y. SIMPSON

P.S.—By the bye, Imlach tells me Dr. P. is to enlighten your medical society about the 'morality' of the practice. I have a great itching to run up and pound him. *When* is the meeting?

The true moral question is, 'Is a practitioner justified by any principle of humanity in not using it?' I believe every operation without it is just a piece of the most deliberate and cold-blooded *cruelty.*

He will be at the primary curse, no doubt. But the word translated 'sorrow' is truly 'labour,' 'toil;' and in the very next verse the very same word means this.

Adam was to eat of the ground with 'sorrow.' That does not mean *physical* pain, and it was cursed to bear 'thorns and thistles,' which we pull up without dreaming that it is a sin.

God promises repeatedly to take off the two curses on women and on the ground, if the Israelites kept their covenant. See Deut. vii. 13, etc. etc. See also Isaiah xxviii. 23; extirpation of the 'thorns and thistles' of the first curse said to come from God.

Besides, Christ in dying, 'surely hath borne our griefs and carried our sorrows,' and removed 'the curse of the law, being made a curse for us.' His mission was to introduce mercy not sacrifice.

Go up and refute him if I don't come.

Simpson sent this note about fashion to his brother, Sandy, who ran the family bakery in Bathgate.

142. Brambles in the hair

To Sandy Simpson   *Erskine House (Autumn 1846)*

My Dear Sandy.—I daresay you will be wondering what has become of the *Scotsman*.

I have been down here for three weeks at Lord Blantyre's, and never thought of the papers till I found a great parcel of them yesterday huddled together. Jessie takes charge of them all at home, and directs them, and I never thought of my neglect till yesterday. I go home to-morrow, and they will all be sent right again.

I have been down dining and sleeping at Mr. Ewing's of Strathleven,—was on the top of Dumbarton, and had a beautiful view.

While here I have been repeatedly at Loch Lomond, Gare Loch, etc., hunting, etc., and feel a great deal stronger of it all. Jessie has been at St. Cyrus with the children.

Erskine House is very large and gorgeous. The hall is 118 feet long. The Duchess of Sutherland, the Marquis and Marchioness of Lorne, and two Ladies Gower have made up, with myself, all the strangers. We have also two very little lords—Lord Albert Gower, three years old; and Lord Campbell, eleven months.

Tell Janet I think *now* artificial flowers very ungenteel. The ladies here wear nothing but real flowers in their hair, and every day come down with something new, and for us males to guess at. Often the Duchess wears a simple chaplet of ivy leaves, sometimes a bracken leaf is all she sports in her head ornaments, and beautiful it looks. Rowans and 'haws' are often worn, beaded into crowns, or flowers, or chaplets. Heather, also, is a great favourite. On Thursday, Lady Lorne came down with a *most* beautiful chaplet tying round and keeping down her braided hair. It was a long bunch of bramble leaves and half ripe bramble berries—actual true *brambles*.

They have been all exceedingly kind to me, and I really feel quite at home among them, though the only *untitled* personage at table.—Yours ever affectionately,

J. Y. SIMPSON

☆ ☆ ☆

The Highland Clearances

Donald Ross (fl. 1854)

On the invitation of friends in Ross-shire Donald Ross, a Glasgow lawyer, visited the area where people had been expelled from their homes to make way for sheep. The effects of the evictions, the Clearances, deeply disturbed him. Throughout the winter of 1853 he protested the case for relief for the destitute Highlanders and assisted practically. Having heard that the author of Uncle Tom's Cabin *was the guest of the Duchess of Sutherland at Dunrobin Castle, Donald Ross wrote a letter to the* Northern Ensign, *with Mrs Harriet Beecher Stowe much in mind. Aunty Kate, aged fifty, was Catherine Mackinnon.*

143. 'Aunty Kate's cabin'

To the Editor of the Northern Ensign   *Glasgow 1854*

 . . . On 18th Feb. last I found poor 'Aunty Kate' under the bush and blankets covering her 'cabin' at Inverie . . . After reaching the spot where I was told it stood I was surprised I could not see it. I went on a little further and then I observed a little mound, like some huge molehill, with some smoke issuing from the end of it. Approaching nearer I was satisfied it was the abode of a human being, for I heard through the openings a hard coughing inside. My friend now came up and we both went to the door of the cabin, and Mr Macdonald (*Father Coll*) asked how Aunty Kate was. At first he got no answer, for the door, which consisted of empty sacks thrown double across a rope, was fast closed down, and two branches were thrown across from the outside, signifying that one of the two inmates was out. Mr Macdonald then went to the other side and having cleared away the snow with his staff, he lifted an old divot and cried—'*A'Cheat, coid an coir a tha airbh an duibh?**' Immediately the poor creature turned round in her bed and putting a little, withered hand out through the hole in the roof, she grasped her friend's hand firmly, telling him at the same time that she felt no better, but worse. I put my eyes to the little opening in the roof . . .

* 'Catherine, how are you feeling this day?'

Aunty Kate has a very miserable look, her face is pale, her eyes black, and as she peaks from underneath the blankets at me the place puts me in mind of where I kept my pet rabbits as a boy. The cabin was in two divisions, one for sleeping, the other for cooking. The sleeping division I already noticed, the other is a small place about four and one half feet long, by four feet broad. The height is two feet nine inches. A small partition of staves and pieces of cloth divides the apartments, and the entrance to the sleeping apartment is just about the size of a door in an ordinary dog kennel . . .

Having heard Mrs Stowe intended to make a comment on the Clearances in a book, Sunny Memories, *where she defended the part the Duchess of Sutherland played in the evictions, Donald Ross wrote to Mrs Stowe but failed to get a reply. He then sent a second letter care of the Duchess of Argyll.*

144. Highland hospitality and Mrs Stowe

To the Duchess of Argyll   *Glasgow 1856*

. . . You are ill-prepared to write anything worthy of being read regarding the clearances and the cruelties to which the Highland people are subjected. At Dunrobin Castle you are in a manner tied to the Duchess of Sutherland's apron strings. You are shown all the glory and grandeur of the Ducal residence. You are brought to see extensive gardens, aviaries, pleasure-groves, waterfalls and all that is beautiful and attractive, and you are occasionally treated to a drive along the coast road for some miles, through rich farms and beautiful corn-fields, and to finish all you are asked to be present at an exhibition of stockings, plaids, winceys, and tartans made up by poor females from a distant part of the country. But you have not visited Strathnaver, you have not penetrated into Kildonan, you have not been up Strathbrora, you have not seen the ruins of hundreds and hundreds of houses of the burnt-out tenants . . .

Father Coll Macdonald (fl. 1855)

Father Coll Macdonald was known to the people around, Catholic and Protestant alike, as Maighstir Colla in admiration for his selfless service. During the evictions from Knoydart, he would leave his home at Sandaig on the shores of Loch Nevis in his little boat and sail to and fro giving help. On one occasion he took seven old people back to his house and built a shelter for them in the garden. He kept Donald Ross informed of developments in his area.

145. 'A regular system of starvation'

To Donald Ross Esq   *16 January 1855*

My Dear Sir,
I received your kind letter some days ago, on returning home from the country. I was yesterday away all day at a sick call, which prevented me from writing you. You have no idea how much good your charity has done here. The Sheriff personally distributed the meal, and bought coals with part of the money. The distribution could not be committed to better hands. I have very distressing accounts from Knoydart. I wrote to Mr McKay immediately, to inform him about the meal you sent there, and telling him to get it divided without delay. I sent a paragraph to the *Glasgow Free Press,* in which I took the liberty of mentioning your impartial labours. It is the first article to which I ever ventured to annex my name. Sheriff Fraser's *Report on the Condition and Treatment of the Poor in Knoydart,* now published, does him great credit. He visited Knoydart twice, and prepared a very able and a very correct report. Nothing could be more carefully or impartially done; and, as Mr. Ellice observed, in his letter to Lord Palmerston, it proves that the poor-law in the Highlands is *'a regular system of starvation'.* Matters are not getting better with us, but worse. Last month,a law officer and assistants from this place were sent, by the proprietor of Arisaig, to turn out a family, and to break down the house of a poor Highlander. The unfortunate man has a wife and twelve children, the youngest at the breast. The children were thrust out on the moor, in a cold winter day, and the roof that covered them was smashed to atoms. This helpless family have been left on the hillside to live as they liked. The place they occupied is to be added to the proprietor's deer forest.

Thomas Maclauchlin (1816-86)

The landlords demanded of the government 'an extensive system of emigration to relieve the destitute poor of the Highlands'. The Inverness Courier *supported the view: 'This excess of population who are for the most part for a period of every year, in a state of great destitution, is variously calculated at from 45,000 to 80,000 souls'. Emigration was the solution, and the landlords painted a rosy picture of the life awaiting the emigrants. The reality was different. The Rev. Thomas Maclauchlin, a Presbyterian minister and Gaelic scholar, published an essay against the Clearances,* The Depopulation System in the Highlands *in*

1849. He also wrote a series of letters to the Witness *excoriating the landlords for their deception in their descriptions of 'the promised land' on the soil of which the emigrants would step on their arrival in North America.*

146. The promised land

To the Editor of the Witness   *No date*

We would bring them to the emigrant sheds of Quebec or Montreal, and we could tell them that during the last great emigration hundreds, we might say thousands, died in these sheds of fearful pestilence. We would bring them to Cape Breton or the district around Pictou in Nova Scotia, and we suspect we could point out an amount of destitution among old settlers not to be outdone by that of the Hebrides . . . We could bring them to the Lewis Highlanders on the Salmon River, who, after ten years of settlement, have hardly been able to pay the small sum due as the price of their lands; and lest they should suppose that this state of things merely existed among *lazy* Highlanders, we could tell them of an English settlement in the same neighbourhood of several years standing where a friend of ours was told within the last year or two, on unquestionable authority, that there were forty families who had not twenty-four hours o' food in their houses at a time, nor the means of purchasing it.

☆   ☆   ☆

David Livingstone (1813-73)

David Livingstone, doctor, missionary and explorer, arrived at the Cape in South Africa in 1840. From there he travelled north as far as the Zambesi. Initially concerned to set up mission stations but frustrated by the Boers, he increasingly became an explorer of central Africa. He discovered Lake Ngami and the Victoria Falls. Latterly his energies, frequently failing through illnesses incurred by tropical conditions, were devoted to finding the source of the Nile. His letters reveal a man of great courage and humanity, with a sense of humour.

147. 'The noble river called Zambesi'

To Mr and Mrs N. Livingstone   *Tette or Nyungue on the Zambesi, Africa*
and daughters   *18 March 1856*

My Dear Parents and Sisters,
Having recieved no letters from any one for years past, I suppose it would be a work of superrogation to apologize to anyone for not having written answers. But I may tell you that my packet of letters from Loanda, written in great weakness from dysentery and fever, went to the bottom of the sea in the Mail Packet 'Forerunner' near the Island of Madeira, and after reaching Sekeletu's I had but a short time allowed for correspondence, in consequence of the Arab who was to carry letters to Angola being about to start immediately.

I am now going down the noble river called Zambesi, and hope in a short time to reach the coast, and I thank God for preserving my life where so many have fallen, and enabling me to do something which I trust will turn out for the true and permanent welfare of Africa. When the door was shut in the South I said and wrote, 'I shall open up another part or perish.' Some of you Scotch canny bawbee-for-the-conversion-of-the-world people, and some grumbling English folks too, think I knew not what I was about. But I guess there have been but a few who resolved to sacrifice their lives & knew not for what. I thank my heavenly guide who enabled me to persevere till success crowned my efforts. I purposed to open up a way from a healthy locality to either coast. I have done that, and now have the prospect of water carriage to within 1° or 2° of the Makololo; and if we can make the passage in during the healthy time of the year, we have the prospect of planting Christ's gospel in a healthy locality, whence though our heads be low in the dust it will radiate to people far more numerous than all you Scotch together, over well-peopled territories, we hope larger than Europe. Was this a small matter? . . .

148. Conscience and Sechele

To the Rev. Charles Livingston   *near Shoshong,*
                              South Africa 6 February 1853

... We had to fight for the water we digged for at Koobe. The rhinoceros and buffaloes would have it in spite of us. We killed two of the former & one of the latter in self preservation. Yet I felt ashamed to take advantage of their necessities. It is such a sneaking cowardly looking thing to lie at the waters, as Cummings did. I felt ashamed to see the moon looking at me. Necessity alone compelled me, and it is only that necessity that will ever force me to take my place by a water again. . .

In 1852 a lion caught a brother of Sechele by the arm, he having run up to it in order to rescue a man who was under it. Afraid to fire lest he should shoot the man, he called for a spear. The lion turned round upon him. The other people rushing forward came to him just as he was caught. Some siezed the lion, others the man. Fancy, if you can, a lot of black fellows pulling one way, viz. the man, the lion holding the arm in his mouth, & others held him so that he could not move. When spears were brought they soon finished him. This is a jumbling account of it, but no white man ever shewed more bravery than some of these people do.

149. Slavery

To Dr. John Kirk   *Webb's Lualaba or Lacustrine River*
                   Across another great bend to the
                   west of about 100° 25 March 1871

. . . The episode I mention was by Muhamad Bogharib's people, and he being the best man of all who have come to trade in Manyema you may, if you can, imagine the conduct of the people of the worst. Bin Hassani, Bin Mbegu and Bin Omar, the heads of the party sent to trade gave the Manyema near to Moene Lualaba 25 copper bracelets worth at Ujiji about 2½ dollars—this was the trap—then went down the river and sold all the rest of their copper for ivory. Coming back they demanded ivory for the 25 rings and began to shoot men in cold blood, and capture women and children and grass, cloth, goats and fowls. They continued their murdering for three days in a densely peopled district and carried off an immense number of women and children because Muhamad does not intend to trade here again. With all his goodness I have no doubt that he knew the plan and will receive his full share of the captives.

They will come into Zanzibar as traders, and the people as *bought* slaves but there is not one slave among them, and to make the matter the more atrocious the very men who murdered and captured repeatedly declared to me that the people now victimised were remarkably civil and kind.

Thousands come over the river every market day to hold markets at various points for flour, cassava, beans, ground nuts, fish, salt, oil, bananas, plantains, sweet potatoes, sugar cane, grass, cloth, earthenware, iron ware as knives, spears, needles, fowls, sheep, goats, pigs, slaves, ivory etc, and it was particularly noticed that when the men of two districts were engaged in actual hostilities the women go from market to market with their wares unmolested. Women were never touched until now by these Muhamadans. As a rule not a slave is sold in Manyema except by the ruffian strangers. It would be only justice if the Sultan would set free all captives from Manyema as soon as they arrive. They were not traded for but murdered for. In talking with these Ujijians I always protest against shedding human blood. They think that rhyming over 'God is great', etc. all sin is forgiven. A slave of Thani bin Suelim of Ujiji named Yahood boasted in my hearing of having with his comrades killed one hundred people and burned 9 villages—all for a single string of red beads which a Manyema man tried in vain to steal. I said to him, 'You were sent to trade not to murder', he replied, 'We *are* sent to kill people, that is our work'.

150. Hardships and trials

To Col. Playfair and Dr Kirk   *Bambarre, Manyema country*
                                                  2 November 1870

. . . I went North with only three [attendants], my feet were torn by travelling in mire and instead of healing kindly as heretofore, an irritable eating ulcer fastened on each foot and laid me up for months—they are common here—a discharge of bloody itch with great pain each night may shew that they are allied to fever. Many slaves are killed by them. I was forced to come to a stand till men came from you and come back to Bambarre. If there had been bad blood as we say between my people and me, I should not have been surprised at their taking advantage when I could get none of the Manyema to carry, but I had a sore longing to finish my work and retire—invited them three times over to take beads and food and said, if they changed their minds, the goods were at their service. When Muhamad Bogharib, a good man, came, they told him that I refused to give them beads! Their only modern accomplishment is to lie without compunction. I am unwilling to get into hot water with Revd. Simon Price, the headmaster of Nassick School, or with the bishop who confirmed them all before leaving, but to send such Africans forth as having been taught trades and being Christians is little less than a public fraud. Mr Price could not have known but the blacksmith confessed freely that he had never welded iron, the carpenter could not cut one piece of wood straight though I chalked it out for him, the mason wanted his stones squared for him. They all believed that when away from the Consul at Zanzibar, no punishment could reach them—'their teachers feared them and never punished'. In this they had correctly judged for the masters dreaded their desertion at Nassick and bringing an ill report on the Institution . . .

Thomas Edward (1814-86)

Thomas Edward, the Banffshire naturalist, was a difficult child at school, for he had a paramount interest in 'creepie crawlies' which he brought into the classroom at Cupar, Fife. He ran away from home, and went to Banff where he settled to the poorly paid trade of shoemaker. Here his zoological interests were fulfilled, especially on the sea-shore. The Professor of Zoology of Aberdeen University visited him and was astonished by his collections. Edward introduced specimens which were unknown to specialists in natural history of his day. He wrote several letters to his biographer, Samuel Smiles, who quotes this early one in his life of Edward.

151. Poverty and the will to learn

To Samuel Smiles   *Banff*

. . . You seem to wonder why I did not mention *books* in my memoir. You may just as well wonder how I can string a few sentences together, or, indeed, how I can write at all. My books, I can tell you, were about as few, as my education was brief and homespun.

I thought you knew—yes, I am sure you knew—that any one having the Mind and the Will, need not stick fast even in this world. True, he may not shine so greatly as if he were better polished and better educated; but he need not sink in the mire altogether.

You may very likely wonder at what I have been able to do—being only a poor souter,—with no one to help me, and but few to encourage me in my labours. Many others have wondered, like yourself. The only answer I can give to such wonderers is, that I had the WILL to do the little that I have accomplished.

If what I have done by myself, unaided and alone and without the help of books, surpasses the credulity of some, what might I not have accomplished had I obtained the help from others which was so often promised me! But that time is past, and there is no use in saying anything more about it. If I suffered privations, I had only myself and my love of Nature to blame . . .

William Melrose (1817-63)

Wlliam Melrose was a member of the well-known Edinburgh family of tea merchants who were the first to import tea from China to Leith in 1835. He spent two periods in China, from 1842 to 1847 as a tea taster and buyer for another firm and then from 1848 to 1853 as buying agent for the family firm. Apart from his business correspondence, he wrote regularly to his father, Andrew Melrose, and a great volume of these letters has survived. The following is an extract from one of these. Perhaps it gives a clue to the success of the Scot abroad, his ability to feel at home anywhere.

152. Lasswade in China

To Andrew Melrose   *Macao 25 December 1848*

About an hour ago I got your letters from Hong Kong. I am glad to hear that you are all well. My poor horse dead! What a pity, it was such a quiet sensible beast. However I should be thankful your letters bring out no worse news. You see I am at Macao again. I did not think when I wrote you last month that I would be able to get down here: but I found, after buying all that I thought worth having, that there was no more to be done at least for a time. And I hate to stay in Canton when there is no business to occupy one's time, so I started for this place on the 17th and got down next day . . .

I am very fond of Macao and really am very comfortably housed and so on. The governor of it has lately made it now quite safe to walk or ride out for miles in the country and a robbery here now is never heard of. I take advantage of this privilege twice every day; I have a long walk in the morning before breakfast and then a long ride in the evening after dinner and come in to tea, just as I used to do before I left. Sometimes I can almost fancy I am at Lasswade, and if you consider that there is a pretty large garden to the house, with cocks and hens and turkeys and sheep and a horse, and that I spend my day and evening in much the same way as I did at Pendreich, it does not take so great a stretch of imagination to suppose I am there, as one would at first imagine . . .

26th 10 o'clock a.m.

Just finished breakfast and a very good one it was. The little fish here are very sweet; as a proof of it I think I must have made from six to eight of them disappear, after that some fresh laid eggs, and wound up with wheat bread and strawberry jam. After all such good things I sit down now to finish your letter in the firm conviction that there certainly are some worse places in the world than China; but you must remember I had at least an hour and a half's walk before breakfast . . .

Allan Octavian Hume (1829-1912)

A.O. Hume was the son of a radical M.P. for Montrose, Joseph Hume. He had a distinguished career in the Indian Civil service from 1849 to 1882 but encountered increasing difficulty because of his outspoken views. After his resignation he devoted himself to campaigning for a democratic voice for the Indians in the control of their own affairs. His famous letter of 1883, from which an extract follows, led to the formation of the Indian Congress Party which eventually achieved independence for India. Scots played a major role in the British government of India and it was a Scot who took the initiative which brought it to an end.

153. The freedom of India

To the Graduates of Calcutta University   *1 March 1883*

. . . Constituting, as you do, a large body of the most highly educated Indians, you should, in the natural order of things, constitute also the most important source of all mental, moral, social, and political progress in India. Whether in the individual or the nation, all vital progress must spring from within, and it is to you, her most cultured and enlightened minds, her most favoured sons, that your country must look for the initiative. In vain may aliens, like myself, love India and her children, as well as the most loving of these; in vain may they, for her and their good, give time and trouble, money and thought; in vain may they struggle and sacrifice; they may assist with advice and suggestions; they may place their experience, abilities, and knowledge at the disposal of the workers, but they lack the essential of nationality, and the real work must ever be done by the people of the country themselves . . .

As I said before, you are the salt of the land. And if amongst even you, the élite, fifty men cannot be found with sufficient power of self-sacrifice, sufficient love for and pride in their country, sufficient genuine and unselfish heartfelt patriotism to take the initiative, and if needs be, devote the rest of their lives to the Cause—then there is no hope for India. Her sons must and will remain mere humble and helpless instruments in the hands of foreign rulers, for 'they would be free, *themselves* must strike the blow.' And if even the leaders of thought are all either such poor creatures, or so selfishly wedded to personal concerns, that they dare not or will not strike a blow for their country's sake, then justly and rightly are they kept down and trampled on, for they deserve nothing better. Every nation secures precisely as good a government as it merits. If you, the picked men, the most highly educated of the nation, cannot, scorning personal ease and selfish objects, make a resolute struggle to secure greater freedom for yourselves and your country, a more impartial administration, a larger share in the management of your own affairs, then we your friends are wrong and our adversaries right; then are Lord Ripon's noble aspirations for your good fruitless and visionary; then, at present, at any rate, all hopes of progress are at an end, and India truly neither lacks nor deserves any better government than she now enjoys . . .

James Clerk Maxwell (1831-79)

As a scientist, Clerk Maxwell ranks with Newton and Einstein. His Treatise on Electricity and Magnetism *was described by James Newman as 'one of the most splendid monuments ever raised by the genius of a single individual'; his work made a fundamental contribution to the development of radio, radar, television and electronics generally. He invented colour photography. When he wrote the first of the letters which follows, he was 13 and at school at the Edinburgh Academy. Only a year later, the first of his scientific papers was read to the Royal Society of Edinburgh.*

154. Hedrons

To his father   *Old 31 (31 Heriot Row, Edinburgh)*
                                                     19 June 1844

My Dear Father—On Wednesday I went to the Virginian minstrels, in which some of the songs were sung, the first line accompanied with clappers, the second on a tamborine, the third on a banjo, like this, . . . played like a guitar very quickly, and the fourth on the fiddle, and the chorus by all together. There were guesses in abundance; and there was an imitation of a steam onion, and other things which you will find in the bill. On Saturday, having got the play for verses on Laocoon, I went with Cha. H. Johnstone so far, and then went to the murain vile till Mrs. M'Kenzie, Ninny, and κυνη * went to visit Cramond, where I played with the boies till high water; and the minister's young brother and the too boies and I doukit in C (big sea as κυνη calls it), and then dried ourselves after the manner of Auncient Greeks; we had also the luxury of a pail of water to wash our feet in.

How is a' aboot the house now our Gudeman's at home? How are herbs, shrubs, and trees doing?—cows, sheep, mares, dogs, and folk? and how did Nannie like bonny Carlisle? Mrs. Robt. Cay was at the church on Sunday. I have made a tetra hedron, a dodeca hedron, and 2 more hedrons that I don't know the wright names for. How do doos and Geraniums come on.—Your most obt. servt.

JAS. ALEX. McMERKWELL
1 2 5   12 7 4 13   3   6   11   8 9 10 14 15 16 17

155. Professor at Aberdeen

To R.B. Lichfield   *129 Union Street, Aberdeen*
                                                     7 February 1858

. . . When I last wrote I was on my way here. Since then I have been at work, Statics and Dynamics; two days a week being devoted to Principles of Mechanism, and afterwards to Friction, Elasticity and Strength of Materials, and also Clocks and Watches, when we come to the pendulum. We have just begun hydrostatics. I have found a better text-book for hydrostatics than I had thought for,—the run of them are so bad, both Cambridge and other ones,—Galbraith and Haughton's *Manual of Hydrostatics* (Longmans, 2s). There are also manuals of Mechanics and Optics of the same set. There is no

* Coonie, who was Colin Mackenzie, then a child of three.

humbug in them, and many practical matters are introduced instead of mere intricacies. The only defect is a somewhat ostentatious resignation of the demonstrations of certain truths, and a leaning upon feigned experiments instead of them. But this is exactly the place where the students trust most to the professor, so that I care less about it. I shall adopt the Optics, which have no such defect, and possibly the Mechanics, next year.

My students of last year, to the number of about fourteen, form a voluntary class, and continue their studies. We went through Newton i. ii. iii., and took a rough view of the Lunar Theory, and of the present state of Astronomy. Then we have taken up Magnetism and Electricity, static and current, and now we are at Electro-magnetism and Ampère's Laws. I intend to make Faraday's book the backbone of all the rest, as he himself is the nucleus of everything electric since 1830.

So much for class work. Saturn's Rings are going on still, but this month I am clearing out some spare time to work them in. I have got up a model to show the motions of a ring of satellites, a very neat piece of work, by Ramage, the maker of the 'top.'

For other things—I have not much time in winter for improving my mind. I have read Froude's History, *Aurora Leigh,* and Hopkins's *Essay on Geology,* also Herschel's collected Essays, which I like much, also Lavater's life and *Physiognomy,* which has introduced me to him pleasantly though verbosely. I like the man very much, quite apart from his conclusions and dogmas. They are only results, and far inferior to methods. But many of them are true if properly understood and applied, and I suppose the rest are worth respect as the statements of a truth-telling man.

Well, work is good, and reading is good, but friends are better. I have but a finite number of friends, and they are dropping off, one here, one there. A few live and flourish. Let it be long, and let us work while it is day, for the night is coming, and work by day leads to rest by night.

156. The Royal Society of Edinburgh

to H.R. Droop   *Glenlair, Dalbeattie 19 July 1865*

. . . There are so many different forms in which Societies may be cast, that I should like very much to hear something of what those who have been thinking about it propose as the plan of it.

There is the association for publishing each other's productions; for delivering lectures for the good of the public and the support of the Society; for keeping a reading room or club, frequented by men of a particular turn; for dining together once a month, etc.

I suppose W———'s object is to increase the happiness of men in London who cultivate physical sciences, by their meeting together to read papers and discuss them, the publication of these papers being only one, and not the chief end of the Society, which fulfils its main purpose in the act of meeting and enjoying itself.

The Royal Society of Edinburgh used to be a very sociable body, but it had several advantages. Most of the fellows lived within a mile of the Society's rooms. They did not need to disturb their dinner arrangements in order to attend.

Many of them were good speakers as well as sensible men, whose mode of considering a subject was worth hearing, even if not correct.

The subjects were not limited to mathematics and physics, but included geology, physiology, and occasionally antiquities and even literary subjects. Biography of deceased fellows is still a subject of papers. Now those who cultivate the mathematical and physical sciences are sometimes unable to discuss a paper, because they would require to keep it some days by them to form an opinion on it, and physical men can get up a much better discussion about armour plates or the theory of glaciers than about the conduction of heat or capillary attraction . . .

I am now getting the general equations for the motion of a gas considered as an assemblage of molecules flying about with great velocity. I find they must repel as inverse fifth power of distance . . .

Andrew Carnegie (1835-1919)

In 1848 Carnegie's father, a weaver in Dunfermline, emigrated with his family to the United States. The young Carnegie worked his way up from a telegraph operator to become a major industrialist in railways and then in steel. He accumulated a vast fortune which he proceeded to distribute systematically to fund public libraries, concert halls, church organs and other social and educational causes in Scotland, the United States and elsewhere. In Scotland, in particular, generations of students and innumerable projects have been assisted by his benefactions.

157. First steps in America

To his Uncle, George Lauder   *Pittsburgh Telegraph Office*
30 May 1852

. . . We have had a flood this year. Every season when the snow melts on the mountains the Rivers raise very high but they have not been so high for 20 years before. It rained for 3 weeks almost constantly and both rivers rose at once. it was up to the ceiling in our house and for 2 days we had to live upstairs and sail about in rafts and skiffs. It was a great time. The lower part of Allegheny was all flooded it caused great destruction of property. Our telegraph was swept away in some places and I had to go down the River 70 miles to take all the Eastern business from Pittsburgh and send to a station below from where the line was all right. I was away more than a week and enjoyed myself first rate.

James Sloan arrived here 2 weeks ago, he has had a hard voyage but he is in good health. he will get along first rate here. he thinks he will go to making shuttles, a great number of them being required for the Steam Cotton works. He has been working before he came here at a place about 100 miles from here. He has gone back to fetch his tools and will be back soon. We were all overjoyed to see him. We have not got all the news from him yet, every day something comes to light that surprises us. He likes this country very well, but as he is going to write he will *gie ye his ain crack.* He says that he knows very little difference in Father and Mother and I was glad to hear him say that Dod and I looked very much alike, far more so than when I was in Scotland. We are also about the same height. He was laughing at me a few days ago because I could not say *sow crae* as broad as he says it. I tried it over and over but could not do it, but although I cannot say *sow crae* just as broad as I once could, I can read about Wallace, Bruce and Burns with as much enthusiasm as ever, and feel proud of being a son of Old Caledonia, and I like to tell people when they ask 'Are you an native born?' 'No, sir, I am a Scotchman,' and I feel as proud I am sure as ever Roman did when it was their boast to say, 'I am a Roman citizen.'. . .

Although I sometimes think I would like to be back in Dunfermline, I am sure it is far better for me that I came here. If I had been in Dunfermline working at the loom it is very likely I would have been a poor weaver all my days, but here I can surely do something better than that, if I don't it will be my own fault, for anyone can get along in this Country. I intend going to night school this fall to learn something more and after that I will try and teach myself some other branches. My paper is nearly done. Please give my kind remembrances to Mr. and Mrs. Martin and John Grant, tell him we were happy to hear that himself and family were getting along. Now my Dear Uncle, please write me soon. I would be so glad to get a letter from you. I will write you regularly. I forgot to ask when you intended coming out. I remain your much indebted nephew

ANDREW CARNEGIE

158. Laird of Pittencrieff

To John Morley   *January 1903*

. . . The greatest event in my life has happened. I am Laird of Pittencrieff, the biggest of all titles to me. King Edward not in it! It's part of the Abbey and Palace ruins at Dunfermline. The Glen, King Malcolm's Tower, St. Margaret's Shrine, *all mine!* Ask Mr. Shaw—he'll explain my transports. He feels it, every Dunfermline child must feel it. I'm going to make it a public park and present it to Dunfermline . . . It's the most sacred spot to me on earth.

Madeleine Smith (1836-1928)

Madeleine Smith is famous for one reputed deed, the murder of her lover, Pierre Emile L'Angelier; reputed because Madeleine Smith was found not proven of the charge of murder, even though a quantity of arsenic, enough to have killed a man many times over, was found in the body at the post-mortem, and though it was known that Madeleine had made several purchases of that poison. L'Angelier died at 11 Franklin Place, Glasgow, a short walking distance from 7 Blythswood Square, the home of the eminently respectable Madeleine, on 23 March 1857. Prayers and propriety were ostensible features of the life of James Smith, architect, and his family. The hidden life of Mr Smith's daughter, Madeleine, was very different. It was she who led the love affair with L'Angelier, even shocking him after they had consummated their love in the garden of the family's holiday home at Rhu. This was hinted in her letter written in June, in which she chooses to address L'Angelier as 'husband'.

My own, my beloved husband,
I trust to God you got home safe, and were not much the worse of being out. Thank you, my love, for coming so far to see your Mimi. It is truly a pleasure to see you, my Emile. Beloved, if we did wrong last night it was in the excitement of our love. Yes, beloved, I did truly love you with my soul. I was happy, it was a pleasure to be with you. Oh if we could have remained never more to have parted. But we must hope the time shall come. I must have been very stupid to you last night. But every thing goes out of my head when I see you, my darling, my love. I often think I must be very, very stupid in your eyes, You must be disappointed with me. I wonder you like me in the least. But I trust and pray the day may come when you shall like me better. Beloved, we shall wait till you are quite ready. I shall see and speak to Jack on Sunday. I shall consider about telling Mama. But I don't see any hope from her—I know her mind. You, of course, cannot judge of my parents. You know them not . . . Darling Emile, did I seem cold to you last night. Darling I love you. Yes, my own Emile, love you with my heart and soul. Am I not your wife. Yes I am. And you may rest assured after what has passed I cannot be the wife of any other but dear, dear Emile. No, now it would be a sin. I dread next Winter. Only fancy, beloved, us both in the same town and unable to write or see each other, it breaks my heart to think of it. Why, beloved, are we so unfortunate? I thank you very much for your dear, long letter. You are kind to me, love. I am sorry for your cold. You were not well last night, I saw you were not yourself. Beloved pet, take care of it. When may we meet (oh that blot) again. A long time, is it not sad. I weep to think of it, to be separated thus—if you were far away, it would not be so bad, but to think you near me. I cannot see you when you come to Miss White's, as you could not be out so late. They cannot keep us from each other. No, that they never shall. Emile, beloved, I have sometimes thought would you not like to go to Lima after we are married? Would that not do. Any place with you, pet.

I did not bleed in the least last night—but I had a good deal of pain during the night. Tell me, pet, were you angry at me for allowing you to do what you did—was it very bad of me. We should, I suppose, have waited till we were married. I shall always remember last night. Will we not often talk of our evening meetings after we are married. Why do you say in your letter—'If we are NOT married' I would not regret knowing you. Beloved, have you

a doubt but that we shall be married some day. I shall write dear
Mary soon. What would she say if she knew we were so
intimate—lose all her good opinion of us both—would she not.

Adieu again, my husband. God bless you and make you well.
And may you yet be very, very happy with your Mimi as your little
wife. Kindest love, fond embrace, and kisses from thy own true and
ever devoted Mimi. Thy faithful.

WIFE

Robert Gardner

*Robert Gardner, Secretary of Queen's Park Football Club, wrote to the
Secretary of the Thistle, a team which the author of* Scottish Football *has not
fully identified, with a view to arranging a match. This was the 'first known
game between two Scottish clubs'. In 1867 the laws had not been formally
established, at least with regard to numbers of players and duration of the
game.*

160. 'Bring your ball'

To the Secretary of the
Thistle Football Club   *Glasgow 9 July 1867*

Dear Sir,
I duly received your letter dated 25th inst. on Monday Afternoon,
but as we had a Committee Meeting called for this evening at which
time it was submitted, I could not reply to it earlier. I have now
been requested by the Committee, on behalf of our Club, to accept
the challenge you kindly sent, for which we have to thank you, to
play us a friendly Match at Football on our Ground, Queen's Park,
at the hour you mentioned, on Saturday, first proximo, with twenty
players on each side. We consider, however, that Two-hours is
quite long enough to play in weather such as the present, and hope
that this will be satisfactory to you. We would also suggest that if no
Goals be got by either side within the first hour, that goals be then
exchanged, the ball, of course, to be kicked off from the centre of
the field by the side who had the origanal Kick-off, so that boath
parties may have the same chance of wind and ground, this we think
very fare and can be arranged on the field before beginning the
Match. Would you also be good enough to bring your ball with you

in case of any breake down, and thus prevent interuptsion. Hoping
the weather will favour the Thistle and Queen's.

I remain,

Yours very truly,

(Sgd.) Robt. Gardner

Secy.

James A. H. Murray (1837-1915)

James Murray spent 35 years on that great work of Scottish scholarship, the
Oxford English Dictionary, *of which he was the first editor. It is a curious
coincidence that he and another great philologist, John Leyden (q.v.), were
both born in Denholm, a small village near Hawick, and that the first
substantial work of both was an edition of* The Complaynt of Scotland. *They
had much else in common, including a strong affection for the Scots language.*

161. 'We were men at 19'

To James Bryce   *Oxford 15 December 1903*

. . . Just to help you to orient yourself, however, and in the
confidence that you—as a brother Scotsman—will not misuse it, I
will try to give an outline answer to your inquiry into my
philological history. I was *always* interested in language, especially
in its *written* forms, since before I remember anything. I am
reported to have known my letters before I was 18 months old, and
when at that age a little brother was born to me, and I was
introduced to him, it used to be told that I brought my primer—or
reading-made-easy, and said 'I will show little brudder "round O"
and "crooked S." ' It was the greatest treat I could offer him. My
mother who died at 80, a grand old Scotch woman, used to treasure
up scraps of paper written in those days in which I had copied out
words of Latin or Greek from books in which they occurred, & a
Hebrew alphabet from the CXIX Psalm in a neighbour's big Bible.
Of these I have only dim memories, but I have seen the scraps. I *do*
remember a vigorous attack at the age of 7 upon a page of the
Chinese Gospel of St. John, reproduced in the *Juvenile Missionary
Magazine*, which I copied many times in very scrawly Chinese, and
learned the characters for *Beginning, God, word, light, life, witness,*

184

man, etc. by observing their recurrence in the columns, which I could write from memory many years after: indeed I fancy I could tell which is which still. Both my father & mother were of good family, but both families had come down in the world, and they were poor, and I had no chance of learning Latin till I was nearly 12, nor French for 2 years later. Greek, I learned mainly by myself two years later still. I was immensely indebted to Cassell's *Popular Educator* when it came out. After this, I had a sort of mania for learning languages; every new language was a new delight, no matter what it was Hebrew or Tongan, Russian or Caffre, I swallowed them all, at least so as to master grammar & structure, but rarely did enough at the vocabulary. Still I at one time or another could read in a sort of way 25 or more languages, at most of which I could still do something with the help of a dictionary. I was Junior Assistant Master in the Grammar School in Hawick for 3 years from the age of 17½ to 20½; then from 20 to 27 Master of the Subscription School called Hawick Academy. That was my great learning time, when I made incursions into nearly all the sciences, botany, geology, entomology, anatomy, chemistry, mechanics, archaeology, electricity. I made Graham Bell, then a boy of 14, I a man of 24, his first electric battery, when I was attending his Father's Vacation Course in Vocal Physiology and Elocution in Edinr.; he had confided to me his desire to know something about electricity, and we set about it in the old garden at Trinity near Edin. He calls me sportively 'the grandfather of the telephone'—a very remote ancestor, I tell him. At the age of 19 (!!) I was one of the founders of the Hawick Archaeological Society, which indeed I named, for the old men who were interested were going to call it the *Antiquarian* Society, when I demonstrated the superior potency of the word *Archaeological,* with such effect that they made me Secy. which I continued to be till I left Hawick in 1864. I am alas the only surviving member of its first years, and the Hawick people greatly want me to go to a Jubilee Celebration in 1906—so you must not bury me yet! In those days we were *men* at 19; I was earning my living, writing articles in the local paper, speaking at public meetings—always on the side of freedom and equality, and corresponding with learned archaeologists, geologists, & naturalists. To that time dates my friendship with Sir A. Geikie, his brother, & Dr Young of Glasgow, all then in the Survey—and a lesson on geology which I gave one day to Sir Roderick Murchison (without knowing who he was)—I took him for a simple tourist who was going to be imposed upon with a sham fossil, that a man wanted to sell him, and pointed out to him 'the utter absence of any organic structure.' How the Geikies did 'roar' when they heard of it! This was at 19; nowadays 'boys' at 19 are leaving school & competing for scholarships, and preparing to begin life at 24. I taught from 17½, & never cost my father a penny thenceforth.

About 1858, I think, the late Prince Lucien Bonaparte began to get versions of scriptural books done into local dialect: a Scotch St. Matthew was done by Henry Scott Riddell. A specimen of the Sermon on the Mount was reprinted in our local paper, and greatly disappointed me; it did not seem *living* Scotch at all. I tried my hand at doing better, had to invent a phonetic spelling for our Teviotdale sounds, abandoned Matthew, did half of Acts, & finally Ruth and Jonah—Ruth I published after as a specimen in my *Lowland Scotch* book. I planned & partly completed a phonetic key to Jamieson's Dicty. Then I noticed that Scottish grammar was not English, and I made a *Scotch Grammar,*showing that all the things that people called 'bad grammar' because they would be so in English, were 'good grammar' in Scotch. I read papers in these linguistic (& many other) subjects to the Archaeol. Soc. A stray copy of Bohn's Alfred the Great by Pauli with the Anglo-Saxon text of Orosius, picked up on a stall in Leith, opened a new world to me. I simply bathed & basked in it. Then at a meeting of the Berwicksh. Nat. Club at Alnwick, at which I represented our H[k]. society, I took part in a discussion of some local names, & showed some knowledge of Anglo-Saxon, on which Canon Greenwell came & introduced himself, asked where I had learned this. I told him and spoke of the difficulty of getting books. He sent me next day a large boxful from his own Library & that of the Chapter—there were Hooker and Lye & Thorpe & Thwaites, & the Heptateuch, & Durham Gospels—it was glorious! I made MS. copies of several whole books; I have them still & have often used them for the Dicty., to save a visit to Bodleian . . .

John Muir (1838–1914)

Muir was born in Dunbar, but his family emigrated to the United States in 1849 and he spent the rest of his life there. He was one of the first to realise the importance of conserving wild life and natural resources, and throughout his life he campaigned for the cause. He is regarded in America as a folk hero and the father of conservation. In Scotland, he is commemorated in the John Muir Country Park at Dunbar.

To his wife   *Dunbar 6 July 1893*

Dear Louie:

I left Liverpool Monday morning, reached Edinburgh early the same day, went to a hotel, and then went to the old book-publisher David Douglas, to whom Johnson had given me a letter. He is a very solemn-looking, dignified old Scotchman of the old school, an intimate friend and crony of John Brown, who wrote 'Rab and his Friends', knew Hugh Miller, Walter Scott, and indeed all the literary men, and was the publisher of Dean Ramsay's 'Reminiscences of Scottish Life and Character,' etc. He had heard of me through my writings, and, after he knew who I was, burst forth into the warmest cordiality and became a perfect gushing fountain of fun, humor, and stories of the old Scotch writers. Tuesday morning he took me in hand, and led me over Edinburgh, took me to all the famous places celebrated in Scott's novels, went around the Calton Hill and the Castle, into the old churches so full of associations, to Queen Mary's Palace Museum, and I don't know how many other places.

In the evening I dined with him, and had a glorious time. He showed me his literary treasures and curiosities, told endless anecdotes of John Brown, Walter Scott, Hugh Miller, etc., while I, of course, told my icy tales until very late—or early—the most wonderful night as far as humanity is concerned I ever had in the world. Yesterday forenoon he took me out for another walk and filled me with more wonders. His kindness and warmth of heart, once his confidence is gained, are boundless. From feeling lonely and a stranger in my own native land, he brought me back into quick and living contact with it, and now I am a Scotchman and at home again. . .

Here are a few flowers that I picked on the Castle Hill on my walk with Douglas, for Helen and Wanda. I pray Heaven in the midst of my pleasure that you are all well. Edinburgh is, apart from its glorious historical associations, far the most beautiful town I ever saw. I cannot conceive how it could be more beautiful. In the very heart of it rises the great Castle Hill, glacier-sculptured and wild like a bit of Alaska in the midst of the most beautiful architecture to be found in the world. I wish you could see it, and you will when the babies grow up. . .

Good-bye

J.M.

Alexander Graham Bell (1847–1922)

Graham Bell was born in Edinburgh, where his father, Melville Bell, who taught elocution, showed an inventive ability which directed his son Graham to his experiments in telephonic speech. Melville was the author of Visible Speech, *a book to instruct deaf-mutes in lip-reading. This interest was continued in the son when he was appointed Professor of Vocal Physiology and Elocution at Boston University. There, despite the expenditure of much time and energy on creating 'an electrical contrivance' which would communicate speech, involving the loss of students from his classes, progress was so slow as to make him despair of achieving a practical invention. In this condition he sought help from the eminent American physicist, Professor Joseph Henry, Secretary of the Smithsonian Institute in Washington. Henry listened with a degree of interest, until Bell described the sound response from the empty coil. What followed Bell described in a letter to his parents.*

163. 'Get it'

To Mr and Mrs Melville Bell   *Boston 18 March 1875*

. . . He started up, said, 'Is that so? Will you allow me, Mr Bell, to repeat your experiments and publish them in the world through the Smithsonian Institute, of course giving you the credit of the discoveries?' I said it would give me extreme pleasure and added that I had the apparatus in Washington and could show him the experiments at any time. . .

He said he thought it 'the germ of a great invention' and advised me to work at it myself instead of publishing. I said that I recognised the fact there were mechanical difficulties. . . I added that I felt I had not the electrical knowledge necessary to overcome the difficulties. His laconic answer was 'GET IT.'

I cannot tell you how much these two words encouraged me. . .

164. The future of the telephone

To the capitalists of the
Electric Telephone Company   Kensington 25 March 1878

... The great advantage it possesses over every other form of electrical apparatus is that it requires no skill to operate ... The simple and inexpensive nature of the Telephone ... renders it possible to connect every man's house or manufactory with a Central Station so as to give him the benefit of direct Telephonic Communication with his neighbours at a cost not greater than that incurred for gas or water.

At the present time we have a perfect network of gas pipes and water pipes throughout our larger cities. We have main pipes laid under the streets, communicating by side pipes with the various dwellings enabling the inmates to draw their supplies of gas and water from a common source.

In a similar manner it is conceivable that cables of Telephonic wires could be laid underground or suspended overhead communicating by branch wires with private dwellings counting houses, shops, manufactories etc. etc. uniting them through the main cable with a central office where the wires could be connected together as desired establishing direct communication between any two places in the City. Such a plan as this though impracticable at the present moment will, I believe, be the outcome of the introduction of the Telephone to the Public. Not only so but I believe that in the future wires will unite the head offices of Telephone Companies in different cities and a man in one part of the country may communicate by word of mouth with another in a distant place ...

Mary Slessor (1848-1915)

Mary Slessor was born in Aberdeen. Her parents moved to Dundee to seek work in the jute mills, where Mary and her brothers were employed twelve hours a day. Having heard of Livingstone in Africa she made up her mind to be a missionary. Despite the handicaps of poverty and lack of training the Foreign Mission Board of the Church of Scotland supported her application. Her courage and devotion to the African tribes which she converted to Christianity and civilised was such that she is venerated by them to this day. She is still known as 'Great Mother' or simply 'Ma'.

165. Converting the heathen

To Mrs Jamie   *Calabar 20 February 1914*

My dear Mrs Jamie,
I must write you a wee scrap to let you know how fickle I am, and
to let you share my joy. You know I think that I have been
exercised in heart about those towns lying in wickedness and sin up
in this remote district. Well, when I came over as far as Odor I just
opened out the Camp bed Miss Peacock loaned me, and sat down in
the Government Rest House and said, I'm not going farther on any
journey, till I have it out with those heathen chiefs who so bitterly
are opposing the Gospel Message. And my opportunity came on
Sabbath Morning when a lot of disciples came early in the morning
in response to my message, and we had service in the yard of the
Rest House, a few from the station coming (with) me and joining.
Then those lads pushed my chair out to Iban — 2 miles distant after
our service, and there we met with the chiefs and hundreds and
hundreds of the towns people, for it was their off work day, and
really the head chief whom I had not seen on a former visit was
more than kind, gave us a warm welcome. We had a long talk and
no repugnance manifested to the Gospel in itself to which they
listen reverently enough, but the results; specially the saving of
twins, and the restoration of twin mothers of their right to live as
women, and not as beasts unclean in the bush,—is too much for
them, their unanimous verdict is, 'Our town will spoil, and we shall
all die.' However, the last word there, was—'Go home, Ma, till we
meet and discuss it, and we shall see you again.' That is the usual
way in native places, and we went back to our gypsy camp very
hopeful. Then in the evening we went into the house . . . on the
outskirts of which we were settled. And again with all the dignity
and all the persuasiveness we could muster made our appeal. After
about an hour's fencing and squashing of bogeys, the tension gave
way, and with a hearty laugh at the demolishing of his arguments,
the old chief said, 'Well, Ma! there they are', with a sweep of his
hand over the crowd, 'Take them and teach them what you like, and
your young men go and build a house for Book.' and etc! and the
citadel was won . . .

*   *   *

R. L. Stevenson (1850-94)

Stevenson is perhaps the most striking example of the power which the idea of Scotland exercises on the mind of the Scot overseas. He was forced by ill-health to spend most of his life abroad, finally in Samoa. His letters, like his novels and poems, reflect a constant preoccupation with Scotland. As he said in a letter of 1 November 1892 to J. M. Barrie, 'It is a singular thing that I should live here in the South Seas under conditions so new and so striking, and yet my imagination so continually inhabits that cold old huddle of grey hills from which we come'.

166. 'Four Great Scotsmen'

To Mrs Sitwell   *Mentone 26 January 1874*

...You have not yet heard of my book?—*Four Great Scotsmen*—John Knox, David Hume, Robert Burns, Walter Scott. These, their lives, their work, the social media in which they lived and worked, with, if I can so make it, the strong current of the race making itself felt underneath and throughout—this is my idea. You must tell me what you think of it. The Knox will really be new matter, as his life hitherto has been disgracefully written, and the events are romantic and rapid; the character very strong, salient, and worthy; much interest as to the future of Scotland, and as to that part of him which was truly modern under his Hebrew disguise. Hume, of course, the urbane, cheerful, gentlemanly, letter-writing eighteenth century, full of attraction, and much that I don't yet know as to his work. Burns, the sentimental side that there is in most Scotsmen, his poor troubled existence, how far his poems were his personally, and how far national, the question of the framework of society in Scotland, and its fatal effects upon the finest natures. Scott again, the ever delightful man, sane, courageous, admirable; the birth of Romance, in a dawn that was a sunset; snobbery, conservatism, the wrong thread in History, and notably in that of his own land. *Voilà, madame, le menu. Comment le trouvez-vous? Il y a de la bonne viande, si on parvient à la cuire convenablement.*

R.L.S.

To Charles Baxter   *Davos 15 December 1881*

My dear Charles

That cheque to Ruedi has been lost; for God's sake stop it and supply another. I lost it. I ought to have written about this before, but we have been in miserable case here: my wife worse and worse, and now sent away, with Sam for sick nurse, I not being allowed to go down. I do not know what is to become of us, and you may imagine how rotten I have been feeling, and feel now, alone with my weasel-dog and my German maid, on the top of a hill here, heavy mist and thin snow all about me, and the devil to pay in general. I don't care so much for solitude as I used to: results, I suppose, of marriage.

Pray write to me something cheery. A little Edinburgh gossip, in heaven's name. Ah! what would I not give to steal this evening with you through the big, echoing college archway, and away south under the street lamps, and to dear Brash's, now defunct! But the old time is dead also, never, never to revive. It was a sad time too, but so gay and so hopeful, and we had such sport with all our low spirits and all our distresses, that it looks like a lamplit, vicious fairy land behind me. O for ten Edinburgh minutes, sixpence between us, and the ever glorious Lothian Road, or dear mysterious Lieth Walk! But here, a sheer hulk, lies poor Tom Bowling—here in this strange place, whose very strangeness would have been heaven to him then—and aspires—yes, C.B., with tears—after the past.

See what comes of being left alone. Do you remember Brash? the L.J.R.? the sheet of glass that we followed along George Street? Granton? the night at Barrymuirhead? the compass near the sign of the Twinkling Eye? the night I lay on the pavement in misery?

> I swear it by the eternal sky
> Johnson—nor Thomson—ne'er shall die!

Yet I fancy they are dead too; dead like Brash.

R.L.S.

168. 'When I was young and drouthy'

To Charles Baxter   *La Solitude, Hyères-les-Palmiers, Var*
May-June 1883

The Solitude, Hi-ears the Pawm Trees, Var

Dear Cherls,
Here's a bit checky, chuckie. It micht hae been mair; and it's His Mercy it's nae less. Hoots. Write to a buddy. Sair, sair hadden doon by the Bubblyjock, and that's wark. I wark frae fower to five hours a day, clerk-clerkin' awa'. It's my idey that mebbe I'll can shupport mysel—that's if I've nae mair damd illnesses.But that's a' to be seen.
    Ye'll hae to acknowledge my checky, do ye ken that?
    Eh, man, ye're grand of it: there's naebody like you, by your way o't. Eh, Thomson.

> When I was young and drouthy
>   I kent a public hoose
> Whaur a' was cosh an' couthy;
>   It's there that I was crouse!
> It's there that me an' Thamson
>   In days I weep to mind,
>
> Drank wullywauchts like Samson
>   An' sang like Jenny Lind.
> We cracked o' serious maitters,
>   We quarrelt and we grat;
> Like kindly disputators
>   Our whustles weel we wat.
>
> A grieve frae by Langniddry,
>   Wha drank hissel to death,
> Was great upon sculdiddry
>   And curious points o' faith.
> The grieve was in the centre,
>   Wi' Thamson close anigh,
>
> An' Doctor Brown's prezentor (pron: presentor)
>   Was often there forby.
> Wi' mair I need nae mention
>   Tho' a' were decent folk—
> That public hoose convention
>   Is now forever broke!
>   Air: Jerusalem the Golden.

For some are died an' buried
    An' dootless gane to grace;
And ither some are married,
    Or had to leave the place.
And some hae been convertit
    An' weirs the ribbon blue;
And few, as it's assertit,
    Are gude for muckle noo!

169. Saxon and Celt

To J.M. Barrie   *Vailima, Samoa February 1882*

Dear Mr. Barrie,—This is at least the third letter I have written you,
but my correspondence has a bad habit of not getting so far as the
post. That which I possess of manhood turns pale before the
business of the address and envelope. But I hope to be more
fortunate with this: for, besides the usual and often recurrent desire
to thank you for your work—you are one of four that have come to
the front since I was watching and had a corner of my own to
watch, and there is no reason, unless it be in these mysterious tides
that ebb and flow, and make and mar and murder the works of poor
scribblers, why you should not do work of the best order. The tides
have borne away my sentence, of which I was weary at any rate, and
between authors, I may allow myself so much freedom as to leave it
pending. We are both Scots besides, and I suspect both rather Scotty
Scots; my own Scotchness tends to intermittency but is at times
erisypelitous—if that be rightly spelt. Lastly, I have gathered we
had both made our stages in the metropolis of the winds*: our
Virgil's 'grey metropolis', and I count that a lasting bond. No place
so brands a man.

    Finally, I feel it a sort of duty to you to report progress. This
may be an error, but I believed I detected your hand in an article—it
may be an illusion, it may have been by one of those industrious
insects who catch up and reproduce the handling of each emergent
man—but I'll still hope it was yours—and hope it may please you to
hear that the continuation of *Kidnapped* is under way. I have not yet
got to Alan, so I do not know if he is still alive, but David seems to
have a kick or two in his shanks. I was pleased to see how the
Anglo-Saxon theory fell into the trap: I gave my Lowlander a
Gaelic name, and even commented on the fact in the text; yet almost

*i.e. Edinburgh

194

all critics recognised in David and Alan a Saxon and a Celt. I know not about England; in Scotland at least, where Gaelic was spoken in Fife little over the century ago, and in Galloway not much earlier, I deny that there exists such a thing as a pure Saxon, and I think it more than questionable if there be such a thing as a pure Celt.

But what have you to do with this? and what have I? Let us continue to inscribe our little bits of tales, and let the heathen rage!—Yours, with sincere interest in your career,

ROBERT LOUIS STEVENSON

170. 'Say a prayer for me'

To S. R. Crockett   *Vailima, Samoa 17 March 1893*

. . . How strangely wrong your information is! In the first place, I should never carry a novel to Sydney; I should post it from here. In the second place, *Weir of Hermiston* is as yet scarce begun. It's going to be excellent, no doubt; but it consists of about twenty pages. I have a tale, a shortish tale in length, but it has proved long to do, *The Ebb-Tide*, some part of which goes home this mail. It is by me and Mr. Osbourne, and is really a singular work. There are only four characters, and three of them are bandits—well, two of them are, and the third is their comrade and accomplice. It sounds cheering, doesn't it? Barratry, and drunkenness, and vitriol, and I cannot tell you all what, are the beams of the roof. And yet—I don't know—I sort of think there's something in it. You'll see (which is more than I ever can) whether Davis and Attwater come off or not.

Weir of Hermiston is a much greater undertaking, and the plot is not good, I fear; but Lord Justice-Clerk Hermiston ought to be a plum. Of other schemes, more or less executed, it skills not to speak.

I am glad to hear so good an account of your activity and interest; and shall always hear from you with pleasure; though I am, and must continue, a mere sprite of the ink-bottle, unseen in the flesh. Please remember me to your wife and to the four-year-old sweetheart, if she be not too engrossed with higher matters. Do you know where the road crosses the burn under Glencorse Church? Go there, and say a prayer for me: *moriturus salutat*. See that it's a sunny day; I would like it to be a Sunday, but that's not possible in the premises; and stand on the right-hand bank just where the road goes down into the water, and shut your eyes, and if I don't appear to you! well, it can't be helped, and will be extremely funny.

I have no concern here but to work and to keep an eye on this distracted people. I live just now wholly alone in an upper room of my house, because the whole family are down with influenza, bar my wife and myself. I get my horse up sometimes in the afternoon and have a ride in the woods; and I sit here and smoke and write, and re-write, and destroy, and rage at my own impotence, from six in the morning till eight at night, with trifling and not always agreeable intervals for meals.

I am sure you chose wisely to keep your country charge. There a minister can be something, not in a town. In a town, the most of them are empty houses—and public speakers. Why should you suppose your book will be slated because you have no friends? A new writer, if he is any good, will be acclaimed generally with more noise than he deserves. But by this time you will know for certain.—I am, yours sincerely,

ROBERT LOUIS STEVENSON

P.S.—Be it known to this fluent generation that I R.L.S., in the forty-third year of my age and the twentieth of my professional life, wrote twenty-four pages in twenty-one days, working from six to eleven, and again in the afternoon from two to four or so, without fail or interruption. Such are the gifts the gods have endowed us withal; such was the facility of this prolific writer!

R.L.S.

171. Robert Fergusson and the 'Edinburgh Edition'

To Charles Baxter   *Vailima, Samoa About 18 May 1894*

My dear Charles,
I have received Melville's report and the very encouraging documents that he encloses. It would really seem to be going ahead. I am sending Colvin some copy. And I have no doubt he will see to my having proofs in time. But the point is, now that the Edinburgh Edition takes shape, that I should try to tell you what I really feel about it. In the first place, don't put in any trash. I would rather die than have *The Pentland Rising* foisted upon any reader as my idea of literature. See my letter this mail to Colvin. In the second place, my dear fellow, I wish to assure you of the greatness of the pleasure that this Edinburgh Edition gives me. I suppose it was your idea to give it that name. No other would have affected me in the same manner. Do you remember, how many years ago I would be afraid

to hazard a guess, one night when I was very drunk indeed and communicated to you certain 'intimations of early death' and aspirations after fame? I was particularly maudlin, and my remorse the next morning on a review of my folly has written the matter very deeply in my mind; from yours it may easily have fled. If anyone at that moment could have shown me the Edinburgh Edition, I suppose I should have died. It is with gratitude and wonder that I consider 'the way in which I have been led'. Could a more preposterous idea have occurred to us in those days when we used to search our pockets for coppers, too often in vain, and combine forces to produce the threepence necessary for two glasses of beer, or wander down the Lothian Road without any, than that I should be well and strong at the age of forty-three in the island of Upolu, and that you should be at home bringing out the Edinburgh Edition? If it had been possible, I should have almost preferred the Lothian Road Edition, say, with a picture of the old Dutch smuggler on the covers.

I have now something heavy on my mind. I had always a great sense of kinship with poor Robert Fergusson—so clever a boy, so wild, of such a mixed strain, so unfortunate, born in the same town with me, and, as I always felt rather by express intimation than from evidence, so like myself. Now the injustice with which the one Robert is rewarded and the other left out out in the cold sits heavy on me, and I wish you could think of some way in which I could do honour to my unfortunate namesake. Do you think it would look like affectation to dedicate the whole edition to his memory? I think it would. The sentiment which would dictate it to me is too abstruse; and besides I think my wife is the proper person to receive the dedication of my life's work. At the same time—it is very odd, it really looks like transmigration of souls—I feel that I must do something for Fergusson; Burns has been before me with 'The Gravestone.' It occurs to me you might take a walk down the Canongate and see in what condition the stone is. If it be at all uncared for, we might repair it and perhaps add a few words of inscription.

I must tell you, what I just remembered in a flash as I was walking about dictating this letter, there was in the original plan of *The Master of Ballantrae* a sort of introduction describing my arrival in Edinburgh on a visit to yourself and your placing in my hands the papers of the story. I actually wrote it and then condemned the idea as being a little too like Scott, I suppose. Now I must really find the MS and try to finish it for the E.E. It will give you, what I should so much like you to have, another corner of your own in that lofty monument.

Suppose we do what I have proposed about Fergusson's monument, I wonder if an inscription like this would look arrogant:

This stone, originally erected by Robert Burns, has been repaired at the charges of Robert Louis Stevenson and is by him re-dedicated to the Memory of Robert Fergusson as the gift of one Edinburgh lad to another.

In spacing this inscription I would detach the names of Fergusson and Burns but leave mine in the text; or would that look like sham modesty and is it better to bring out the three Roberts?

I shall send—no, come to think of it, I send now with some blanks which I may perhaps fill up ere the mail goes—a dedication to my wife. It was not intended for the E.E. but for *The Justice Clerk* when it should be finished, which accounts for the blanks.

To my wife
I dedicate
This Edinburgh Edition of my works.

I see rain falling and the rainbow drawn
On Lammermuir; hearkening, I hear again
In my precipitous city beaten bells.
Winnow the keen sea wind; and looking back
Upon so much already endured and done
From then to now—reverent, I bow the head!

Take thou the writing; thine it is. For who
Burnished the sword, blew on the drowsy coal,
Held still the target higher, chary of praise
And prodigal of counsel (censure?) —who but thou?
So now, in the end, if this the least be good,
If any deed be done, if any fire
Burn in the imperfect page, the praise be thine!

☆   ☆   ☆

R. B. Cunninghame Graham (1852-1936)

Cunninghame Graham was one of the most dashing and colourful characters in modern Scotland. He was described by MacDiarmid as 'the damned aristo who embraced the cause of the people', and was widely known as 'Don Roberto' because of his aristocratic and Spanish connections and South American experiences. Bernard Shaw modelled characters in two of his plays on him. He was once jailed for six weeks because of his part in a banned demonstration on behalf of the unemployed. He was in turn a Liberal M.P., first President of the Scottish Labour Party, President of the National Party of Scotland and then first President of the Scottish National Party on its formation in 1934. His short stories and sketches are set both in Scotland and in South America.

172. Perverted sentiment

To R. E. Muirhead　　　　　　　　　　　　*British P.O. Tangier*
　　　　　　　　　　　　　　　　　　　　　8 February 1930

. . . There is certainly much apathy at home, and a sort of self content, that indisposes people to act. The absolute neglect of Scottish *national* affairs by the Labour Party should open peoples eyes, if anything can open them. What makes me despair at times, is the (I think) perverted channels into which Scottish sentiment runs. Burns Clubs, St Andrew's Nights, Whisky, and talk about the Misty Hebrides (by men who speak no Gaelic) are all very well in their way, but practical matters cut no ice, and England treats Scotland as a dependency. It is very galling to one's national pride, and I wonder all Scotsmen do not resent it . . .

173. The real enemies

To R. E. Muirhead　　　　　　　　　　　*Ardoch, Dumbartonshire*
　　　　　　　　　　　　　　　　　　　　　8 November 1930

. . . Many thanks for the *Scots Independent*. How right Thomson is that the enemies of Scottish Home Rule are in Scotland and not in England. The English have usually reacted generously to national demands. It is your McBawbee Type, the successful man of money, who is against us. Give the old Tory time to see the sentimental side and we shall have him with us, I think. The Labour crowd are sitting on the fence. Socialist measures conceived and controlled at Westminster would be nothing but a curse to Scotland, as I see the matter . . .

Sir Patrick Geddes (1854-1932)

Geddes is recognised as the founding father of modern town planning, but his interests and influence were far wider than that. He was, in the words of Hugh MacDiarmid, 'one of the outstanding thinkers of his generation'. He sought to free Scotland from 'the intellectual thraldom of London' and to make Edinburgh once again a great European capital of the arts and intellect. He wrote of a 'Scottish Renascence' long before the term was applied to the movement associated with MacDiarmid.

174. New York

To his wife at Lasswade   Boston, Mass. USA
                                                17 March 1899

Darling Winsome,
This is just a wee line for yourself. (I wrote today already by ordinary mail; and while I am waiting for a cab for a return journey to New York for Brooklyn lecture I am thinking of you, and so take pen.)

What shall I say? That absence does make fonder: that it constantly makes me realise how great and rare our happiness is; how delightful and beautiful our home, how noble our city and country—for oh, woe's me! this vast wealth and energy as yet produces little save a pandemonium city; its very luxuries, of hot blasts and ice, of whirling electric cars, of decoration and the Press, of feasts and flare, making up an impression which is generally more painful than pleasant—and which forces the impression that America is the martyr of her own progress ... Yet there are better things here, in part beginnings, too, of neotechnic future. And it is coming, too, a great ferment of changes ...

People are moving fast in thought, and are more ready for what I have to say than at home; their own thought too, is often more congenial and complementary than I find at home, and as I said today, I have found no such mine of ideas as at Worcester.

But, Oh, dear lassie, how I long with it all for you, and to have you in my arms again—and all, and all—and *all*. And the dear little ones too. I wish often I could see them at play and asleep and round the table.

I am glad to be coming home in time for my session, etc., though not, I fear, for much of Crauford. Still, I hope for Sunday—but one must not hope too much, for steamers are apt to be late.

Always your loving

P.

To Victor Branford   *Outlook Tower, Edinburgh*
                                        16 September 1910

. . . Bovril you know is from Edinburgh Infirmary beef tea; hence its butcher and its chemist Lord Playfair so long bossed that great Company.

But not always are science and industry kept together thus. A generation ago we expatriated Prof. Melville Bell, and his Visible Speech. True, he was only a professor of elocution, and in this city of the letter that killeth it was only natural to give but the humblest status to the exponent of the living word. Now however this invention of visible speech is better known as his son's Telephone, and also as Edison's Phonograph. (So by the way Dundee threw away its local inventor's initiatives of electric lighting and of wireless telegraphy.) Returning to Edinburgh: so we lost the Student's Microscope (designed here) to Germany; and so on in other cases.

Of this process there is a great instance just now, a new loss of the first magnitude. But this, it is some compensation to read, may wake up the community as nothing has ever done before—the University, City Fathers and all—masters and workmen too, as they grasp its present meaning, and still more its significance for the future. Even West End lawyers will understand it!

What can this be which can rouse our sleeping city, you will ask? Get from your bookseller the prospectus of the *Encyclopaedia Britannica*, now advertised as acquired by the Cambridge University Press, and to be re-edited there in a new (11th) edition.

Now so strangely and fixedly asleep are my fellow-citizens that no one whom I have met since this announcement appeared in the 'Scotsman' lately, has noticed anything more in this than in any other ordinary business transfer; no more indeed than did that great newspaper itself—(all the more evidently our appropriate organ, you will say!) Yet as you know, my acquaintance is not among those whom you would consider the most comatose, but quite otherwise; in fact among the positively or relatively awake and open-minded! And as so far consolatory evidence of this, they have seen as I pointed it out (and so would have come to see without me,)—what a loss this means (a) for the printing trade of Edinburgh in future years, as compared with past ones; also (b) for the authority of Edinburgh science, medicine and other faculties. When we edited or wrote in it from Edinburgh, Cambridge was not left out—witness Ward's great article on Psychology for instance—but who in Cambridge will come to Edinburgh?

Again in personal detail you will see how this is the fitting nemesis of the expulsion of Robertson Smith, and a reward of Cambridge's worthy acceptance of him, both officially as their University Librarian, and more especially as their Professor of things in general. It is quite dramatic, how a personal persecution evolved this large civic loss—this still greater academic one.

Nor is this the only way in which we compare—and how we fail to compare—with Cambridge! Recall the Darwin celebrations at Cambridge and London, and how here we had no celebrations whatsoever. Yet this was the University of three generations of Darwins—first Erasmus, then his sons: first Charles, the boy genius who killed himself in his enthusiasm of discovery, and then his other son Robert, father of the great Charles (so called after the lost uncle) who was naturally therefore sent here in his turn. Here too, like his lost uncles, he read his first papers to the Edinburgh Medical Society hard by: there the connection ended. No notice was taken of Darwin in his lifetime, though there was time and again occasion for honouring him, and when he would have appreciated it. So here the next generation of Darwins have never set foot—and no wonder!

Again, you and everybody else know what Cambridge owes to Lord Acton, and how wisely she commemorates him. But no Edinburgh man I have ever met knows (do you?) that the one and only British University Acton attended was Edinburgh! So far from encouraging him when he was young enough to appreciate it, recall our Edinburgh treatment of his subject. Just as it refused Carlyle before Acton's day, so I can remember their refusing Robert Louis Stevenson, the first historical imagination of his generation, just as Acton was its Encyclopedist! We want 'safe' men here you know, and so we generally get them. Since Blackie, Masson, etc., no more such fiery spirits have been admitted to the Faculty of Arts; just as since Goodsir and Forbes, Lister and Simpson, the greatest care has been taken of the Faculty of Medicine; and though it is fair to note that good men still manage to slip through the inspection, they are pretty free from the stigmata of genius which characterised the older generation . . .

James Keir Hardie (1856-1915)

James Keir Hardie was born in the mining village of Legbrannock in Lanarkshire. He never went to school. At the age of ten he began working in the mines and became interested in the Trade Union movement at an early age. He was the major influence in the founding of the Scottish Labour Party. In 1900 he was elected M.P. for Merthyr Tydfil, which he remained until the end of his life. His socialism had a religious and ideal base, as may be gathered from the letter which he wrote as Secretary of the Ayrshire Miners' Union.

176. 'Not party politicians'

To Lord Randolph Churchill M.P.   *Ayrshire Miners' Union, Cumnock*
6 December 1889

My Lord

I am instructed by the Executive of the Ayrshire Miners' Union to invite you to deliver one or more addresses on the Labour Question under our auspices.

We are not party politicians in any sense of the word. As working men we are prepared to give support to any candidate for parliamentary honours who will when returned support measures for the shortening of the hours of labour and the general social elevation of the masses.

Your lordships recent utterances on these points have met with more favour than those of any other prominent politician in the country, Sir Charles Dilk alone excepted.

Should you find it convenient to respond to this invitation you will easy understand that such controversial topics as Home Rule must be rigidly excluded from your speeches. We have had Liberal Members of Parliament addressing us and they have had in every case to come under a similar obligation.

You are I believe the first Conservative Member of Parliament ever invited to take part in a miners' meeting in Scotland.

To show that the social question is not the exclusive property of any political party I trust you will strain a point to come down on the earliest date which can be made convenient.

Respectfully yours

J KEIR HARDIE

Sir James Barrie (1860-1937)

Barrie had all the successes his heart desired, it would appear. His immense popular success was first achieved on the stage by Peter Pan *or the Boy who never grew up (1904), though he was more interested in applause from the 'best' people. He had many honours, a baronetcy, an O.M., Chancellorship of Edinburgh University, and he was received in the houses of the English aristocracy. Yet there remained an unresolved complication of affections. He was the boy who had to take the place of his dead brother, David, his mother's favourite: he was a failed husband, the boy who could not grow up being tied to his long dead mother. Out of these complications he made his dramas and stories about Scotland from the distance of London. In 1933 Barrie invited Lady Asquith to discover his place and 'the boy' (himself). On her return to England Barrie wrote her a confessional letter.*

177. 'London that eternally thrills me'

Lady Cynthia Asquith

Adelphi Terrace House
9 September 1933

. . . I am so glad you did enjoy Glen Prosen; I had similar fears to yours about the experiment, but in a day or two I knew it was to be one of the happiest holidays of my life, and so without any doubt it proved. Fain would I have lingered. For the first time perhaps I was 'sweir' to return to the London that eternally thrills me and has been to me all the bright wishes of my youth conceived. I have often felt a wish that Branwell Brontë who yearned for it so much and never reached it had been plunged in as I was. In being able to live in London by my pen I achieved my one literary ambition; I never sought the popularity that is mostly fluke, I would have been as satisfied though I had remained in a nice two-pair-back to the end, quite unknown round the corner so long as it was a London corner. And now I am still best here, but nevertheless I do love my native parts with almost a ferocity of attachment. I could send my love even to all the side-boards in Balnaboth and indeed try to count them if that would warm their hearts. The house and its hills and little bridges over the burns had a very steadying effect on me. They were the only things that stood still. All else we saw as in a flashing cinema. I never showed you anything. We were always in cars and a mile in front of whatever I had to say. The only way to have shown you the boy I was looking for of whom you write would have been to steal off in Michael's car in the night-time and to leave it hidden in Caddam wood while we wandered through a sleeping

Kirriemuir. There is a window in one of the mills where I once thought I should have to live my life as a clerk, the window where my father sat for many years. There is the Lozie grounds I did most miserably frequent (and the Ben too) haunted (what would Michael think!) by the dread that there was nothing for it but to become a doctor. My chief memory of that birthplace is of playing with Maggie under a table upstairs on which stood the coffin containing my brother. I have no recollection of him . . .

Helen Bannerman (1862-1946)
William Bannerman (1858-1924)

Helen Brodie Cowan Watson, Mrs Helen Bannerman, wrote and illustrated Little Black Sambo *and many other popular children's books. She spent a large part of her life in India with her husband, William, an army doctor who became Surgeon-General. They sent their children, at school at home in Edinburgh, a long series of letters, all illuminated with Helen's delightful watercolours. They now fill many volumes in the National Library of Scotland. Helen's biographer, Elizabeth Hay, says of these letters that they show how the 'Scots participated in the Empire as Scots. They did not in any way feel it was England's Empire . . . Will thought of himself as Scottish first and then British. "Scotland and the Empire", was his rallying call.'*

178. St Andrew's Day in India (1)

William to Robin Bannerman

Barel, Bombay
3 December 1910

. . . Last Thursday we had the St. Andrews Dinner and there were 92 at it. It was held in the Freemason's Hall, and we had a band and pipers to keep us lively.

We had the Pipe-Major and three pipers from the Gordon Highlanders, all the way from Cawnpore, and it was delightful to hear how they played, and to see how they danced. And we had very good speeches all about Scotland and the great men who have gone out of it to help to rule great lands and to do good in all parts of the world.

It is surely a great privilege to belong to such a land, and we must try to be good and great men for Auld Scotland's sake . . .

Helen to Day Bannerman   *Madras 3 December 1914*

My own dear Day

Last Monday Dad, Janet and I were invited to a St Andrew's dinner at a Mr Mackay's. Mrs Mackay is not Scotch, but all the same she gave us little bunches of white heather to wear, tied with little bows of Mackay tartan ribbon, and she made the two haggises. (The one Janet and I were offered was very good, the one Dad got was more like soup, as it had burst in the boiling). And we each had a real little wooden quaich, and the kind of menu dad has sent Opa with his letter (I didn't drink out of my quaich but I noticed other people's quaiches absorbed quite a lot of whiskey, and some even dripped through) and after dinner we had all the toasts given on the menu. Dad's was quite the best speech of the evening. He took as his text the three reasons given by Rob Roy, why Bailie Nicol Jarvie would not speak the word would lead to his capture, and he pointed out how auld lang syne and early memories held Scots together, how blood was thicker than water, and how in an emergency the Scot was ready, and he quoted Ludovic Grant 'fechtin at funerals' and said he thought the race that would fecht at funerals would give a good account of itself anywhere—just at first he was tired and did not seem interested himself, and I was afraid he was going to be very slow and very dull, and I reproached myself for not telling Mr Mackay he was too busy to make up a speech. But it was just like launching a boat. Suddenly he got off the shingle, and set off sailing before the breeze, and he had his hearers in shouts of laughter, especially over Ludovic Grant and that tale of the old academy boy in the last chronicle, taking the German prisoners 'He was a poor spirited animal, and put up his hands the minute I poked my gun in his face'!!!

Many thanks for your letter of 36th!! That 'willing' people to do things sounds quite wonderful.

Many thanks for the photo. It is very good, and very like what you were when we were last at home. It is *mine* but Dad has swapped it for *his* table.

YOUR OWN MOTHER

☆   ☆   ☆

The Creation of the Scottish Office (1885)

Lord Salisbury's Government decided in 1885, in response to agitation in Scotland about the neglect of Scottish interests, to restore the office of Secretary for Scotland. Salisbury offered the new post to the Duke of Richmond and Gordon, and the following correspondence ensued.

180. 'Approaching to Arch-angelic'

Salisbury to Richmond   *7 August 1885*

. . . What are your feelings about the Secretaryship for Scotland? The work is not very heavy—the dignity (measured by salary) is the same as your present office—but measured by the expectations of the people of Scotland it is approaching to Arch-angelic. We want a big man to float it—especially as there is so much sentiment about it. I think you seem pointed out by nature to be the man. Lothian's health would not be up to it—& Balfour of Burleigh or Dalrymple are too insignificant. The Scotch people would declare we were despising Scotland—& treating her as if she was a West Indian Colony. It really is a matter where the effulgence of two Dukedoms and the best salmon river in Scotland will go a long way.

181. 'Quite unnecessary'

Richmond to Salisbury   *9 August 1885*

. . . I am quite ready and willing to take the office of Secretary for Scotland if you would like me to do so and think that by doing so I can be useful to you. You know my opinion of the office, and that it is quite unnecessary, but the Country and Parliament think otherwise—and the office has been created, and someone must fill it. Under these circumstances I am quite ready to take it, and will do my best to make it a success (if this is possible!).

182. 'Wounded dignities'

Salisbury to Richmond   *13 August 1885*

. . . I really am very grateful to you for your kindness in taking the Scotch Office. It makes it a success at once—for the whole object of the move is to redress the wounded dignities of the Scotch people—or a section of them—who think that enough is not made of Scotland: & your taking the office will make all the difference between the measure being a compliment to them, or a slight.

183. Dover House

Salisbury to Richmond   *20 August 1885*

. . . I am very glad you are settling the matter so quickly—it will impress your vainglorious countrymen the more. I signed away Dover House for you to reside in. I believe I have as much right to sign away Westminster Abbey—but the Lord Advocate seemed to take it very easy. No doubt the freebooting instincts of his ancestors hang about him. Anyhow it is better than twelve rooms over a Post Office. I wonder Plunket did not offer you the second pair back over a gin-shop.

James Ramsay MacDonald (1866–1937)

The first Labour Prime Minister was born in Lossiemouth, Morayshire. A fluent and attractive speaker, a talented writer, he quickly rose through the ranks to become leader of the Labour Party, but in 1914 he made an anti-war speech which at first was applauded by members of the Party and then derided so that he was compelled to resign from the Commons. He used the time to study, write and increase his knowledge of public affairs. In 1924 as Prime Minister he seemed to be totally in control. But under him the Labour Party split and in 1929 he formed a coalition government, a move which many of his former colleagues regarded as a betrayal of Socialism. The two letters, written while he was out of office, indicate a buoyant spirit and a man believing in the justice of his position.

184. 'I a Bolshevist!'

To Arthur C. Murray M.P.   9 Howitt Road, Hampstead
                                            11 January 1919

My Dear Murray

Thank you very much indeed for your nice friendly letter. Of course I am somewhat grieved to have my work broken by this misfortune, especially in view of the scandalous misrepresentations which brought it about.

I a Bolshevist! I a pro German! I am truly sorry that [Lloyd] George condescended to that kind of thing. It was not quite the game—even to play it pretty low down. I stood by him as you know in bad times, and though he and I profoundly disagree with each other now, he might have criticised severely without joining in a howl which he knows quite well is one of ignorance. What the future is to bring I know not, but the pressure of economic circumstance may compel me to take up work which will be inconsistent with public work. However, it is good to look back upon the days that have been, and it is well not to trouble too much about the days that are to be.

I was in the country of our hearts a week ago and had a great time—hundreds of people turned away, great cheering and so on. But for the moment I rest on my oars, I belong neither to the Right nor the Left. I am neither Tory nor Jacobin, neither traditionalist nor revolutionist, and so there is perhaps no place for me. I have seen my great political creation fall into other hands and my friends reduced to praying in my support and that is the last phase in the saintly life here. Your friends do not pray that your oil ventures will succeed and so they do succeed! I am now merely a spectator and I see the ragged pageant process in front of me—whither bound, God only knows. I am particularly sorry to be out of the Indian reconstruction—but here I must stop or you will think I am only bitter and persistent, and indeed I am little of either. I am finishing a book on Indian government, editing a half dozen volumes Civil History of the War which is to put our case and work it right through events to the Peace Settlement, and reading the works of our Benefactor John Knox on a study on him and his work for Scotland. I wish you were in history and political philosophy and not in oil—the only reason for the wish being that we might meet oftener for a gossip.

Yours very sincerely

J. Ramsay Macdonald

Dear Mrs Graham Murray
I have been in Paris and Berne for a month and am just back. Your letter has had to be patient and wait for my return as I had nothing forwarded. For the moment I am 'haughty' with Departments and am not addressing a word of wisdom to any of them unless I can do so privately. 'Tis best so. They will have the Box o' Tricks about their ears if they are not careful.

Edinburgh—my beloved capital city—seems far away at present and God knows when my feet will walk it. I must go back to the Continent—perhaps for months:— perhaps I shall not go at all. Everything is uncertain.

Do you like this little story? It fits in with some of the charitable defences which you have put up for me.

Scene railway sleeper south of Paris: irate and pompous Canadian Colonel enters and finds someone else (a friend of mine) in a compartment which he believed should be given all and exclusively to his dear precious self. Result a row which I went from the adjoining compartment to pacify. I talked sweetly to the Colonel as David did to Saul and left the two reconciled for the night. When I left: *Colonel* to friend: Wall I guess that is a fine type of old Highland gentleman of fine pedigree. *Friend* (giggling) Comes from Adam. Do you know who he is? C No but I guess he's somebody. Going to the South for the winter. Monte Carlo maybe. F. Off the board, old man. Do you know him? C. Somebody famous? F. Notorious. Name in every paper. C. No! Who is he? F. Ramsay MacDonald. C. Hell and Blazes!!!!!!!XX

Having recovered under the medical attention of my friend who appears to have outworn him and taken the wind out of him, the Colonel thought he would like another look. We spent a pleasant hour and as I turned in a knock disturbed me and a voice: 'Say! By God I'll never believe a newspaper again'.

I am back, old and broken and bagged out. For years I have been doing little and made up my mind to have one real good old splash before I retired to my cave so I put my back into Berne, worked night and day, finished up with influenza, soaring temperature and speeches: In Paris I did not sleep for two nights with a kind of fever and was within an ace of pneumonia but was up and out every day; and now here I am at home once more rapidly getting better.

Berne is wonderful. Spies, agents—jewellery, dresses, smiles, sighs—a cinema show from 'Ouida'. It filled my eyes with splendour, my head with interest, and my heart with pity. But it was an experience. I sit and dream of it with a pipe, cheap tobacco and a book on theology. I have just read John Knox's love letters so as to give me a mental background.

Yours very sincerely

J. RAMSAY MACDONALD

Charles Rennie Mackintosh (1868–1928)

The genius of Charles Rennie Mackintosh, which found its finest expression in Glasgow School of Art, proved to be too original for ready acceptance in his native land or elsewhere in the United Kingdom. As a consequence his achievement in architecture is confined to the work of ten years, 1896-1906. Now Glasgow School of Art and Mackintosh's other buildings are universally admired. His interior furnishings and designs were lauded at their first viewing in the 8th Secessionist Exhibition in Vienna. This led to exchanges of correspondence and visits from continental designers. One of these, Josef Hoffman, sought advice from Mackintosh on setting up a metal workshop in Vienna, to which Mackintosh replied in German. The extract is a translation.

186. 'Artistic success must be your first aim'

To Josef Hoffmann   *Glasgow 1903*

. . . If your programme is to achieve artistic success (and artistic success must be your first aim), then every object you produce must have a strong mark of individuality, beauty and outstanding workmanship. Your aim from the beginning must be that every object is created for a specific purpose and a specific place. Later on, when the high quality of your work and financial success have strengthened your hand and your position, you can walk boldly in the full light of the world, compete with commercial production on its own ground and achieve the greatest accomplishment ('Werk') that can be achieved in this century; namely the production of all objects for everyday use in beautiful form and at a price that is within the reach of the poorest, and in such quantities that the ordinary man on the street be forced to buy them because there is nothing else available and because soon he will not want to buy anything else. But until that time many years of hard, earnest, honest work by the leaders of the modern movement will be required before all obstacles will be removed either totally or partially. For a beginning the 'artistic' (excuse the term) detractors must be subdued and those who allow themselves to be influenced by them must be convinced through continuous effort and through the gradual success of the modern movement that the movement is no silly hobby of a few who try to achieve fame comfortably through their eccentricity, but that the modern movement is something living, something good, the only possible art for all, the highest achievement of our time . . .

George Douglas Brown (1869–1902)
(George Douglas)

From a difficult and impoverished childhood in Ayrshire, Brown won his way to Ayr Academy, Glasgow University and Oxford. His reputation rests on a single novel, published in the year before his early death, The House With The Green Shutters. *It is a savage reaction, or over-reaction, to the rural sentimentalities of the so-called Kailyard School of Barrie, Crockett and Maclaren.*

187. 'Bletherin awa'

To Tom Smith   *Munday (March 1894)*

Dear Tam,
We are a' sittin thegither cheek by jowl bletherin awa like Biddy McAnally when the soo piggit. Bella's on ma richt, Mary's on ma left, and the snores o' Maggie Steen are sughin out through the kitchen door. I hae been stravaigin in aboot the kintraside an' as Hugh McMillan wad say 'have taken up my domicile for the night at the schoolhouse.' Thanks for your last letter which I o't to have answered before but they put us through our paces at the last you know and leave little time for anything. However I faked up an excuse and got home about a week before the end of term and have transplanted my household gods to Crofthead—for the benefit of the sea air. Man it's glorious tae hae the big quate fiels, and the peesweeps, and the mavises an' the Arran sunsets at yer door insteed o' the damned yammerin' and skirlin' o' the weans aboot Ochiltree. I was up at a pairty at McTeedieston on Friday nicht. When twal' o

clock came we had champit tatties, ham, deuk, grapes (o' a kin's)
lemonade for the lassocks and whisky for the men, and Will
Lindsay nae less tae ladle it oot till us. A' the ——s were
there—Billy scunnerin' me tae ma bowels whammet in my inside
an' Bess liltin' awa' like a mavis in a dauchy gloamin'. I cam
daunering doon the road on Saturday mornin', gaed straucht tae
Ayr, roon by Affleck and feenisht aff wi' a nicht wi' Downie. A fair
programme, I'm thinkin. I hae verra little min' o' ony mair tae write
to noo and so subscribe masel yer sincere frien

GEORDIE BROON

188. 'A brutal and bloody work'

To Ernest Barker   *London 24 October 1901*

... Well, I suppose you have read the *Green Shutters* by this
time. 'Tis a brutal and a bloody work; too sinister, I should think,
for a man of your kindlier disposition. There is too much black for
the white in it. Even so it is more complimentary to Scotland, I
think, than the sentimental slop of Barrie, and Crockett, and
Maclaren. It was antagonism to their method that made me embitter
the blackness; like old Gourlay I was going 'to show the dogs what
I thought of them.' Which was a gross blunder, of course. A
novelist should never have an axe of his own to grind. If he allows a
personal animus to obtrude ever so slightly, it knocks his work out
of balance. He should be an aloof individual, if possible, stating all
sides and taking none.

I have taken to reading Virgil of late with appreciation. The
fourth book of the Aeneid was always my favourite, even when
Latin to me was a mere thing to be crammed, and I've read so much
of it of late that I know screeds of it by heart ...

Why do you pedagogues in high places not teach the classics as
instinct with supernatural beauty and significance, and not as mere
composts of gerunds and absolute ablatives? Why, Oxford might
have made something of me even, if the hook had been baited
properly. But I'm willing to admit that it was less the fault of the
angler than the fish ...

J. D. Fergusson (1874-1961)

J. D. Fergusson was the most radical of the Scottish Colourists and the most dramatic in his treatment of subjects. He was also active in promoting artistic activities other than painting and sculpture. He was at one with the modern movement in France. He made his home there until 1939 when he returned to settle in Scotland. Here, aided by his wife, Margaret Morris, who founded Celtic Ballet, he set about creating a more congenial environment for artists. He associated with the Saltire Society (founded in 1936), which arranged an exhibition of contemporary art in 1939. He founded the New Art Club in Glasgow, which was opened by Alison Sheppard, because she as Secretary of the Saltire Society, according to Fergusson, 'had devoted herself to freedom for Scottish art'. Fergusson's own lack of inhibition is evident in the spontaneity of his letters.

189. The coalman and the sculptor

To Margaret Morris   *Edinburgh 27 September 1915*

. . . Talk about your financial worries—yesterday was the limit. Cold, bleak, pouring rain, so I managed to get these prints done—took all day. This feeling of Sunday. A good enough day of course for painting, drawing, bed or the sofa before the fire in the studio, but otherwise, my God! I tried going a walk the other Sunday, but people made me want to blow hell out of everything. In their Sunday clothes and faces to match—again a shower of M. . . s! Today I got back to the sculpture, not so bad. Very cold, wonderful moon tonight. Lately huge moon; great harvest here, fine crops and good weather. Have been out at night looking at the fields, the country is splendid in movement—really amazing.

Altogether, the place since I came has been delightful because of the weather, the people, the village blacksmith (I took my chisels to him tonight), the joiner, the builder—all of these people are most human and sympathetic.

The other morning my sister burst into my room about 8.30 to say that the coalman had arrived (I work in the part of the garden where thé cart comes in, right in the middle of the 'drive'; not carriage drive, coal-cart drive.) I said hell!!!! of course, because I'd stuck the head of my mother on a base of cement. I thought of the coalman. I dressed and my sister said the man had put my stuff to one side. . . ! I rushed down, here was a splendid looking giant, very good looking, he said good morning and, 'I moved them, they're all right, very interesting, very good carving, I lifted it up a bit and looked at it.' He looked more like a sculptor than I do, by a long way, oh yes! Had seen what it was—the head of my mother. He'd lifted it by the bottom so it couldn't be damaged. I lifted it later and broke the cement. He's a great chap. So is the man I bought the stone from. All that is dèja quelque-chose, n'est pas? I said to the coalman, 'Stone carving is most interesting.' He said, 'Yes, and you've got such a fine place to do it in', which was a marvellous thing to say, for its's *the place that makes me do it.* Seeing things against the foliage . . .

Cheer-oh, Yours JDF

190. Praise for the maker of haggis

To Margaret Morris   *Edinburgh 19 October 1915*
(pet name—Gosse)

Dear Gosse. . . My God, let me have artists for friends—I mean people who feel, even if they're grocers, coal-heavers, anything you like except people devoid of sense of time, colour and sound.

The man I called on, on Sunday night, was discussing painting and has a real feeling for it. I mentioned Burns (of course) and he told me he was at a Golf Club dinner and a butcher who was a great admirer of Burns recited 'Address to a Haggis'. He put so much into it that he nearly collapsed at the end.

Being a squeamy veg, of course you'll think that most ludicrous and disgusting. I think it splendid and inspiring. The man making haggis, selling haggis and reciting the haggis address with real feeling of sympathy with Burns's understanding and sympathy, seems to me to be really getting near the real thing. I'm sorry you can't see it. Think of this disgusting person, a dealer in meat! Worse still, a dealer in tripes—that is, entrails, innards, or guts. A stuffer of tripes, entrails, innards or guts. A maker of haggises, or haggi. That is, a person who stuffs intestines of animals, with chopped livers, in fact the large and small stomach-bags of sheep, stuffing them with a mixture of lights, liver, heart and oatmeal, Jamaica peppers and black peppers and salt and the juice the pluck was boiled in, stirrred into a consistency and stuffed into the large stomach-bag, sewn up with a needle and thread and boiled for hours and prodded from time to time with a large needle—to let out the gas and keep it from bursting.

Imagine him over a cauldron of boiling haggises, watching them and prodding them with a needle, moving them about rhythmically while Burns's words run in his head and at moments of intense emotion, at the *sight* of their fullness of form and the *knowledge* of their fullness of food, of real food that nourishes both through feeling and fact—at these moments, feeling the continuity of idea that comes from having conceived created and completed the work—at these moments this frightful person will get into the fourth dimension, so to speak, and recite with the fullness of emotion derived from this comprehensive experience, marking the rhythm with the needle, and punctuating the time with prods . . .

Yours JDF

John Buchan (1875-1940)

John Buchan, the first Lord Tweedsmuir, the son of a Free Church minister, was born in the Border village of Broughton. His fame rests on his adventure novels, such as The Thirty-Nine Steps *(1915),* Greenmantle *(1916) and* Mr Standfast *(1919). His biographies of* Montrose *(1928) and* Sir Walter Scott *(1932) show more of the mind of the statesman who became Secretary to Lord Milner in South Africa (1901-03) and Governor General of Canada (1935-40).*

191. 'Wood Bush—a kind of celestial Scotland'

To Anna Buchan   *Pietersburg 4 January 1903*

. . . One day I rode down into the fever country—appallingly hot but very interesting. I slept New Year's Night there in the house of a German called Altenroxel where I ate the most wonderful tropical fruits and saw a lot of snakes. Yesterday coming home I was nearly done for. I sent all my party out on different routes and arranged to meet my waggons at a certain place. And I somehow missed my waggons and had to ride straight in here. My horse was dead-beat, the night pitch dark and I had nothing from 6 one morning till 1 the next morning when I got in. I lost my road and was really rather scared for a little. I rode over 70 miles, say the distance from Glasgow to Selkirk, under a blazing sun, without food or drink, and was altogether 14½ hours in the saddle. I had a long sleep and am perfectly well and fresh today . . .

This Wood Bush has really fascinated me—a kind of celestial Scotland and I am very keen to have a bit biggin of my ain in it. I wish I could take you to see it. Hardly anybody knows anything about it. To reach it you sail 5000 miles, travel 1500 in a train and then drive 60 on the worst mountain roads in the world. So it's fairly inaccessible to the tripper for Saturday to Monday . . .

A. Thresh (fl. 1915)

This letter, eloquent in its simplicity of the tragedy and wastage of war, is sadly representative of the experience of countless thousands. It was sent to us by Bruce R. Tyrie who writes, 'The letter was written by a friend of my uncle's to my uncle's girlfriend in Forfar and is self-explanatory. My uncle's name was John Pennicuik Tyrie and I hold his medals along with those of his brother, William, who was also killed in the First World War.'

192. A soldier in a foreign field

To Miss Ramsay *British Mediterranean Expeditionary Force*
17 July 1915

Dear Miss Ramsay

I suppose by the time you receive this you will know of the terrible news of poor Jack. I am more sorry than I can tell you. Don't worry more than you can help, as I know he would not wish you to worry too much. It was the will of God that he should go. I'm afraid it is very poor consolation I can give you, but I can assure you that you have the heart-felt sympathy of all his chums. One consolation I can give you is that he suffered no pain, as he died immediately the bullet struck him, and that he had as decent a burial as it was possible to give him under the circumstances. I only wish I could get a photograph of his grave, but I am afraid it is impossible. I did not hear of it until the day after: it occurred on the 13th. When we got back from the trenches, I had a look through all his things, and found three letters he wrote just before he went up. I have put a line in so that you will know them, and I must ask you to forgive me if I did wrong, but before doing so, I asked the advice of the rest of his chums, and they all agreed it was the best thing to do. I believe Fleming is sending home the things he had in his pockets, and there was nothing in his kit-bag except clothing and tobacco and writing paper. Do you mind if I keep his Bible? It was all I could get that belonged to him. Fleming gave it to me: he was with poor Jack when it happened. Fred is writing you as well. I honestly believe

Jack's death has touched the lads more than any other man's death out here. I have lost the best chum I ever had, but deep as my sorrow is, I know it is nothing compared with yours. Is there anything I can do for you? If so, do let me know, and I shall only be too pleased to do it. I will conclude now hoping that you will not grieve too much, and try and find consolation in the knowledge that he died as he lived, every inch a man, and doing his duty.

Hoping you will regard me as,

Ever your friend

ARTHUR THRESH

John Fraser (1894-1985)

The Very Rev. Dr John Fraser was Moderator of the General Assembly of the Church of Scotland in 1958. During the Second World War he served as a chaplain with the 52nd (Lowland) Division. He was a combatant in the First World War and, when he wrote home before the 3rd Battle of Ypres, he was a second lieutenant in the 7th Battalion of the Gordon Highlanders.

193. 'Inferno let loose'

To the Rev. Mr Fraser   *B.E.F. France 2 August 1917*

My dear Father

I suppose you will be reading in the Scotsman just now of the great Flanders advance. I did not tell you definitely for more than one reason that during our last long rest we were training very minutely to take part in the advance. However, it is all over now and I can tell you something about it.

Our Battalion went into the line on Monday night and formed up in assembly trenches alongside many other Battalions of the Highland Division. At 3.50am on Tuesday morning we went over the top being preceded by the most magnificent artillery barrage that there has ever been. What a spectacle it was—inferno let loose!

If you had yelled till you were hoarse you couldn't have made the man walking beside you hear a word you were saying. Our artillery barrage was 100 yards deep and crept on in front of us preparing the way, while the infantry moved on behind wave after wave. It was still pitch dark, and the bursting shells, thermite and liquid fire was

218

an awful sight. But it gave us great confidence and we swept on like true Highlanders. Our battalion took the first 4 lines of German trenches and other 2 Batts of our Brigade passed thro' us and took other systems of trenches right as far as 2 miles ahead. The Bosch were absolutely demoralised and held up their hands at once. We were very lucky and got off with about 2 killed and 50 wounded in our Company. We had tanks and cavalry and aeroplanes all taking part. Immediately in reaching our objective we dug ourselves in and formed a defensive position. It was ghastly to see the dead Bosch lying thick around. I have lots of little souvenirs which I took off various Huns. I will send them home by degrees and you might keep a careful collection of them.

It is wonderful what a lot of the Germans can speak English. One came up to me later on on the morning of the show and said 'Excuse me, Sir, I am wounded, where shall I go to?' They all seemed delighted to be taken prisoner. I have a pair of fine field glasses which I got off a Hun, whom we bombed out of his concrete dug out.

The terrible rain we have has spoilt the further advance there was to have been—but everything up until now has been splendid.

We are now in a camp in a field—up to the knees in mud, not far from where we were before i.e. near Forbes—

We came out of the new positions on Wed. night. There was not a sq-inch for 3 miles that hadn't been battered—shell holes & craters—nothing else! You can imagine what the ground was like after we had advanced over this turned up soil—nothing but mud!

I am sure you will find this letter very incoherent—but you may gather from it some idea of what this show has been like—

Much love to all

Ever your loving

JOHN

Francis George Scott (1880-1958)

Francis George Scott's distinctive contribution to music was in the wedding of Scots poems to a musical idiom which took full account of their national characteristics as well as their individual message. He created an idiom which introduced a subtlety and verve, an ironic comment, drama and an intensity of feeling new to Scottish music. His influence on the Scottish Renaissance went beyond his music. Born in Hawick, he had the same pride in his native place as that other Borderer, Christopher Murray Grieve alias Hugh MacDiarmid, whose lyrics Scott set to music with perceptive skill. At Langholm, Scott became MacDiarmid's teacher. The relationship of mentor remained. MacDiarmid profited especially by the help Scott gave him in the construction of his masterpiece, A Drunk Man looks at the Thistle. *Despite Scott's sometimes abrasive comments, MacDiarmid returned to him for advice on literary matters and sent him his work,* Mature Art. *The poem grew from the time Scott saw it in 1938 to 20,000 lines by 1940, when its name was changed to* A Vision of World Language. *Oppressed by the threat of impending war, Scott's exasperation is understandable.*

194. 'Mature Art'

To Christopher Murray Grieve   *44 Munro Road, Glasgow*
                                                       12 June 1938

. . . You asked me to give it the once-over but as a matter of fact I gave it the *twice-over* and a bit, and even then couldn't feel sure that any opinions I had come by were worthy of putting before you. If I could convince myself that I knew exactly where the world is going at this moment I might be emboldened to tell you straight back that your reading of the situation is a correct or a totally absurd one. But I don't know . . . Idiosyncrasy!—that is the word I would like to harp on—but how does that sound in a world swung between Hitlerism and Stalinism? You said in one place, I remember—'I am a Communist', and had to add a little later that you would have none of it when all the world would accept it. So why are you a Communist? Why not say, 'I am an Anarchist'? It would certainly be nearer the truth than the other. Your trouble then comes from how you are going to equate Anarchial Art with dialectical materialism à la Stalin and not find yourself at a Moscow trial . . . So there, Christopher, I have done the best I can for 'Mature Art' . . . It's probably that I'm hardening in old age—but somehow I don't feel it. I have found myself, on the contrary, more concerned with the future of my own work than with the merit of anything I have done in the past. I believe like you that everything, life, literature, morality and everything else is in the melting pot, that there are no standards of criticism, no rules of composition etc., etc. but maybe I'm more conscious than you of the need to keep swimming, even against the stream. I can't credit, being a real sceptic, that Communism or any other -ism is going to transform life so much that the art of the next hundred years will obliterate all we today know as art, or create life of such a kind that ours will look flat, stale and unprofitable. In my gloomier moments I can foresee a human society that has reached a veritable heaven (or hell) of mediocrity—and uniformity, with bread and circuses, picture houses, wireless, television, aeroplanes, clinics, tractors, wi' nae bother at a', all free, gratis and for nothing, trying to figure out what kind of lunatics the Beethovens and Grieves and Scotts were, who had such fantastic notions about life and who in reality knew so little about how to live. Art will then be purely utilitarian, something to amuse and entertain. It's some notion, this Marxism. I can see whiles that it places value only on the living present—and unfortunately you and I are both getting older and older. Never mind—keep up your pecker—we'll hae munelicht again! . . .

Tom Johnston (1881-1965)

In the special conditions of the wartime coalition and political truce, Churchill in 1941 offered the post of Secretary of State for Scotland to Johnston, who had been a Labour MP for many years. He accepted on conditions which gave a measure of de facto, if undemocratic, autonomy to Scotland. Johnston made good use of his power and became something of a legend as the man who had achieved more for Scotland than any other individual in this century. He was a staunch supporter of the Saltire Society.

195. Weary of London

To Emrys Hughes   *House of Commons, London*
                              Sunday ? 1937

Dear Emrys
Herewith my stuff! I asked the office to post my papers here, this, and next week so that I could get them on Saturday forenoon at the H of C. But nothing arrived. Will you please see that they post in time for next week-end.

A miserable dreary, health damning life this! Would to God I were away from London and like you, getting the wind of the hills.

Ask Miss Hamilton to send out to Kirkintilloch some time, three or four copies of the new edition of the History of the W/Classes.

Am hunting the share pusher swindlers (see next Tuesdays Hansard!) International Poles (and trying thereby to keep the L.P. from voting for re-armament against Fascism!) digging out material for a History of Kirkintilloch, hunting Lawyers-Judges who seek increases looking after Scots business, doing my French society job, dodging the flu, and asking myself if I am sane in trying to do it all.

Yours aye   TJ

James Maxton (1885-1946)

James Maxton was born in Glasgow, and educated at Hutcheson's Grammar School and Glasgow University. He was a teacher from 1906 to 1916, in which year he was imprisoned for an anti-war speech, which took the form of calling for a strike on the Clyde. Despite his radical politics — he was a member of the Independent Labour Party, and for a time a paid organiser of it — his sincerity and geniality won him friends in all parties. He was referred to as 'a beloved rebel'.

196. 'Stick to teaching'

To Mr Ibbotson *House of Commons 3 April 1944*

Dear Mr Ibbotson

Pardon my delay in answering your letter but I've been very busy. It is very difficult for me to advise you because it is so much a matter of one's own personal beliefs as to what is the right thing to do.

With reference to myself, you say I abandoned the teaching profession. That is scarcely the correct description. I was dismissed through matters arising out of my political activities. I do not believe in professional politicians, that is men who set out to make a career for themselves in politics. I believe in men and women throwing themselves into the Socialist movement wholeheartedly. If that should result in throwing them into parliament or prison. Good enough, but neither of these should have a primary objective.

With reference to a job in the political movement of the left, I think you'd find that socialist organisations, are like other prospective employers, they like to see some previous record of work in their line that indicates you have the qualities and capacities they want. My advice to you for what its worth is stick to teaching. It's a job worth doing, and although the first two or three years may be a little irksome till you've adjusted yourself to it, you'll probably find it getting more congenial. I would however transfer into some area which offers better opportunities than Worcester for work in your leisure time in Socialist politics, Cooperate movement or Trade Unionism, where you would gain knowledge and experience, and if you have the qualities necessary earn the reputation, esteem, and regard of your fellows, which might lead to responsible position in the working class movement.

Yours sincerely

JAS MAXTON

Edwin Muir (1887-1959)

Edwin Muir was a sensitive poet and critic obsessed with a personal vision of the fall from Eden, not unconnected with his own early experience: a sudden move from a farm in Orkney to poverty and family misfortune in Glasgow. Muir's personal circumstances—as it were having been driven out of Eden—and the social and political circumstances in the years before the outbreak of war in 1939, tended to give him a pessimistic view of the survival of Scottish literature and of Scotland as a nation. His expression of these views in Scott and Scotland *led to a notable controversy with Hugh MacDiarmid. Muir's sense of there being a spiritual dimension in human existence led him to write visionary poetry, some of it of great beauty. In the letters both sides of the man find expression.*

197. 'Scotland worth living in'

To George Thorburn   *Menton 14 May 1927*

. . . When we were in Scotland last time we heard a lot about Scottish Nationalism from C. M. Grieve (Hugh MacDiarmid) who wrote *A Drunk Man Looks at the Thistle*. It seems a pity that Scotland should always be kept back by England, and I hope the Scottish Republic comes about; it would make Scotland worth living in. Grieve is a strong nationalist, republican, socialist, and everything that is out and out. He thinks that if Scotland were a nation we would have Scottish literature, art, music, culture and everything that other nations seem to have and we haven't. I think that would probably be likely; but I feel rather detached, as I've often told Grieve, because after all I'm not Scotch, I'm an Orkney man, a good Scandinavian, and my true country is Norway, or Denmark, or Iceland, or some place like that. But this is nonsense, I'm afraid, though there's some sense in it, as Lizzie will agree. . .

Yours ever,

EDWIN

198. 'All great art is a wrestling with life'

My dear Sydney,
What can I say about your letter except that fundamentally, completely, when you talk about your attitude to life, I agree with you? Of course all great art is a wrestling with life, a facing, realisation, of everything in the artist and in the world outside him that he can see and that torments him and is a problem to him. From that surely comes the joy and the freedom which we find in great art. We feel that Shakespeare never turned aside from anything, and not because he did not suffer—he must have suffered monstrously —but because he had a passion greater than his suffering. We feel this too about Proust, to take an example much nearer us. I agree, too, that the people who only take art seriously, and not life, and especially themselves, can never produce significant work. And I feel absolutely sure of this, that only those who face the great issues of life, who enter into and therefore suffer with humanity, the struggles of their time, the whole thing, great and small, and put their witness, as if it were their signature, to it, can attain that joy which the great artists have felt; which I believe Baudelaire and Dostoevsky must have felt as much as Mozart. . .

As for your last point, what can I say? To myself I make no contradiction when I say that the artist should not be solitary and that his centre should be within himself. It is like saying that we are mankind and yet individuals. You mentioned the other day how galling it sometimes is that we cannot talk to all sorts of people; that we are cut off by modern life from all sorts of experience. I take this to mean finally that we all have a tremendous impulse to be united with humanity in some way; we get it, according to our natures, in becoming drunk, in joining societies, in becoming socialists, in working for 'humanity', in a hundred different ways. Union is as essential as separation, and the most profound union that can exist is that between a man and a woman in love. But the most essential thing in that union, it seems to me, is the unconscious out and in flowing of life between the two, which postulates both a physical and a spiritual correspondence between them, and is very like a process of nature, and is in any case as old as the hills. But this process strikes me as more like a free give and take, the freedom of two people who are united in one thing (their feeling towards each other) than like a unity. What is it that gives one thoughts, images and so on, in the centre of oneself? It is one's unconscious which is one's own from the cradle, but which a great experience can set free—a union with someone one loves, for instance. If marriage can do that, it does not matter how extreme may be what you call the tyranny of love, it is an entirely good thing. If it does not, then it is not good. But this is a very crude statement of the subtlest thing in the world. I do not agree here with your terms, and I have tried to put mine clearly. . .

199. The elimination of Scotland

To James Whyte   *Crowburgh 10 September 1931*

Dear Whyte,
Many thanks for your letter. I did not think that there was much immediate hope of an economically self-supporting Scottish literature—and it may be that there isn't ever any ultimate hope of it. You are on the spot, and far more in touch with things than I am; and your findings—with which I can do nothing but agree—are pretty hopeless. But if there is no ultimate hope of such a consummation—or even no hope of it in our life-time—I think I am clear too on this further point; that Scottish literature as such will disappear, and that London will become quite literally the capital of the British Isles in a sense that it has never yet quite been; that, in other words, it will become our national capital in just as real a sense as it is the capital of an ordinary English man to-day. How long it will take for this to happen it is impossible to say—a few centuries, or only one, what does it matter? 'Hugh McDiarmid' will become a figure like Burns—an exceptional case, that is to say—an arbitrary apparition of the national genius, robbed of his legitimate effect because there will be no literary tradition to perpetuate it. Scottish literature will continue to be sporadic—and being sporadic, it will be denied the name of a literature, and it seems to me rightly so. But for myself I feel so detached, when I look at this possibility objectively, that I cannot even quite exclude the thought that this resolution of the Scottish spirit, its disappearance finally into a larger spiritual group, to which it would inevitably contribute much, may be a consummation to be hoped for. At any rate, all things seem to me to be working for it: the fact that Scottish energy has gone mainly into international forms of activity, finance, industry, engineering, philosphy, science—forms of activity where one's nationality is irrelevant; the fact Scotsmen have helped to shape the industries of so many other countries and neglected their own: their almost complete blindness or indifference to the forms of activity in which the spirit of a nation most essentially expresses

itself—poetry, literature, art in general: all this, looked at from outside might almost make us imagine that Scotland's historical destiny is to eliminate itself in reality, as it has already wellnigh eliminated itself from history and literature—the forms in which a nation survives. But the really awful phase is the present one: we are neither quite alive nor quite dead; we are neither quite Scottish (we can't be, for there's no Scotland in the same sense that there is an England and a France), nor are we quite delivered from our Scottishness, and free to integrate ourselves in a culture of our choice. It was some such dim feeling as this that made me take up the question. The very words 'a Scottish writer' have a slightly unconvincing ring to me; what they come down to (I except Grieve, who is an exception to all rules) is a writer of Scottish birth. But when we talk of an English writer we do not think of a writer of English birth: we hardly think of such things at all. A Scottish writer is in a false position, because Scotland is in a false position. Yes that's what it comes down to; and now that I think of it, that is what fills me with such a strong desire to see Scottish Literature visibly integrated in a Scottish group living in Scotland for that would make the position unequivocal, or at least would be a first step towards doing it; it would not merely be a gesture, or an expedient, but a definite act, and therefore with a symbolical value. England can't digest us at the present stage, and besides one does not want to be digested—it is a shameful process—one wants to be there. And there is no there for Scotsmen. And the idea that there might be is, I feel sure, a dream. Like Scottish Nationalism and the great digestive act, Scotland will probably linger in limbo as long as the British Empire lasts. It seems inevitable.

All the same, at suitable opportunities, and when I feel like it, I am going to have a shot at advocating an indigenous Scottish school of literature in Scotland. I'm glad that you are thinking of writing an editorial about it. I think it should be pressed in the B.B.C. Don't you occasionally speak for them? The weekly review I pin little faith to: it would be inadequate for the purpose in any case. And I don't know why I brought the matter up at all except as a protest. It will have no effect in my own life, which will go on pretty much as it has gone, except for the possible accident that I may manage yet to write something better than I've written so far. Which is quite a praiseworthy wish.

To Sydney Schiff   *St Andrews 16 January 1939*

. . . Thanks for Broch's letter; Broch is a great man and a very good man. I don't know whether I agree or not with your opinion: that the only hope of the world lies in the gospel of Christ. As you know, I have believed for many years in the immortality of the soul; all my poetry springs from that in one form or another; and belief of that kind means belief in God, though my God is not that of the churches; and I can reconcile myself to no church. I have as little use for the materialistic doctrines of Communism as you have, and Fascism seems to me definitely evil. I look upon myself as an anti-Marxist socialist; a man who believes that people are immortal souls and that they should bring about on this earth a society fit for immortal souls. Immortality, unfortunately, does not make them good, and hardly any of them are conscious of immortality; they act for immediate and generally private and petty ends. Most of them no doubt have to do so for reasons of necessity; that should not be. I am quite clear in my mind that society must change, that Capitalism must be transcended; but if the change comes through the terrible Marxist machine of Materialist Determination, it will be a major calamity, for it denies the soul, and there cannot be a more fundamental denial than that. But everything is dark, and is getting darker: the horrible persecution of the Jews is the most obvious symptom of the madness which tinges all the new movement in Europe, but the movement itself threatens us all, threatens everything that we not merely hold dear, but everything necessary for a real living as apart from an ostensible one. There is a real denial of humanity here, as Broch says; there is more, a contempt for humanity, hatred of anyone with a separate, unique life of his own. The capacity to recognise immaterial realities is almost dead, it seems to me; is quite dead in the sphere of action at any rate, the sphere in which Hitler, Mussolini and Chamberlain move. And in the last resort we live by immaterial realities; that is our real life; the rest is more or less machinery. We are moved about, caught, wedged, clamped in this machinery; and that is what is called history.

I wish you both well and think often of you. I don't know when I shall see you again. I am as sick, I think, as you can be, over the dreadful things that are being done to the Jews, and the darkness that has fallen over them. I am ashamed, as every citizen in this country should be, of the part England has played. And I share, with everyone else, the part of the responsibility for it; for we have all been too easy-going and thoughtless and hopeful.

My love to you both,

To Willa Muir   *Bristol 12 March 1958*

My dearest Lamb,

Happy Birthday to Thee, and better and better ones as the years go on for us. I love thee, I shall always love thee, and I'm so happy that I shall see thee the day after thy birthday, so keep it for me. I would have preferred the 13th (dear old 13th) to the 14th: I put out a tentative feeler, but in vain. I must lecture to the students on the 14th at 10 a.m., and on nothing more exciting than T. S. Eliot. I shall get the 11.45 from here; if I'm lucky and the train is up to time I shall get the 2.24 Liverpool Street train to Cambridge, arriving at 3.24. If I miss that I shall have to put up with the 3.48 arriving at 5.15. Blessings on thee, my Jewel, and my love to thee. It's been very cold here; there was fresh snow on the ground this morning; now (I'm writing this before 12) it has all melted away, and the paths and the ground are wet and sopping. This milder weather is on the way to thee, and will reach thee, I prophesy, by the blessed Thirteenth.

How wonderful to think I'll see thee on Friday

Thy P.B.

I hope the necklet has arrived and that thu likes it.

Willa Muir (1885-1970)

Edwin Muir described his marriage to Willa as 'the most fortunate event of my life'. She commented at the end of Belonging, a memoir, 'we came to a lasting wholeness and joy in each other'. Yet two more different temperaments could hardly be imagined: Willa the extrovert, assertive, bustling, outspoken, giving the impression of dominating Edwin; and Edwin the introvert, sensitive, shy, avoiding conflict. Yet their collaborations in the translations of Kafka and of other European writers resulted in .what Willa described as 'a seamless garment'. The balance in the nature of the lovers may be observed in the contrast between Edwin's Birthday Letter, and Willa's response to a publisher's request for a description of her husband and of his life, even allowing for the one letter being private and the other a public communication.

202. Edwin Muir

To the Editor of The Bookman   *The Sonntagberg July* 1924

. . . Lived on a small island containing one tree (known as The Tree) till he was fourteen, avoiding school, ostensibly herding his father's cows (i.e. dreaming in the pasture while they ravaged the corn and turnips) and being spoilt by his mother because he was the youngest.

At the age of fourteen went to Glasgow; saw trains, elevators and street cars for the first time in his life. Learnt to use a knife and fork, and to wash daily. Attended church and was twice 'saved' before he struck Pascal and Nietzsche. Acquired a minute knowledge of the seamy side of Glasgow life, and a remarkable vocabulary. Developed a natural gift for contradictiousness.

Wrote his first book 'We Moderns' in the office (during office hours) without being discovered by his employers. Notoriously unpunctual, but seldom brought to book, because his fellow clerks spoilt him a little, just as his mother did. Received brilliant testimonials when he left to go to London, certifying that he could above all things be trusted with cash.

Went to London with 60 dollars, abetted by his wife, a reckless woman from the Shetland Islands, with whom he speaks in the barbarous dialect of these regions. In London he learned to choose wines and order drinks in Soho; escaped whenever possible to the country for week-ends.

Went to Prague because it was in the middle of Europe, and he knew nothing about it. Perhaps also because he could speak neither German nor Czech. After eight months of Prague, went to Germany, and succumbed to its influence completely. Stayed there for a year, began to write poetry, take sun-baths and wear sandals. Tried Italy next, and learned to swim; but driven by a longing for the North (disguised mother complex) returned to Salzburg and to Vienna. Can't live in a city in spring-time; and so is at present marooned on a mountain in Lower Austria. Future movements completely uncertain.

Personal Characteristics. Gives a general impression of quietness, gentle kindliness, and a little reserve. Black hair, blue eyes, very slim, small hands and feet, looks ridiculously young and won't say how old he is. Has an enormous forehead, like a sperm whale's; a fastidious, fleering and critical nose; an impish and sensuous mouth, a detached, aloof, cold eye. Witty when at his ease: elegant when he can afford it: sensitive and considerate: horribly shy and silent before strangers, and positively scared by social functions. Among friends, however, becomes completely daft, and dances Scottish reels with fervour. Smokes cigarettes continually: likes to lie in the sun by the hour: enjoys being petted: and is beloved by cats, dogs, small children, and nearly all women. (Women always want to mother him when they see him; but he has a horror of having his independence encroached upon.)

Passionately devoted to football, although now too short-sighted to play. Watches football matches for hours.

An unusual combination of clear thinking and passionate intuition.

Has a very Scottish look about him! But has been mistaken for Irish and Russian.

This is a true and (I believe) unprejudiced portrait.

James Bridie (O. H. Mavor 1888-1951)

Dr Osborne Henry Mavor practised medicine in his native city, Glasgow, until 1938, by which date, as James Bridie, he had two London theatre successes, Tobias and the Angel *and* The Anatomist, *followed by other witty, ingenious plays, such as* The Sleeping Clergyman, Mr Bolfry *and* Dr Angelus. *Bridie considered the critic of* The Observer, *St. John Ervine (who was also a dramatist), had failed to understand him and made the point in a correspondence that stretched over several years. We enter it with Bridie bristling.*

203. Bridie bristles

To St. John Ervine
          Gateside, Drymen, Stirlingshire
          3 December 1936

. . . As to the matter of my dramas, while I defer, naturally, to your enormous knowledge of the business, I still remember what one man thinks funny another thinks imbecile; that what St. Paul was excited about the intelligent Greeks thought foolishness; that there are I don't know how many ways of constructing tribal lays; and that only God knows whether I am right in inviting the customers into a plain decent-looking wagonette and then letting the horses bolt . . .

Two and a half years later feelings are still running high, Bridie having accused St. John Ervine of 'having a tendency to fall back on a snub, which is not in my book of Queensberry rules'. The accusation was rejected and Bridie lets the matter pass in a quip in his letter from North Berwick, but there are other matters of complaint.

204. Glasgow will not be patronised

To St. John Ervine   *North Berwick 5 June 1939*

Dear St. John Ervine

For SNUB read BUNS and forgive me.

But when you class me with the bruised and whining ones, you lie. London has treated me very well indeed, considering that it hasn't the faintest idea what, if anything, I am talking about.

That is why you must not attribute to me a series of mutton-headed opinions I do not hold. That is why you must not look down on Yorkshire from the Holy City of Belfast—nor on Glasgow which gave the world the internal combustion engine, political economy, antiseptic, aseptic and cerebral surgery, the balloon, the mariner's compass, the theory of Latent Heat, Tobias Smollett and James Bridie.

And pardon this long and illegible letter. I am having a holiday with sea-breezes and uneatable food. I wished to tell you that I respect you as an artist though not all your work rings bells in me. I think also the qualities that make you an artist absolutely invalidate you as a dramatic critic; but what do dramatic critics matter anyhow?

I also want you to know that I may be a B.F. but that I am entirely different from the kind of B.F. you have visualised from time to time in your fertile Irish imagination.

And further, if *Bridge Head* had been about a Higher grade Civil Servant in Kensington or Napoleon or Kubla Khan and had been as well written and as badly neglected, I should have been all for it. Good God, what makes you think I admire the Irish for their own sakes? I live in Glasgow, I tell you.

Ever yours,

JAMES BRIDIE

The correspondence had a happy ending. Bridie met St. John Ervine at the Edinburgh Festival and they became good friends.

205. 'Rabelaisian decency'

To Neil Gunn   *6 Woodlands Terrace, Glasgow*
9 January 1932

. . . it might amuse me and perhaps you if I put into 100 words what I think of Rabelaisian decency.

Talking smut is a relief to what I suppose are one's pent-up reproductive instincts, and a very pleasant and harmless one too. Smut is the by-product (useless) of the phantasies, and ideas and impulses that go to the reproduction mill. Talking smut is therefore analogous to the pleasant but unseemly act of defecation. . . . But hypocrisy, in moderation, is oil to the wheels, a concession to society, lots of other excellent things.

Now copulation is a sweet and necessary act . . . It is, like defecation, an exceedingly interesting process; but it is much better described in physiological text books than in all the works of all the novelists ancient and modern who ever existed. What is interesting is the emotional colouring that mankind has added to the act; and this, making all allowances for differences in craftsmanship, is as well understood by Miss Annie S. Swan as by Mr A. Huxley. So while it may occasionally be an artist's job to describe these oddities which make man, the animal, such an entertaining contrast (in some ways) to man, the spirit, I do deprecate the perpetual recurrence in every bloody book I pick up of serious attempts to shock old ladies. Now old ladies have made much greater progress in the art of living than most young novelists, and what is repellant to them is not improbably inconsistent with an orderly development of society.

And so to bed . . .

☆ ☆ ☆

A Flyting of Novelists

Neil M. Gunn   v   Naomi Mitchison
(1891-1973)   (1897-   )

Neil Gunn, the son of a fisherman from Dunbeath, Caithness, told his stories with zest and directness, with close observations of his place—land and sea—and of his people. His most famous novel, The Silver Darlings *(1941), has been described as 'a folk epic'. He is fascinated by the completeness of a child's life, which he celebrated in the story of a boy in* Morning Tide *(1931). Ultimately he draws attention to the mystery of life. When the boy in* Highland River *(1937) sets out on his journey in the strath, it becomes a symbolic journey. This view coloured Neil Gunn's politics, as may be sensed in the dialogue between the novelists in the letters. First Neil Gunn states the limitation of administrative change.*

206. 'Beyond revolution'

Gunn to Mitchison   *Braefarm House, Dingwall*
                                              18 April 1943

. . . As to your three ways of changing things profoundly—cheers. There are probably a dozen methods of attack. And we should be beyond revolution in the bloody sense. We have had about enough blood for our lifetimes. At least that's the way I feel. But then I have always been a little repelled by the materialist interpretation of history and all the rest when it becomes the new religion. Religion and ideals and what not. Fine. But oh God they do manage to prosecute them to the nth in cruelty. A drunk man with a revolver is a happy child compared with the fellow who has power to convert you. Anyway, if history is to have any meaning at all, surely hundreds of years of understanding of the democratic concept as we have had it in Scotland must count for something. If not—if we have to copy Russia or somebody else—then don't expect us to be impressed. After all, take the organisation of the Scottish church, from kirk session or local soviet up to the General Assembly and you might say it gave Russia its governmental pattern. What a wealth of belief and enthusiasm and shedding of blood went to that foundation! And what do you enlightened revolutionaries think and say of it today? At least we have something to go on. Which is my whole case for Scotland. I know what you mean when you say that it's no good just altering things so that folk can go twice a week to the films instead of once. But that's precisely what they'll do however you alter things. What could be altered for the better is the community spirit and the kind of flicks. Though here again I am not sure that the highbrows should have it their own way. Before you came to Carradale and found what country living really meant, would you have been a sound person to have been placed in charge of their entertainment? And could we have relied on you to have shown generally the model behaviour pattern for such a reformed community? Of course we can now, I know . . .

The wide range of counselling and practical activities of Lady Naomi Mitchison—she was awarded the Palmes de l'Académie Francaise and adopted as Tribal Adviser and Mmarona (mother) to the Baggatha of Botswana—may have obscured her achievement as a novelist. Like Neil Gunn she has an interest in folk material and in childhood but her approach is different. She has written children's books, The Big House *(1950), and she has used the history of the Haldanes—her brother was the scientist, J. B. S. Haldane—as material for her historical novel,* The Bull Calves *(1947). Her most notable novel is* The Corn King and the Spring Queen *(1931). Her home has been at Carradale, Kintyre, since 1937.*

207. 'Bloody centralising'

Mitchison to Gunn   *Carradale 31 May 1944*

. . . Do you ever feel with a book, sometimes by an author you've never met or even heard of before, this book was written for me? I feel that awfully with the Green Land and I keep wondering how many people are going to get it. It certainly isn't for the same audience that you appear to have been writing for earlier (I say appear advisedly, because the most unexpected do read you). I don't expect I've got it entirely on a first reading, indeed that's not likely, and I don't know whether, for instance, Merk and Axle—Axel?— are other people. And I don't know if your girl is a girl I met at a party at the Soviet Embassy and she looked at us all the time as if we weren't real but rather frightening kinds of images. But you've laid down a challenge which I feel bound to take up.

I think first, all the same, I ought to say what you no doubt know already, that it's a damn good piece of writing. You are amazingly good at describing the pleasures of the senses, particularly eating. It wouldn't surprise me, though, if you thought eating was slightly wicked—somewhere far back in your mind no doubt. And it's full of the loveliest winged bits.

But it is in effect the anarchist case. Now in so far as it is saying: power corrupts, that's fine. I think it also says purely intellectual power corrupts, the worst thing is the power of the bureaucrat, the planner at head-quarters. And you are completely contemptuous of the idea that anything can be planned 'from the bottom up'. Well, it seems to me that it's got to be, and very largely has been, and where the Communist party has failed, the thing they planned has failed too. And it's pretty essential that your members should not be a secret society but open prodders—liable to be bumped off if they annoy people too much. And all the big people, especially Lenin, knew that they themselves couldn't plan alone or with an elite, they had to have the 'correct contact with the masses' which is as real a thing as direct contact of the mystic—or the electric cable. There is a good deal of this in a recent Penguin 'Soviet Light on the Colonies', some of it very applicable to Scotland. You won't read it, I suppose? In war this bloody centralising is probably inevitable, but you don't get a Red Army made up of people whose souls have been killed or are in the process of being killed.

I think they probably have killed the soul considerably in Germany and town people go, for the reasons you suggest, more easily than country people. But I think we'd better all go to Russia after the war and have a look at some fishing co-operatives.

The thing is, you've got to have something as strong as the Communist party to stand up to the other side, even in the Highlands. Here are all your grand anarchists, the civilised peasants, the men like my Denny MacIntosh here who have a kind of gentleness and nobility that makes one feel one would die to defend it, and they are at the mercy of capitalism and are quite incapable of not being crushed, for the old shifts won't serve. The economic base will be changed under them while they are busy poaching a salmon and they won't be able to evade change, and the old delights will cease to seem worthwhile.

Here now is Carradale which is a step nearer Glasgow than Clachdrum — but that is only a matter of a generation or so. Now it is all disintegrating, not because of the pressure of totalitarian war (the boys would probably have left anyhow as there are no houses for them, and in general they are rather prosperous) but because of the pressure of the values of good old Liberal competitive capitalism — of course turning rapidly towards monopoly capitalism, as they'll find when a few more of them have sold their boats (I saw you had a bit about that in the Record). Their women aren't like

Highland Mary, at least ninety per cent of them aren't. They don't have generous impulses, they are out to grab every little advantage like the girls who get the boys in the strip advertisements. Underneath, but getting increasingly deep under, there is the remains of the other standards of value, but I see no chance, Neil, none, of that surviving without a revolution. If we could organise Carradale with a soviet (or call it anything else, the name doesn't matter), making people take responsibility and run their own lives which is the beginning of democracy, and discussing every kind of thing with some chance of being effective, then the place would come alive. Just now the farmers are all co-operating more or less — more since we had the big thresher which meant working in a team — but after the war are we to go back to bargaining and cheating and struggling for points? Can't we be allowed to be the servants of the community, giving the best we can grow, not having to think of everything in cash terms? We can't be as things are. There's been a correspondence in the Scottish Farmer lately, about how lovely it is to be a crofter, such a good life for the children and all that — fine so long as crofting is subsidised! But it isn't real. We've got to get capitalism off our backs, and I don't see how we can do it by just being anarchists. The individual may, but what's the good of being free if our neighbours whom we love aren't free? And how can we defeat capitalism except by some weapon such as the communist party.

I suppose I must remind you again that I'm not a communist. I may be yet, but I don't for various reasons care for the party in this country. Perhaps I'm wrong though . . .

208. 'Dehydrated potato'

Gunn to Mitchison   *Brae, Dingwall 9 June 1944*

. . . If I'm a queer devil, Naomi, you're an incalculably charming woman. And that's it in a nutshell, in this literary business anyway. Unless we're concerned with life in its vivid living moments, we should take to pamphlets. Incalculably living, aware that it should be beneath everything, the reason for everything, and its last meaning. Hellsbells, woman, I've just been listening to the news, and have been told with triumph that we shall soon be able to get dehydrated potato which we can mix with a little water and find indistinguishable from normal mash. And you—even you—acted upon unconsciously by psycho-analytic news, suggest that I—me— think eating wicked, somewhere far ben! Really appalling. When I consider the number of women who don't know how to boil a potato. When I think of the food we have in the Highlands and how it isn't cooked. Lord, the flavour of a golden wonder, steamed in its jacket, until it bursts its coat in laughter. An oatcake that is really crisp. Butter, real butter on that oatcake. Heather honey. Our berries. Our game. Our prime herring. Hill mutton . . . I refuse to talk to you about it. You'll be calling me a gourmet next. Go away.

How delightful of you to utter the ultimate compliment by saying that you think the Green Isle was written for you. That sort of living response would make anyone write a book. In fact I wrote the Green Isle right off, just because an old friend of mine in Ireland, who has mostly for company now his little grandson, was so affected by what he considered the inner truth of YOUNG ART that he said I mustn't leave them at the River. So I didn't. Can you think of any better reason for writing a book?

And when you accuse me of anarchism, do you mean the anarchism of Kropotkin or just individual chaos? There's a mighty difference. That the herring fishermen should be in a cooperative is anarchism. That they should be run by a State herring industry Board is — what? I have been a socialist all my life, and still am, but I have always been aware of the servile state.

. . . Think of what your criticism amounts to. My book is against fascism. You take it as being against Communism. Now isn't that a thought! . . .

☆   ☆   ☆

Hugh MacDiarmid
(Christopher Murray Grieve) (1892-1978)

It is not surprising that the present century in Scotland has been described as the Age of MacDiarmid. He was a powerful, if uneven, poet who enlarged the intellectual range of Scottish poetry and gave fresh vitality to the Scots language. His tireless campaign for Scottish independence and the renaissance of Scottish culture transformed the intellectual and political atmosphere in Scotland. David Murison wrote of him: 'There is one other Scot, at first blush an unlikely candidate for comparison, who is his spiritual ancestor—John Knox; in him we have the same extremist absolutism, the same unrestrained vituperative argumentativeness. . . After MacDiarmid, as after Knox, Scotland will never be the same place again.' Of course, not everyone approved of him.

The publication in 1984 of an edition by Alan Bold of MacDiarmid's letters (900 pages, but far from complete) revealed him as a prolific and vigorous letter writer. The letters show a fundamental consistency beneath the surface contradiction, and kindess and courtesy behind the extremity and vituperation.

209. His early life

To George Ogilvie

Somewhere in Macedonia
20 August 1916

Dear Mr Ogilvie:-
The Sergeant-Caterer of the Officers' Mess (that's my new post in our little military world here) has to go 'on deck' at dinner—dinner commencing at 7.30 p.m. and running to some five courses—freshly shaven, boots and buttons mirror-bright, properly dressed with belt and all. He does nothing, of course, save supervision. A spot of tarnish on a knife or fork—lack-lustre of a wine glass—uneven flaming of one of the hanging lamps—slackness on the part of the waiters—slow, slovenly, or uneven dishing-up on the part of the cooks—what an eye one develops for detail on such a job! Between the Mess-Marquee, and the Mess cook-house, is a strip of open hillside over which the waiters run backwards and forwards in the moony Macedonian night. Brightly the beams fall on platefuls of white vegetable soup, patum peperium entrées, portions of cottage pie enlivened with rice-stuffed peppers, liberal helpings of rice and raisins, coffee pots and later when the Mess has come to the walnuts and almonds and the wine-steward is busy supplying Vin Blanc, Vin Russe, or Vin Muscat de Samos (my favourite wine, recalling with every sip the wonderful tribute of a poem of Mr Sturge Moore's and unreservedly endorsing every adjective therein), the Sergeant-Caterer and his staff dine too. (What an awful war, to be sure!). . .

210. The death of Lewis Grassic Gibbon
(Leslie Mitchell)

To Mrs Rhea Mitchell   *Whalsay, Shetland Islands*
                                          12 April 1935

My dear Rhea,
Valda (who will be writing to you herself) and I were very glad to
get your letter on Wednesday. We were worrying about you and
wearying to hear what was happening. Do not take this as any
reproach for not writing us sooner. We did not expect that knowing
the shattering grief and subsequent burdens you have had. I know
of the Scottish PEN's effort to help and I knew about the Royal
Literary Society hope. I am more than relieved to hear of the latter's
grant: I know of course that alas! it won't go far—but it is a great
help at the moment—and the Scottish PEN will do their best too. I
haven't heard from Helen for a week or two but she had told me
you thought of getting back into the Civil Service—it is terrible to
think that even if you do the pay is so inadequate. It is impossible in
circumstances like yours to say or do anything that does not seem
horribly helpless and irrelevant. I agree with all you say about the
wanton cruelty and utter senselessness of such a bereavement—and
personally I can accept that; it squares with my irrationalist
philosophy of life—but what I do find absolutely appalling and
unendurable is not the ultimate meaninglessness from any human
standpoint, but the fact that within our human scheme of things it
should be added to by readily preventible ills which are in many
ways still more immediately torturing and terrible. However
brutally and unintelligibly the blind forces of nature cut across all
that seems decent and reasonable, there is no earthly reason why to
such unspeakable outrages on human sensibility should be added
horrible economic jeopardies and humiliation, and obligations of
drudgery and anxiety superimposed on the irreparable loss. The
latter—the thrust-back of the hapless victims into toil and need, and
the intolerable savaging and neutralising of the best human hopes
and efforts—is perfectly avoidable. In other words, I can face up to
the inhuman cosmic course of things and have no religious belief of
any sort or any consolation derived from from a philosophy that
relies on ultimate good in any human sense of the term; but every
fibre of my being protests to the uttermost against the needless
degradations and difficulties that arise from a remediable economic
system. I am terribly touched by all you say of the children and the
sudden reversal and circumscription of their happy and promising
lot. It is sheerly damnable and I have, I am afraid, no point of
contact with those who find any means of comfort in religious or

other fugues from reality; and yet I know how supremely difficult it is while refusing to relapse on such false consolations to tackle the day-to-day burden bravely. But it is useless, at least in a letter, to try to pass on such an attitude. I am glad, anyhow, that Muir, Linklater, Ivor Brown and others have rallied to your support and I feel sure that they, and others of the Scottish PEN and outside it, will continue to stand by you and the children in any and every way they possibly can. . .

Kisses to the children from all of us and every warm good wish to yourself.

Yours,

CHRIS

P.S. I have said nothing of Leslie, or about the details you give of the illness which a better doctor or prompter treatment might have kept from being fatal. I agree with all you say yourself and find myself instinctively trying not to think about it all—it has hit me very badly too. I cannot trust myself to say more.

211. The literati in war-time

Douglas Young (1913-73), classical scholar, poet and polemicist, has been described as 'Scottish Nationalist and patriot, internationalist and polyglot, physically and intellectually a big man, . . . one of the most original and gifted Scotsmen of his generation'. MacDiarmid sent the following letter to him when he was in Saughton Prison in Edinburgh under sentence for his refusal to accept the right of a British government to apply conscription in Scotland. See also Letters 224, 225.

To Douglas Young   *35 Havelock Street, Glasgow*
                                                      17 January 1943

My dear Douglas,

It was a great treat to have your letter and your own assurance that you are, all things considered, in such excellent health and spirits. As requested, I have written to your mother and to David Murison. I hear from MacLellan that the latter has at last returned the proofs of *Auntran Blads* and hope this book will be forthcoming speedily now. Sorley was wounded in both feet at the Battle of El Alamein and is in hospital in Egypt. I hope that while entailing no permanent crippling these wounds may secure his return to this country and his discharge from the Army soon. I am writing him tonight. MacLellan tells me Sorley's poems are now in book form and expresses his satisfaction with Wm. Crosbie's illustrations thereto. I am looking forward keenly to this volume also. I have not heard of or from Hay for a long time now, but Scott's settings of some of his lyrics were included in the recent Edinburgh concert programme of Scott's songs and scored a great hit. They are really magnificent . . .

As you perhaps heard some months ago I had a very serious accident at work—pulled a pile of copper plate down on myself and disabled both legs and one of my arms. I was extremely lucky not to be killed. My injuries responded excellently to treatment and while I was off work for weeks and even after I returned was a pathetic sight hobbling about with the aid of walking sticks, I was speedily O.K. again except for a slight limp of the left leg, which since it is due to a severe rupture of the muscles, will probably continue to affect me for years—but happily does not prevent my working, entail any pain, nor impede my movements.

It is splendid to think that if all goes well you'll be amongst us again in a matter of eight weeks now. We must have a real celebration. It will be a great occasion.

Congratulations on your great spirit, and every cordial greeting and good wish.

Au revoir

Yours,

CHRISTOPHER

212. 'Not only flame, but a lot of rubbish'

To George Bruce   *Brownsbank, Candymill, by Biggar*
                                        1 July 1964

Dear George,
Many thanks for the script of the discussions on Walter Keir's review of Buthlay's book. What you say in your note in expansion of Alex Scott's remark re my being 'the worst poet' I of course understand perfectly. The necessity of being honest with oneself—i.e. exhibiting one's weaknesses as well as one's strengths—is not generally understood. Alex Scott is quite right—but it is part of the image I have always tried to project that it should be so. It would not have suited my book at all to be faultless. My job, as I see it, has never been to lay a tit's egg, but to erupt like a volcano, emitting not only flame, but a lot of rubbish.

All the best.

Yours,

CHRIS

The Rev Anthony Ross OP   *Brownsbank 22 September 1967*

Dear Father Ross,
Many thanks for your letter of 20th inst. re *Scottish International*,
and inviting me to become one of the five trustees. I note that Alex
Gibson of the SNO is also being invited to be one of the trustees.

You say: '*When you have more information about what is aimed
at* we hope you will honour us by becoming one of the five
trustees.' I will certainly need a great deal more information.
Pending that, please regard this reply as merely provisional. My
suspicions may not be well founded but I think it necessary to be
quite frank and to say that I regard the whole matter with the
gravest suspicion.

I have devoted many years to seek to overcome the inability of
the academic authorities and literary circles in many countries to
recognise that Scotland is a separate and a very different country
from England, that Scotland has an independent literary tradition at
odds in many vital respects with the English tradition—and that it
has always been, and remains, the aim of the latter to eliminate the
former and assimilate Scottish Standards completely to English.
Government agencies like the Arts Council, the British Council,
British consulates, etc. have pursued this policy and been largely
responsible for the general identification abroad of what is merely
English as British, and these agencies have actively endeavoured to
frustrate my efforts to give foreign countries a true sense of
Scotland's difference, of the need for Scotland to build on its own
separate traditions without regard to England, and in particular to
revive our native languages, Scots and Gaelic . . .

I think you will agree that I cannot lend my name and influence
to a project which does not accept as of prime importance the
encouragement of Scots and Gaelic, the necessity of Scottish
Independence, and the recognition that in contradistinction to the
situation in England a deep-seated Radicalism is the chief, and an
irreversible, element of the Scottish political tradition and a prime
requirement of Scottish conditions today and henceforth.

Unless therefore I can be assured that these matters are all
safeguarded in a way in keeping with the programme I have pursued
for the past half-century I am not only unable to be associated with
the project in any way but will be obliged to expose its real aims and
to oppose its development in every way I can.

Also, I note you stress that the new organ is designed to be
essentially encouraging to the under thirties. Personally I have
always sought to encourage and help new Scottish writers no matter

of what age. But I view with deep suspicion the stress laid on the young. There are always thousands of literary aspirants, not one per cent of them ever come to anything of consequence, and the effect of encouraging young writers generally is simply to ham-string the development with an ever-heavier weight of mediocrity. I am quite opposed to the way in which the Arts Council's bursaries for writers operates. I am sure no good can come of it, and certainly the objectives for Scotland with which I am mainly concerned cannot be served in this way.

Ever since you gave the memorable lecture on my poetry I have hoped we might meet again and get to know each other better. I am therefore all the more sorry to have to give a reply to your letter which may seem churlish and unhelpful. But on reflection I am sure you will agree that I have no option, and that the tenor of my letter in no way runs counter to my high regard and good wishes for yourself.

Yours sincerely,

CHRISTOPHER GRIEVE

214. 'Nothing popular'

To George Bruce   *Brownsbank 9 May 1971*

Dear George,
Just a line to congratulate you on the Glasgow University Fellowship and wish you the best of luck with it. I've just been listening to the Bookmark discussion on Arts Council grants to authors. I think University fellowships much better—tho' I would never have liked one myself . . .

Anyhow so far as encouragement of Literature is concerned I think one criterion should be that nothing popular or likely or designed and intended by the author to give the public what it wants should be encouraged at all but on the contrary discouraged by every possible means. Literary value is not a matter of opinion— there are objective standards independent altogether of whether many people or indeed any like or dislike a particular work or not.

All the best to Mrs Bruce and yourself.

Yours,

CHRIS

Joe Corrie (1894-1968)

Corrie started work in the Fife coalfield at the age of 14 in 1908. The labour troubles of the 1920s, when Corrie found himself on the dole, made him a writer. He wrote articles, poems and short stories for The Miner, *the newspaper of the Fife miners. He turned to plays, including* In Time O' Strife, *which toured Scotland with a company composed of miners and their wives from Corrie's own mining village.*

215. 'Hewers of Coal'

To J. Archibald Henderson   *25 November 1949*

Dear Archie,

Hoo the hell are ye gettin' on. I often think aboot ye but it's ay when I'm writin' a play and my typewriter is engaged, and I say 'when I get to the end o' this page I must write to Erchie and see hoo he' gettin' on'. But I forget and afore I mind again I'm half way through anither page. And that's hoo it's been gaun on for weeks. But I ha'e been thinkin' aboot ye maist o' the day the-day, for some reason or ither, and altho' I'm ready to pop into my bed, and I'm in my pyjammies, I feel it a duty to drap ye this wee note just to hope that ye keep weel and happy and wish that you'll bide like that for a lang time to come.

When are ye gaun tae Ameriki? And what are ye dain' wi' the dramatics—if onythin'? Drap me a wee note some time sune and let me hear aboot your ongauns.

I ha'e been a hell o' a busy man since I wrote tae ye last—plays, by God!—they're jist spewin' frae me, and nane o' them what ye could ca' tripe either, altho' that has become sic a luxury that we'll need to be gettin' anither word to tak' it's place in the literary world—sossidge, I think, would be mair appropriate.

Is the wife keepin' weel? And the weans? And are ye still teetotal? And hoo is your freen', the gaffer up by, and his faim'ly? A'weel, I hope, and lookin' furrit to the New Year to forget aboot what wee worries they may ha'e ower a dram.

The festival'll sune be awa' again and there'll be a wheen determined to murder some o' my plays nae doot—but there's nae guid o' me bein' angry wi' them for the puir sowls dae their best. (There's naebody does bad if they ken hoo tae dae guid—and that I think, gets to the core o' the hale thing—damned ignorance). But nae doot some o' them'll blame my plays, and in some cases they'll be justified. But what does it maitter. A hunner year' efter this there'll be nane o' us here. Of coorse there's ay the chance that Auld Nick rins a dramatic club—a body never kens. If he does I'll ask to get to Heaven oot o' their road.

It's a guid lang while since I felt sae weel mysel' and sae happy forby. The better I can work the happier I am. It would just be terrible for me if somebody forced me to work a five day week.

Seein' you're on the back shift if ye listen to the wireless on Friday forenoon at eleven forty in the Schules programme you'll hear somebody tryin' their hand at HEWERS OF COAL. But dinna let it keep ye frae gaun to the pit for I wadna like to ha'e the name o' keepin' ony man frae enjoyin' himsel'. Just tak' a good stiff dram to yoursel' and say 'To hell wi' that man Coarrie, he just leives for daithes and distasters' . . .

Weel, I canna sit a' nicht here in my pyjammies, for the fire's gaun doon and I can feel a wee cauld in pairts, so I'll just bid ye a' guid nicht—I mean, guid mornin', and leive in hope o' gettin' a latter frae ye afore the year is oot.

Maist Sincerely,

JOE

John Grierson (1898—1972)

Grierson was one of the great creative forces in the evolution of the documentary film, through his work for the Empire Marketing Board, the GPO Film unit, the Films of Scotland Committee and the National Film Board of Canada. His influence was world-wide and modern television technique owes much to it. Most of his adult life was spent outside Scotland, but, as his biographer Forsyth Hardy says, he 'was never in spirit far from his native country'. He was direct, egalitarian, unpretentious, kindly and convivial in a manner that is essential Scottish.

Saltire Review, to which the following letter was sent, was a quarterly published by the Saltire Society (1954-61) and continued as New Saltire (1961-64). It is a valuable source for work by most of the important Scottish writers of the time.

216. 'A Scottish film industry'

To the Editor, Saltire Review   *Glasgow 14 June 1960*

Sir,—You ask me: is a Scottish film industry possible? My own answer is no. You remember the burghers of Calais who, poor souls, failed to fire a salute for the English King and were up, hats off, on the royal mat. They said they had seven good reasons to advance. They duly advanced them cogently and in great detail, one by one. The seventh was that they had no guns. Don't let us fool ourselves. It is not in the Scottish mind or heart these days to risk the necessary dough. Ask that old warrior Compton Mackenzie.

My own experience in seeking money from Scotsmen has been short, swift and, I am happy to say, slight. I only once tried and I suspected from the beginning I was being a damn fool. I wanted to make a Scottish picture on a straight-forward commercial basis. The funny thing was that I didn't really need the money. I was at the outset offered all I needed in London. But no, I wanted to do it the hard way. I thought it was good in principle to get my fellow citizens gambling on pictures and on the end-money moreover. So I insisted and I persisted and, boy, did I come unstuck.

I never tried again or ever would. Film-making belongs like all show business to that magical world in which two and two can make five, but also three or even less. It is, by that token, not a business to which the presbyterian mind is natively and naturally attuned.

Just in case you get things mixed up and think of the honourable Scottish names associated with the film industry, let me say that I am aware of none at the risking end of the business, which is where the good producer dies a little. We have turned out able exhibitors and distributors and the *Cosmo* and the *Cameo* are specialised cinemas of European repute which have taken many a shot in the dark. But their kind of risk is a short-term risk and I never saw either an exhibitor or a distributor suffer from heart-break.

Give him a money book with a couple of columns and he will stop the tear-drop dead in its tracks. 'Go down the middle, go down the middle,' John Maxwell used to say to me. It was Scottish advice at its best. I am sure John Maxwell was sorry that I never went about it the right way and quite unhappy that I wasn't making as much money as he was. But going down the middle doesn't make pictures: at least the pictures you would wish to put to your country's credit. . .

The only true analogy is the role of the old village dominie whose honour lay in backing the lads o' parts and obscuring his own role in the encouraging of others. Find two or three of these and you will have your Scottish films; and I see no reason why the country which once produced dominies shouldn't find them again for our film purposes. It involves a certain measure of selflessness but it has its compensations. As with the old dominies, the opportunities for dedication—and even a certain calculated arrogance—are considerable.

I won't go much further than this for the present. We have a Films of Scotland Committee which guides the making of several Scottish films every year. They have done well in an ordinary sort of way. I am a member and cast this cabbage happily in my own face. I am not worried about The Films of Scotland Committee, even if you say, as I do, that what mostly it has to be proud of is the Scottish scenery in its films, which it owes strictly to the Almighty . . .

It is of course the example that counts. It is the example in method, the example in approach, the example in understanding between patronage and the creative effort, which a single success can sanctify. Get the basic conditions right, as Kant said long ago, and the reality follows. At least in the long run it follows. You want Scottish films? Tell the Scottish Development Council, tell the public authorities, tell the industries to imaginate about themselves and you will get your Scottish films. But please forget all that business about traditions as such, as Scottish culture as such and, yes, even Scottish writers as such—forget all about them. There are many ways of skinning a cat and these may not be the most immediate considerations for the imaginative knacker.

Yours faithfully,

JOHN GRIERSON

William Soutar (1898–1943)

The indomitable spirit of William Soutar, the Perth poet, triumphed over an illness which confined him to bed for nearly thirteen years until his death. His main achievement was in his poems in Scots which ran from humorous character creation to singing lyrics. His diaries, journals and letters are also to be valued. Naturally he had a special interest in the growing body of poetry in Scots. When Edwin Muir gave his verdict in Scott and Scotland *that the only way forward for a Scottish poet was to give up Scots, Soutar reviewed the book in MacDairmid's* The Voice of Scotland *(June-August 1938) in a remarkably detached way: 'One can sympathise with the critics who maintain that the Scottish poet must accept the ready-made vehicle of English as his only solution. . .' In a letter Soutar describes the different uses of English and Scots.*

To George Bruce   27 Wilson Street, Perth
13 August 1941

. . .You also convince me, if I yet require it, how much of Rilke is beyond the compass of Scots. This is not altogether a deficiency in vocabulary but because Rilke is so individual an artist, and Scots by historical necessity is essentially communal. Purely as a linguistic movement I see no promise of a growing revival, merely a temporary outcropping; and Muir's analysis in 'Scott & Scotland' is in the main correct within this orbit. What Muir failed to apprehend was that the re-awakened interest in Scots, such as it is, was symptomatic of social forms of government. Even from the aesthetic viewpoint it can be regarded as a protest against the over-erudite, esoteric, private and intellectualised tendencies in contemporary verse: a gesture feeble enough in practise but significant in its alignment. For it is a false assumption that a complicated age conditions a complicated art: in the end what we mean by complexities are but the excrescences upon a central problem; and ours is the re-establishment of community.

I have always thought it paradoxical that Auden & Co. should have come forward to speak for the ordinary man in the accents of Hopkins and Eliot: Yeats, in his later work, as I now realise, could have taught them otherwise; for I am convinced that contemporary art, if it is to be the voice of brotherhood, must become direct, bare, and simple in the true meaning of the word. . .

Lewis Grassic Gibbon (1901-35)
(James Leslie Mitchell)

The outstanding achievement of Lewis Grassic Gibbon is now recognised in his trilogy, Scots Quair, *and especially in* Sunset Song. *His genius is seen in the dramatic and flexible use to which he puts his Aberdeenshire speech, in his characters and in his powerful Scottish-English prose through which he expressed a passionate indignation at cruelties, injustices and bigotries, and his deep feeling for the land. Helen Cruickshank wrote to Gibbon complaining about his dwelling on cruelty in* Sunset Song. *In this letter he responds.*

218. 'Horrors do haunt me'

To Helen Cruickshank   *107 Handside Lane, Welwyn Garden City*
18 November 1935

... Yes, horrors do haunt me. That's because I'm in love with humanity. Ancient Greece is never the Parthenon to me: it's a slave being tortured in a dungeon of the Athenian law-courts; Ancient Egypt is never the Pyramids; it's the blood and tears of Goshen; Ancient Scotland is never Mary Queen; it's those serfs they kept chained in the Fifeshire mines a hundred years ago. And so on. And so with the moderns; I am so horrified by all our dirty little cruelties and bestialities that I would feel the lowest type of skunk if I didn't shout about the horror of them from the house-tops. Of course I shout too loudly. But the filthy conspiracy of silence there was in the past!—and is coming again in Scotland, in a new guise, called Renaissance, and Objectivity, and National Art and what not. Blithering about Henryson and the Makars (whoever these cretins were) and forgetting the Glasgow slums. . .

Moray Maclaren (1901-71)

Moray Maclaren made his first television broadcast on St Andrew's Day 1953 from the manse of Dunbarnie in Perthshire. A prolific writer, he was at his best when he described with gusto and affection his native city, Edinburgh, in his book, Capital City *(1950). It was characteristic of the man that when he decided to write* The Highland Jaunt, *as Samuel Johnson called the tour of the highlands of Scotland which he made with his biographer, James Boswell, he not only covered the ground of the eighteenth-century travellers, he went on horse from Inverness. He identifies himself with both characters with relish. When, however, he describes the impact of the broadcast on himself in a letter to Gordon Gildard, Head of BBC Scottish Programmes, we hear the effusiveness of Boswell as Moray Maclaren savours the applause for himself. It is a pity James Logie Baird (1886-1946) did not live to know the impact of his invention on a fellow countryman.*

29 Inverleith Row, Edinburgh
                                          4 December 1953

My dear Gordon

Now that the heat and dust of the TV broadcast is dying down, I am beginning to get a clearer view of the picture. Let me say at once that I thoroughly enjoyed doing it and that I think it was really worthwhile. The usual spate of letters is arriving, and so far none but the most loudly congratulatory. But what really does impress me is the impact sight broadcasting seems to make as compared with sound. I must have broadcast on sound some 400 to 500 times, and a number of times at peak listening hours, i.e., immediately after the news, etc., but never have I experienced such an immediate result. I can scarcely walk down Princes Street without being stopped every 200 yards or so by perfect strangers who wish to say something pleasant about it.

I had occasion to go into the High Court of Session two days ago. The Judge obviously recognised me, though I did not know him: the Advocates in Parliament Hall crowded round me afterwards. And so it goes on. I won't belabour the point, but certainly as far as Edinburgh goes, it seems that everyone has a television set and everyone saw and heard me. It is quite fantastic, and very agreeable, except that it puts paid to any private life, and I shall have to watch my step about any, even the mildest, misbehaviour in future . . .

Eric Henry Liddell (1902–45)

Eric Liddell, athlete and missionary, was born at Tientsin in China, where his father was a missionary. His education began in the village of Drymen, Stirlingshire, on the return of his parents on leave. His major athletic achievements were recorded while he was a student at Edinburgh University and Heriot Watt College, culminating in his winning the Gold Medal for the 400 metres, breaking the world record for the distance, in the Paris Olympics of 1924. He deliberately missed the chance of a second gold medal by refusing to run on Sunday, which was the climax of the film about Eric Liddell, Chariots of Fire.

He saw such achievements as of secondary importance. First he was a missionary Christian, in which capacity he returned to China in 1925. By 1938 communications about Tientsin were disrupted by the Japanese and travel was dangerous, as will be gathered from this letter describing a return journey to the hospital at Siaochang.

220. A good Samaritan

... When journeying back from Tientsin to Siaochang my colleagues and I heard of a wounded man, lying in a temple, 20 miles from our Mission Hospital. No carter would take the risk of taking wounded men, for fear of meeting the Japanese troops on the way. However, one Chinese carter said he would go, if I accompanied him. They have a wonderful confidence in us!!! It would be quite dangerous for him, but I think there was no danger so far as I was concerned.

On Saturday, February 18th, the carter started on the journey, and some hours later I cycled after him. By evening the carter reached Huo Chu, 18 miles from Siaochang, where we had our Mission premises. I cycled on to Pei Lin Tyu, 3 miles further on, to see the Head-man of the village and make arrangements for the wounded man to be removed. He lay in the temple about 100 yards outside the village. The temple is a filthy place open to the wind and dust. No one ever comes along to clean it.

No home was open to the wounded man, for if the Japanese descended on them and found that a home had anything to do with the military, it would be destroyed at once, and the lives of those in it would be in danger.

For 5 days the man had lain in the temple. A friend came there daily to feed him. He lay on a thin mattress on the ground. When we remember that the nights and days are cold and that every night the temperature would be at freezing point, if not well below it, we marvel that he was still alive. The Japanese (a tank and 10 motor lorries) were at the next village a mile away.

I told the wounded man we would be back early the next day, and then I returned to Huo Chu. That night, as I lay down, wrapped in my old sheepskin coat, my thoughts turned to the next day. Suppose I met the Japanese, what would I say? I felt for my Chinese New Testament, a book I constantly carried about with me. It fell open at Luke 16. I read until I came to verse 10, and this seemed to me to bring me my answer. 'He that is faithful in that which is least is faithful also in much: and he that is unjust in the least is unjust also in much.' It was as if God had said to me, 'Be honest and straight.' I turned and went to sleep. We started early next morning. As we approached the first village, there was a man standing in the entrance to it, beckoning us in. We entered the village and as we passed through it the Japanese mechanised troops went round it. We fortunately missed each other.

Many of the roads had been dug up, and were like enlarged trenches, and in clambering out our cart overturned.

We reached Pei Lin Tyu early in the day and went to the temple. It was Chinese New Year's Day. People were in the temple burning incense. They were even burning it at the side of the wounded man. I asked the people to come out. I gave them a talk on fresh air being of more value to sick or wounded than air laden with incense smoke. Then I turned to those great words from Micah—'Wherewith shall I come before the Lord? Shall I come before Him with burnt offerings . . . He hath shewed thee, O man, what is good; and what doth the Lord require of thee, but to do justly, and to love mercy, and to walk humbly with thy God?' . . .

Robert Garioch (1909-81)
(Robert Garioch Sutherland)

Robert Garioch wrote as if he was putting on paper his natural speech, though in fact he was a careful, skilled craftsman, much as was Burns and his predecessor, Robert Fergusson. It was the mantle of Fergusson that he wore as he noted the follies and absurdities of the people of his native city, Edinburgh. Yet we always hear his own individual voice, that of a modest man whose gentle satire includes himself. He spent most of his life as an unwilling schoolmaster.

221. Unwillingly to school

To J. K. Annand   *Bromley, Kent 1 October 1955*

. . . But it is an awful strain, this Deacon Brodie sort of life, Sutherland by day and Garioch by night, schoolmastering and making poetry being such different things, and yet both tiring you out in the same way, that's the damn thing about it. So for the last fortnight I've had a kind of revulsion or scunner and can't bear to read or write or do anything serious in the evenings. Usually I'm half-gyte with the thought of so much to do and only the evenings to do it in, so that the day seems an irrelevant and maddening interruption, however quietly it may be got through; 10 lines done between 7 and 9, and pick it up again next evening at 7. What a life.

Surely the Burns Prize should not damn you in the view of the long-haired boys. I'm one of them myself, though most of the hair has been pulled out in tufts long ago. They're all trying to write Scots the best way they can, and do you realise that you and I belong to about the last age-groups to have spoken Scots as laddies in the ordinary way of life? I'm not sure, but I fear that must be about true, at least in places like Edinburgh. Perhaps not. But the great thing is that they keep on trying. Have you met Tom Scott? . . . He toils very sedulously in Scots, having deliberately changed over from English. There must be some younger fellows, but I don't know them. But you should meet Tom Scott and discuss things. This resurrected word *Lallans* surprised me when I came home from the war, but the accompanying activity surprised me even more, and there seemed to be an exciting atmosphere that we never used to have. . .

222. 'I like being in Edinburgh'

To a Friend   *4 Nelson Street, Edinburgh*
                                                             8 November 1961

. . . I like being in Edinburgh, and I like meeting the literary boys, who are to be found in a strictly limited set of howffs. Not much visiting at houses seems to go on, instead one mills about in a crowd, getting a word in here and there. There is a good deal of sojourning to Callum Macdonald's late at night of a Friday; he is very robust in his hospitality, and that says a lot for him; he works on Saturdays. . .

There was a poetry-reading ploy, with which these people were connected, in a deep and dark cellar in North St Andrews Street, where I went and read *Embro to the Ploy* beneath a wee light to a lot of shadowy figures who laughed loudly at the funny bits, and it was good fun, but I can't tell you who they all were, as it was too dark. This seems to have been a Festival ploy, as the cellar is always closed when I pass now. A curious business, with poetry mixed up with jazz and various other things that seem incompatible. Someone announced a forthcoming event at which Somebody would be swingin his poems. Critical judgment on my effort was that the audience had been *sent*, i.e. had enjoyed the performance. Well, that's O.K. by me, though I think this expression is out of date. Queer business, altogether. Also there is a good deal of guitar-playing and singing of Scottish folk music as it is called, with Hamish Henderson stirring it all up in great style. Trouble with me is that I can no longer stand the guitar three-chord-trick (tonic, dominant, subdominant). I greatly enjoy the playing of Segovia, so it can't be the instrument that gives me the jim-jams. . .

223. The invite

University of Edinburgh
School of Scottish Studies
17 January 1972

Dear Sir, or Madam, as the case may be,
We request the pleasure of yir companee
At the

21ST BIRTHDAY PAIRTY

of the Schule of Scottish Studies

DRESS INFORMAL. i.e. the usual orra duddies,

ON THE 29TH JANUAR AT 7 P.M.

Sae ye can easy get there efter the gemm.
We'd better tell ye, no to be mair circumstantial,
That ye'll maist likely get something gey substantial,
For beit said, the Schule of Scottish Studies
Kens mair about cookery than jist hou to byle tatties
　　　　　　　　　　　　　　　　　　　and haddies
There's to be Haggis and Clapshot, Stapag, and
　　　　　　　　　　　　　　parritch caad Brochan,
That thick, ye'll maybe can tak some o't hame in yir
　　　　　　　　　　　　　　　　　　spleughan,
Atholl Brose, very nice, to mak yir thochts mair
　　　　　　　　　　　　　　　　effervescent,
Frae a genuine Atholl recipe—we mean the Forest,
　　　　　　　　　　　　　　　no the Crescent.

R.S.V.P. BY THURSDAY, 27TH JAN.

Or maybe sometime suiner, if ye can,
And if ye come to

27 GEORGE SQUARE, EDINBURGH

　　　　　　　　　　　　　　　frae aa the airts,

Ye'll find parking space fir yir cawrs, caravans and
　　　　　　　　　　　　　　　　　cairts
Richt forenenst the Schule of Scottish Studies,
And, in the Meedies, guid grazing fir yir cuddies.

254

Thanks fir the invite til yir pairtie,
We're keen to come, no on a cairtie,
But in a Twintie-seevin bus;
That will dae weill eneuch fir us.

My wife and I read wi delyte
The letter wi yir kind invite,
And houpe to win, be't wind or weet,
Til this byordinar Schule-treat.

Yours aye,

ROBERT G. SUTHERLAND

Sorley Maclean (1911-   )
(Somhairle MacGill-Eain)

Sorley Maclean's poetry, 'because it is great poetry,' wrote John Murray, leaps over the barriers of culture and language to run freely 'across eternity, across its snows'. He led the other Scottish Gaelic poets to make a new Gaelic poetry, which is now recognised as a central achievement in the Scottish Renaissance of this century. Something of the humanity which is expressed in his poetry, along with a good-humoured tolerance of the oddities of human behaviour, is to be found in the letters he wrote to Douglas Young, when he was in training camps in England as Signalman S. Maclean, before being posted to North Africa.

224. 'A "unit" of the "British" Imperial forces'

To Douglas Young   A. *Coy 1st Depot Battalion,*
                                    Catterick Camp, Yorks. 1 October 1940

Dear Douglas
I am here a 'unit' of the 'British' Imperial forces and am reacting not at all as expected. To begin with I like the rude physical exertion and the feeling of becoming fit and hardy in the body which I feel developing every day. The barrack room life gives no privacy but then I don't mind that very much as I have I think the capacity of covering myself with a tough shell. Half of our squad of 25 are

Scots, mostly from the central belt, the rest are Yorkshiremen. I can't pronounce on the English yet but my first impression is that I do not at all dislike the proletarian Englishman much as I loathe the bourgeois Englishman. Perhaps that is all to be expected from me. I am not sensitive to national differentia but very to class differentia. I loathe the English bourgeois and more the Anglo-Scot bourgeois but honestly I like the English privates here. Most of them too I suppose are not proletarians but petty bourgeois, people of the same class as that in which I am at present myself but some are genuine proletarians . . . Again I am not finicky about food and there is plenty of it here at least and the cooking is to my uncritical taste remarkably good. As for my conscience, well! Am I being a traitor to Scotland and more so to the class struggle? Am I just in the army because I haven't the courage to object? All I can say is that I have such an instinctive loathing and fear of Naziism and such a distrust of its demagogy that I cannot accept for myself the responsibility of refusing to resist it even with the cooperation of English imperialist capitalism . . . Even if Naziism is not a capitalist dictatorship, even if it is only the aristocracy of a 'strong, warrior caste' I loathe the inhumanism of that. If it won I am afraid it would make its triumph far too permanent. I may be wrong but for myself I cannot take the risk of treating it even as the equal of British imperialism . . . my attitude to the Nazis . . . is that they are just the very devil. You have Grieve on your side but I cannot lean much on his political judgment. What worries me far more is that I fear you have too the example of John Maclean; but is the case the same? I believe he would have taken your line in effect and that fills me with misgiving about myself. You see I am not a pure conscript. I am afraid I did not tell you that I asked the Edinburgh corporation to release me for military service in September 1939. I did that because I took it to be the C.P. line then. At that time I did respect the political line of the C.P. I am afraid I don't now . . . I am not impressed by their subsequent arguments that the situation has really changed . . .

George Campbell Hay (1915-84)
(Deorsa MacIan Deorsa)

George Campbell Hay was the son of John MacDougall Hay, the author of the powerful novel, Gillespie. *He was described by Sorley MacLean as 'a most rare poet and patriot, . . . intensely obsessed with the sufferings and aspirations of his own compatriots and of human beings in general'. He was an accomplished linguist who wrote poetry in Gaelic, Scots, English and other languages. The following letter is from his early days in the army. He never fully recovered from his later wartime experiences in North Africa and the Middle East.*

225. Army recruit

To Douglas Young   RAOC, Earl Shilton, England 1941

Dear Dia

At last I can snatch a moment from my unremitting duties to let you know a little about my self and my surroundings. There's no great need to discourse about my opinions or feelings as I have hardly time to have any, and the ones I have are unchanged.

Tha sinn 'san t-seann nàdur

'S a bha sinn roimh àm an achda*

as the good Mac Mhaighstir Alasdair said (whose works I carry around in my left breast pocket, the one usually reserved for the traditional pocket bible which invariably stops the inevitable bullet. I wish Alasdair had written enough, for his works as I have them wouldn't even stop a .22 bullet).

My surroundings are a section of the Midlands of SB. Fields with heavy green soggy grass in them separated by heavy green trees and hedges from more fields of the same kind. A careful observer will discover, if he is attentive, a few faint folds and convolutions in the landscape, sometimes running to the vertiginous height of a hundred feet. Earl Shilton is a biggish village which can be analysed into several thousand bricks, all of the same parched red (except for the kirk and the war memorial which consist of clach or stone). In this brickery are to be found seven pubs which sell a peely-wally beer tasting of tepid ditches and railway stations, between the frequent periods when they run dry. In this place are also to be found the 5th company of the Second Training Battalion (tho' you're not meant to mention that last) of that warlike unit, the RAOC, and this Company is being dragged by the collar thro' an intensive cramming course of Infantry Training and Departmental Training (which they call School. As a matter of fact life in the khaki hordes is startlingly like life at boarding school, except it's not so bad. It's also like life at Sauchton Jail Midlothian, only more exhausting). The Infantry training is bearable. It started with a physical grill on hot tarred roads under a blistering sun, marching to and fro, stamping the heels with unnecessary violence, and striking

---

*We are in our old condition and we are before the time of action

various postures (with all of which I had made my acquaintance at that piece of 'forever England', Fettes College) with the usual Lee Enfield. Now it's more interesting however — anti-gas training, Bren Gun (which is marvellously simple for an automatic weapon), anti-aircraft fire for winging dive-bombers, and (still to come) hand grenades and the good old romantic-archaic bayonet. I enjoy learning all these things, tho' not for the regulation reasons, but don't infer from my enjoyment that I'm reconciled to the Arm Lachdunn*. Today I surprised myself and everyone else by scoring seven bulls with ten shots and the corporal said he didn't suppose that any bloody jerries had better loiter about in front of me. But I wasn't thinking of 'bloody jerries'.

Luckily the NCOS are decent souls, including our own Sergeant, one algar, a Geordie from near Alnwick who had the pleasure of being carted thro' Dunkirk as a casualty from Flanders. As he is from the North and speaks what is almost a kind of Lallans I can understand him when he opens his mouth. But some of the NCOS (only the CSM and one sergeant are Scots) are a continuous puzzle to their men, and vice versa. One corporal told his platoon that the first letter of the alphabet was 'Oi' (or more 'oi'). On the other hand a quiet soul of 39 years from the Broch went and asked his sergeant if he would 'bide ahint' where we paraded. The funniest instance of language fog was caused by a Glesca boy who, being a great consumer of beer, was puffing and panting at PT and screwing up his face in anguish. 'Wot are you pantin' and makin' fices for?' asked the instructor 'If you don't loike to be 'ere we don't want cher'. When Glesca had interpreted this to himself he was deeply insulted and howled 'Ah wisnie mekin' faces ah wiz pechin'. The instructor gazed blankly at him, but was too mindful of his dignity to ask what 'pechin' meant.

The Caledonians and South Britons mix no better than oil and water. If you ask about anyone and what sort of person he is the first classification is always 'He's wan o they bloody Englishmen' or 'He's a Scotch bastard' and that's the natural attitude you get. If you strike up an acquaintance with an Englishman (excepting a small minority) you feel it's abnormal and provisional. The most noticeable characteristic about the English is how docile they are, and it's not a docility with after-thoughts or reservations. But most of my compatriots, God be thankit, haven't the faintest trace of the spirit of subordination and they are incredibly outspoken for poor bloody privates. A Fifeman I know well (a piper) once caught one of the Regimental Police washing with the official armband of authority off. 'Ye ken' he said to him 'ye're a dour sort of bugger'. 'I

*Khaki Army

258

don't understand you Scotch people', said the dumbfounded RP. 'What do you mean, I'm dour?' 'I mean ye're an awfu' sulky kinna bugger'. 'I'm not sulky' (he must have been thrown quite off his balance to demean himself by going into explanations) 'I've got a lot of worries on my shoulders'. 'Ach, I hae mair worries in the arse of my troosers'. One Aberdonian (we have plenty) eyed a nagging kind of sergeant significantly and said 'Did anyone ever hit ye afore, sergeant?' These people are naturally direct. An Englishman would go into a huddle in a dark corner and grouse about what he would do to that 'bloody bastard', but he would click his heels smartly and say 'yes sergeant' when he had the bastard face to face with him.

My departmental work is learning how to make red tape and documents grow fruitful and multiply and how to think and talk in jargon and innumerable abbreviations. It's a six months course, and we have five weeks to do it in. Everything here is scamped work and cramming. 'You're trained soldiers now' quotes the CSM last week.

Sometime I'll write a decent long letter, but my Time Allocated Letters (for purpose of writing off) is about expended.

I'm still a Scotsman, not a N.B., so write me and tell me about yourself and Scotland, particularly what the decent Scotsmen are doing and thinking.

*Leis a h-uile deagh dhùrachd,

DEORSA

PS A pal of mine called Steward Taylor, who worked in the Enbro GPO, invariably uses 'thir' for 'these.' It's drole I should hear what I thought a dead word for the first time in Sasunn.**

Sydney Goodsir Smith (1915–75)

Two long poems in Scots, MacDiarmid's A Drunk Man looks at the Thistle *and Sydney Goodsir Smith's* Under the Eildon Tree, *may be claimed as the only masterpieces in this genre in this century. Smith's extraordinary love poem, including comment on domestic and historical dramas in Auld Reekie, and ranging in allusions from John Knox to Stalin, was hardly to be expected from his erratic, spontaneous, but brilliant, pen. The twenty-two page letter, from which a relatively small portion is quoted, and which gives a flavour of the unbuttoned natural Smith, was a response to a request by Lindsay for a note (a hundred words or so) for the back cover of Smith's* Selected Poems, *one of the series,* Modern Poets, *edited by Maurice Lindsay and Douglas Young, published by the Saltire Society in 1947.*

*With every good wish   **England

To Maurice Lindsay   *50 Craigmillar Park, Edinburgh*
                                              3 April 1947

. . . As to my biographical history: I was born in October (under
the sign of Scorpio in Mars I think or Venus, I forget. Scorpio
children have dual personalities, are artistic and suicidal. Frequently
also they lead double lives), the year 1915, the place Wellington,
New Zealand. My first memory is of an earthquake from which I
awoke and announced that the pictures in the room were crooked.
Crooked pictures have always been an abomination of mine. In
youth I had (though you would not believe it from my raddled and
dissipated countenance) extreme beauty which led onlookers to
prognosticate an early death. This was within an inch of occurring
in Malta. In some cathedral, which I visited with my mama, they
were burning incense which brought on a violent spasm of asthma, a
distemper to which I had and have been subject from babyhood.
When purple and black in the face and all hope lost, however, my
deity intervened and I recovered as you can see.

My mother and I left N.Z. to join my father who was then in the
RAMC in Egypt. Our ship was unfortunately torpedoed by the
German raider Emden and we were put ashore by the chivalrous
captain of that ship at Singapore, where I idled away several months
in rickshaws and no doubt contracted habits of sloth from which I
have never since wholly recovered. In fact, as I grow older, they
become, if possible, intensified. I am writing this in bed, where most
of my writing is done—in beds or in pubs. . .

At the age of 6 or so . . . I was sent to school in the pleasant,
secluded and sea-dashed village of Swanage in Dorset. Within the
next half-dozen years I suppose I became more distinguished than I
shall ever be again, being at the end Head of the School, Captain of
Rugby Football, Champion Athlete, Prizewinner in English
Literature (an essay on Milton) and holder of various great and high
positions—included amongst which was a record of being beaten
three times in twelve hours by the Headmaster . . .

My holidays during this period of 7-13 years were spent in the
village of Moniaive, Dumfriesshire, where I was the leader of a gang
of ragamuffins, which terrorised the neighbourhood with our
reiving of eatables from the only shop, and chickens, rabbits and
other legitimate game from the backyards and farms of the district.
My poetic Muse awoke for the first time about now. I must have
been between 8 and 10 when I conceived my first passion for a
member of the opposite fair sex (apart from my sister Betty, of
course and the matron of the school, a buxom young thing of about

18 with enormous breasts which I delighted to grip from behind and squeeze to the accompaniment of her delighted and mock-indignant shrieks—but this, I freely admit, was lust more than love!).

But my passion for May Maxwell, the daughter of the keeper of the only grocer's shop in Moniaive, was of the heart, and it possessed that peculiar melancholy that always goes with love—at least, so it seems to me. May Maxwell, as I clearly remember to this day was a thin (no 'thin' is wrong, for she was plump in places) slight (that's better), a slight, dark and precociously developed lassie of about eight years, with dark, deep swimming eyes and lips of the purest cherry colour. This may bore you somewhat but to me it is infinitely touching to recall her. I expect she is now a strapping, great husky bumpkin and mother of six. Sunt lacrimae rerum. Tempora mutantur et nos mutamur in illis*. Dear May. We quarrelled in the end and I remember the terrible scene so vividly though the cause of the quarrel is quite forgotten. We were standing by the white-washed coalhouse and I struck her. The expression in her eyes was one of amazement. Then she burst out greiting, her head in her hands, her long black hair over her bent head and leaning against the white wall of the coalhouse. Jean MacNab, who lived next door and was a little older than the rest of us started to shout at me to stop but I would not stop pummelling with my fists the bent back of May as she leant against the wall.

I never saw her again. She would never come out to play with me, she would accept no apologies. I was never forgiven, and my heart was broken. Before this I had written her many verses, oddly enough, in the ordinary dialect we used. We used to sing them together. There was one which went to the tune of 'My bonnie is over the ocean', which was a favourite song of ours.

After our quarrel, and in secret, I gathered all these little scraps of paper together and solemnly made a bonfire of sticks and burnt them. (My eyes have grown quite wet at the recollection.) These were my first serious verses. . .

*These are the tears of things. Times change, and we change with them.

James Kennaway (1928-68)

James Kennaway is probably best known for his novel Tunes of Glory *(1956), which was made into a film; but* Some Gorgeous Accident *(1967), published the year before his death in a car accident, reveals a deeper understanding of human motives and particularly of the drive of egotism. He wrote to George Bernard Shaw, the Irish dramatist, just before his discharge from the army.*

227. Proposal . . .

To George Bernard Shaw　　　　　　　　*48 Hollywell Hill, St Albans*
　　　　　　　　　　　　　　　　　　　　　25 September 1947

> Sir
> I am no fond regarder
> 　　Of pompous interview
> But I come from Auchterarder
> 　　And I'd like to chat with you.
>
> I know you're getting older
> 　　And have little time for me
> But the army's made me bolder
> 　　So I'd like to call for tea.

. . . and Shaw's riposte

To James Kennaway　　　　　　　　　　*Ayot Saint Lawrence*
　　　　　　　　　　　　　　　　　　　　28 September 1947

> Would you, by Gum! I'm sorry,
> 　　But many thousands more
> Are in the self-same hurry
> 　　So I must bar the door.
>
> I have not tea enough for you
> 　　Nor teacakes in my larder
> And so send this rebuff to you
> 　　Dear lad from Auchterarder.

Sources

1. Th. A. Fischer, *The Scots in Germany* (Edinburgh 1902) *p.* 3.
2. Sir James Fergusson, Bart., (ed.), *The Declaration of Arbroath* (Edinburgh University Press: Edinburgh 1970) *pp.* 7-9.
3. Agnes Mure Mackenzie & James Kinsley (eds.), *A Garland of Scottish Prose* (Grant: Edinburgh 1956) *p.* 153.
4. P. Hume Brown (ed.), *Vernacular Writings of George Buchanan* (STS: Edinburgh 1892) *pp.* 58-59.
5. W. C. Dickinson, Gordon Donaldson and Isobel A. Milne (eds.), *A Source Book of Scottish History*, Vol. II (Nelson: Edinburgh 1953) *pp.* 91-92.
6. *The Last Letter of Mary, Queen of Scots*, NLS, Adv. MS 54.1.1 (Edinburgh 1971).
7. D. Laing (ed.), *The Works of John Knox*, Vol. VI (Edinburgh 1895) *p.* 47.
8. ibid. Vol. III, *p.* 338.
9. J. K. Hewson (ed.), *Certain Tractates by Ninian Winzet* (STS: Edinburgh 1888) *p.* 138.
10. G. P. V. Akrigg (ed.), *Letters of King James VI & I* (University of California Press: California 1984) *pp.* 84-85.
11. ibid.
12. ibid.
13. Th. A. Fischer, *The Scots in Germany* (Edinburgh 1902) *p.* 104.
14. David Reid (ed.), *The Party-Coloured Mind* (Scottish Academic Press: Edinburgh 1982) *p.* 58.
15. ibid. *p.* 48.
16. George Blake (ed.) *Scottish Treasure Trove* (Molendinar Press: Glasgow 1979).
17. Duncan Thomson, the catalogue of *A Virtuous & Noble Education* (National Gallery of Scotland: Edinburgh 1971) *p.* 18.
18. Agnes Mure Mackenzie & James Kinsley (eds.), *A Garland of Scottish Prose* (Grant: Edinburgh 1956) *p.* 107.
19. W. C. Dickinson, *Two Students at St. Andrews 1711-1716* (Edinburgh 1952) *p.* 39.
20. W. T. Johnston (ed.), *The Best of Our Owne: Letters of Archibald Pitcairne* (Saorsa Books: Edinburgh 1979) *pp.* 43-44.
21. ibid. *p.* 53.
22. *Manuscripts of the Earl of Mar and Kellie* (HMC: London 1904) *p.* 436.
23. *Scottish History Society*, Vol. X (Edinburgh 1965) *p.* 170.
24. ibid. *pp.* 170-172.
25. *Manuscripts of the Earl of Mar and Kellie* (HMC: London 1904) *p.* 270.
26. British Museum Add. MSS 34, 180.
27. *Manuscripts of the Earl of Mar and Kellie* (HMC: London 1904) *pp.* 494-495.
28. A. M. Kinghorn & Alexander Law (eds.), *The Works of Allan Ramsay*, Vol. IV (STS: Edinburgh 1970) *pp.* 204-205.
29. ibid. *pp.* 205-206.
30. ibid. *pp.* 206-207.
31. Hugh Douglas, *Charles Edward Stuart* (Robert Hale: London 1975).
32. Maurice Lindsay (ed.), *Scotland – An Anthology* (Robert Hale: London 1974) *p.* 124.
33. Donald Nicholas (ed.), *Intercepted Post* (The Bodley Head: London 1956) *pp.* 19-20.
34. ibid. *p.* 48.
35. ibid. *p.* 70.
36. Robert Forbes (ed.), *The Lyon in Mourning*, Vol. III (Edinburgh 1846) *pp.* 12-14.
37. Elizabeth Gray Vining, *Flora MacDonald in the Highlands and America* (Geoffrey Bles: London 1967) *p.* 90.

38. J. Y. T. Grieg (ed.), *The Letters of David Hume,* Vol. I (Oxford University Press 1932) *pp.* 169-171.
39. ibid. *p.* 255.
40. R. Klibansky & E. C. Mossner (eds.), *New Letters of David Hume* (Oxford University Press 1954) *pp.* 68-69.
41. J. Y. T. Grieg (ed.), *The Letters of David Hume,* Vol. I, (Oxford University Press 1932) *p.* 436.
42. ibid. *p.* 470.
43. ibid. Vol. II, *pp.* 206-207.
44. ibid. Vol. II, *pp.* 208-209.
45. ibid. Vol. II, *pp.* 209-210.
46. R. Klibansky & E. C. Mossner (eds.), *New Letters of David Hume* (Oxford University Press 1954).
47. Alison Cockburn, *Letters and Memoir of her own life* (Edinburgh 1900) *pp.* 124-125.
48. ibid. *p.* 187.
49. Agnes Mure Mackenzie & James Kinsley (eds.), *A Garland of Scottish Prose* (Grant: Edinburgh 1956) *p.* 85.
50. Lewis M. Knapp (ed.), *The Letters of Tobias Smollett* (Oxford University Press 1970) *p.* 33.
51. John Hill Burton (ed.), *The Autobiography of Dr Alexander Carlyle* (Edinburgh 1910) *pp.* 567-577.
52. John Small, *Biographical Sketch of Adam Ferguson* (Edinburgh 1864) *p.* 4.
53. J. Y. T. Grieg (ed.), *The Letters of David Hume,* Vol. II, *pp.* 450-452.
54. W. R. Scott, *Adam Smith as Student and Professor* (Glasgow 1937) *pp.* 281, 283, 284.
55. Jean Jones, *Annals of Science* 40 (1983) *p.* 82.
56. ibid. *p.* 85.
57. SRO GD 18/4840: by permission of Sir John Clerk of Penicuik.
58. Barbara L. H. Horn, *Letters of John Ramsay of Ochtertyre* (SHS: Edinburgh 1966) *p.* 39.
59. ibid. *pp.* 80-82.
60. ibid. *pp.* 203-204.
61. ibid. *pp.* 262-264.
62. Eric Robinson & Douglas McKie (eds.), *Partners in Science: Letters of James Watt and Joseph Black* (Constable: London 1971) *pp.* 232-235.
63. ibid. *pp.* 272-273.
64. ibid. *pp.* 317-319.
65. Frederick A. Pottle (ed.), *Boswell on the Grand Tour, Germany and Switzerland 1764* (Printed with permission of Yale University and the McGraw-Hill Book Company (William Heinemann, Ltd.): London 1953) *pp.* 213-215.
66. C. B. Tinker (ed.), *Letters of James Boswell* (London 1924) *pp.* 169-170.
67. ibid. *pp.* 194-196.
68. J. W. Reed & F. A. Pottle (eds.), *Boswell: Laird of Auchinleck* (Printed with permission of Yale University and the McGraw-Hill Book Company (William Heinemann, Ltd.): New York 1977) *pp.* 66-68.
69. Frank Brady & F. A. Pottle (eds.), *Boswell in Search of a Wife* (Printed with permission of Yale University and the McGraw-Hill Book Company (William Heinemann, Ltd.): London 1957) *pp.* 232-235.
70. Kirk Session Records, Foveran.
71. Matthew P. McDiarmid (ed.), *The Poems of Robert Fergusson,* Vol. I (STS; Edinburgh 1954) *pp.* 99-101.
72. *Historical Records of the Cameron Highlanders,* Vol. I (Edinburgh 1904) *pp.* 45-46.
73. W. H. Wilkins, *South Africa a Century Ago* (London 1901).

74. Jean MacDougall, *Highland Postbag* (Shepheard-Walwyn: London 1984) *pp.* 96-97.
75. Edinburgh University Library MS La II 62.
76. Agnes Mure Mackenzie & James Kinsley (eds.), *A Garland of Scottish Prose* (Grant: Edinburgh 1956) *p.* 56.
77. J. De Lancey Ferguson (ed.), *The Letters of Robert Burns*, Vol. I (Oxford 1931) *pp.* 66-68.
78. ibid. *pp.* 94-95.
79. ibid. *pp.* 105-107.
80. ibid. *pp.* 133-134.
81. NLS MS Acc. 8810.
82. J. De Lancey Ferguson (ed.), *The Letters of Robert Burns*, Vol. II, *pp.* 194-196.
83. ibid. *p.* 330.
84. Edward Hughes (ed.), *The Scottish Historical Review*, Vol. 35 (1956) *pp.* 34-35.
85. *The Introduction by Tamara Talbot-Rice to the catalogue for the Arts Council Exhibition: Charles Cameron, Architect to the Imperial Russian Court* (1967) *p.* 19.
86. *The Journal of Mrs Calderwood.*
87. Sir Walter Scott, *Biographical Memoir of John Leyden*, Edinburgh Annual Register, Vol. IV (1811).
88. David Douglas (ed.), *Familiar Letters of Sir Walter Scott*, Vol. I (Edinburgh 1894) *pp.* 12-15.
89. NLS MS Acc. 8879.
90. Norah Parr, *James Hogg at Home* (Dollar 1980) *pp.* 94-95.
91. ibid. *pp.* 95-96.
92. Douglas Mack, MS in Alexander Turnbull Library (transcribed) (Wellington, New Zealand).
93. Norah Parr, *James Hogg at Home* (Dollar 1980) *p.* 106.
94. ibid. *pp.* 107-109.
95. ibid. *pp.* 109-110.
96. H. J. C. Grierson (ed.), *The Letters of Sir Walter Scott*, Vol. I (London 1932-37) *pp.* 320, 321, 322, 323, 325.
97. ibid. *pp.* 342-343.
98. ibid. Vol. IV, *pp.* 206-207.
99. P. H. Scott (ed.), *Sir Walter Scott's Letters of Malachi Malagrowther* (Blackwood: Edinburgh 1981) *pp.* 136-138.
100. H. J. C. Grierson (ed.), *The Letters of Sir Walter Scott*, Vol. IX (London 1932-37) *pp.* 468-470.
101. J. G. Lockhart, *Life of Sir Walter Scott*, Chap. 5.
102. H. J. C. Grierson (ed.), *The Letters of Sir Walter Scott*, Vol. XI (London 1932-37) *pp.* 113-115.
103. Ronald Miller (ed.), *Travels in the Interior of Africa* (Dent: London) *p.* 282.
104. NLS MS 19806, *pp.* 133-134.
105. ibid. *pp.* 38-40.
106. Henry Cockburn, *Life of Lord Jeffrey*, Vol. II (Edinburgh 1852) *pp.* 140-141.
107. ibid. *pp.* 292-293.
108. David Douglas (ed.), *Familiar Letters of Sir Walter Scott*, Vol. I (Edinburgh 1894) *pp.* 344-345.
109. ibid. *pp.* 305-306.
110. Sir Walter Scott, *Biographical Memoir of John Leyden*, Edinburgh Annual Register, Vol. IV (1811).
111. D. M. Moir, *Biographical Memoir of John Galt*, *pp.* xlvii-xlviii.
112. Harry A. Cockburn, *Letters of Henry Cockburn* (Edinburgh 1932) *p.* 33.
113. ibid. *pp.* 34-35.
114. NLS MS 9688 *ff.* 59-62.
115. NLS MS 9688 *ff.* 124-129.

116. *Memoirs of Dr Chalmers* (Constable 1852) *p.* 281.
117. Science Museum Library, Fox Talbot Collection.
118. NLS MS Acc. 7967/1: by permission of Mrs J. W. Stanton.
119. The Royal Observatory, Edinburgh.
120. John A. Doyle (ed.), *Works of Susan Ferrier*, Vol. IV, *pp.* 163-164.
121. Wilfred Partington (ed.), *The Private Letter Books of Sir Walter Scott* (London 1930) *pp.* 247-251.
122. Leslie A. Marchand (ed.), *Byron's Letters and Journals*, Vol. 10 (London 1980) *pp.* 237-240.
123. ibid. Vol. 9, *pp.* 85-87.
124. ibid. Vol. 10, *pp.* 189-190.
125. Ian Campbell (ed.), *Thomas and Jane* (Friends of Edinburgh University Library: Edinburgh 1980) *pp.* 43-46.
126. Alexander Carlyle (ed.), *The Love Letters of Thomas Carlyle and Jane Welsh*, Vol. I (London 1909) *pp.* 366-367.
127. ibid. *pp.* 367-369.
128. *The Collected Letters of Thomas and Jane Welsh Carlyle: Duke-Edinburgh edition*, Vol. IV (Durham, N.C., 1970-) *pp.* 39, 42, 43.
129. ibid. *pp.* 46-49.
130. Ian Campbell (ed.), *Thomas and Jane* (Friends of Edinburgh University Library: Edinburgh 1980) *pp.* 53-55.
131. ibid. *pp.* 62-63.
132. *The Collected Letters of Thomas and Jane Welsh Carlyle: Duke-Edinburgh edition*, Vol. VIII, (Durham, N.C., 1970-) *pp.* 75-77.
133. Hugh Miller, *Letters*, Vol. I, *p.* 110.
134. John Brown, *Rab and his Friends and other Papers* (Dent 1907) *p.* 93.
135. ibid. *p.* 104.
136. H. A. Kennedy, *Professor Blackie: His Sayings and Doings* (London 1895) *p.* 215.
137. John Brown, *Letters*, *p.* 318.
138. A. R. B. Haldane, *Three Centuries of Scottish Posts* (Edinburgh University Press: Edinburgh 1971) *p.* 301.
139. Samuel Smiles, *Robert Dick* (John Murray, 1905) *p.* 64.
140. ibid. *p.* 172.
141. J. Duns, *Memoir of Sir James Y. Simpson, Bart.* (Edinburgh 1873) *pp.* 215-216.
142. ibid. *pp.* 199-200.
143. John Prebble, *The Highland Clearances* (Secker & Warburg, 1963) *p.* 300.
144. ibid. *p.* 309.
145. Donald Ross, *A Plea for the Famishing* (Glasgow 1855) *p.* 7.
146. John Prebble, *The Highland Clearances* (Secker & Warburg, 1963) *p.* 212.
147. T. Shapera (ed.), *David Livingstone – Family Letters*, Vol. II (Chatto & Windus: The Hogarth Press, 1959) *p.* 278.
148. ibid. *p.* 210.
149. R. Foskett (ed.), *The Zambesi Doctors – David Livingstone's Letters to Dr John Kirk* (Edinburgh University Press: Edinburgh 1964) *p.* 145.
150. ibid. *p.* 140.
151. Thomas Edward, *The Life of a Scottish Naturalist* (John Murray: London 1875) *p.* 381.
152. Hoh-cheung Mui & Lorna H. Mui, *William Melrose in China* (SHS: Edinburgh 1973) *pp.* 31-34.
153. Sir Walter Wedderburn, *Allan Octavian Hume* (London 1913) *pp.* 50-53.
154. Lewis Campbell & William Garnett, *The Life and Times of James Clerk Maxwell* (London 1882) *p.* 60.
155. ibid. *pp.* 301-302.
156. ibid. *pp.* 342-343.
157. Burton S. Hendrick, *The Life of Andrew Carnegie* (London 1933) *pp.* 39-41.

158. ibid. *p.* 589.

159. Jack House, *Square Mile of Murder* (Molendinar Press: Glasgow 1975) *p.* 13.

160. Kevin McCarra, *Scottish Football, A Pictorial History from 1867 to the Present Day* (The Third Eye Centre and Polygon Books) *p.* 6.

161. The Bryce Papers, Bodleian Library, Oxford. Reprinted in *Andrew Cruikshank's Scottish Bedside Book* (Johnston and Bacon: London & Edinburgh 1977) *pp.* 166-168.

162. W. F. Badé, *The Life and Letters of John Muir*, Vol. I (Boston & New York 1924) *pp.* 272-275.

163. Helen Elmira Waite, *Make a Joyful Sound* (Macrae Smith Company: Philadelphia 1961) *p.* 265.

164. ibid.

165. Mary Slessor, NLS MS.

166. Sir Sidney Colvin (ed.), *The Letters of Robert Louis Stevenson*, Vol. I (London 1926) *pp.* 157-158.

167. De Lancey Ferguson (ed.), *Stevenson's Letters to Charles Baxter* (Yale & Oxford 1956) *pp.* 97-98.

168. ibid. *pp.* 116-117.

169. Sir Sidney Colvin (ed.), *The Letters of Robert Louis Stevenson*, Vol. IV (London 1926) *pp.* 15-16.

170. ibid. *pp.* 193-196.

171. De Lancey Ferguson (ed.), *Stevenson's Letters to Charles Baxter* (Yale & Oxford 1956) *pp.* 353-356.

172. MSS Dartmouth College Library (New Hampshire).

173. ibid.

174. Philip Mairet, *Pioneers of Sociology: The Life and Letters of Patrick Geddes* (Leonard Humphries: London 1957) *pp.* 93-94.

175. ibid. *pp.* 132-134.

176. NLS Dep. 176/1/1.

177. Viola Meynell (ed.), *Letters of J. M. Barrie* (Peter Davies: London 1942) *p.* 230.

178. NLS MS Dep. 325/Letter Book I.

179. ibid. Letter Book VIII.

180. Quoted by H. J. Hanham in an article in the *Juridical Review* (1965) *pp.* 229-230. MSS in Goodwood MS 871 (West Sussex Record Office) and Salisbury Papers.

181. ibid.

182. ibid.

183. ibid.

184. NLS MS 8808 (Elibank Papers).

185. ibid.

186. Thomas Howarth, *Charles Rennie Mackintosh and the Modern Movement.* Preface to the Second Edition, XXXVIII (Routledge and Kegan Paul: London).

187. James Veitch, *George Douglas Brown* (London 1952) *p.* 72.

188. ibid. *pp.* 153-154.

189. Margaret Morris, *The Art of J. D. Fergusson* (Blackie & Son: Glasgow 1974) *p.* 107.

190. ibid. *p.* 110.

191. Janet Adam Smith, *John Buchan* (Rupert Hart-Davis (Grafton Books): London 1965) *p.* 130.

192. Family papers.

193. 1914-1918 Archive, Sunderland Polytechnic.

194. Maurice Lindsay, *Francis George Scott and the Scottish Renaissance* (Paul Harris Publishing: Edinburgh 1980) *p.* 200.

195. NLS MSS Dep. 176/26/Z.

196. NLS MSS Acc. 8895.

197. P. H. Butter (ed.), *Selected Letters of Edwin Muir* (Chatto & Windus, The Hogarth Press: London 1974) *p.* 64.

198. ibid. *p.* 49.
199. ibid. *pp.* 70-71.
200. ibid. *p.* 107.
201. ibid. *p.* 202.
202. Willa Muir, *Belonging* (Chatto & Windus, The Hogarth Press 1968).
203. Winifred Bannister, *James Bridie and his Theatre* (Rockcliffe 1955) *p.* 32.
204. ibid. *p.* 34.
205. NLS MSS.
206. NLS MSS Acc. 5813.
207. ibid.
208. ibid.
209. Alan Bold (ed.), *The Letters of Hugh MacDiarmid* (Hamish Hamilton: London 1984) *pp.* 7, 8, 11, 12, 13.
210. ibid. *pp.* 560-563.
211. ibid. *pp.* 599-600.
212. ibid. *p.* 531.
213. ibid. *pp.* 871-873.
214. ibid. *p.* 699.
215. Linda MacKenney, *Joe Corrie: Plays, Poems and Theatre Writings* (7:84 Publications: Edinburgh 1985).
216. *Saltire Review,* Vol. 6, No. 21 (Edinburgh: Summer 1960) *pp.* 83-91.
217. NLS MSS Acc. 8787.
218. Munro, *Leslie Mitchell: Lewis Grassic Gibbon* (Oliver and Boyd: Edinburgh 1966) *p.* 107.
219. MS BBC Archives.
220. D. P. Thomson, *Eric H. Liddell* (The Research Unit: Crieff 1971) *p.* 151.
221. Fulton (ed.), *A Garioch Miscellany* (Malcolm Macdonald: Edinburgh 1986).
222. ibid.
223. ibid.
224. NLS MS Acc. 6419/38.
225. ibid.
226. Family papers.
227. NLS MS: by permission of Mrs Susan Kennaway.

Index

Letter numbers are in bold type, author references in italic.